AFRICA'S HEALTH CHALLENGES

Global Environmental Governance

Series Editors: John J. Kirton, Munk Centre for Global Affairs, Trinity College, Canada and Miranda Schreurs, Freie Universität Berlin, Germany

Global Environmental Governance addresses the new generation of twenty-first century environmental problems and the challenges they pose for management and governance at the local, national, and global levels. Centred on the relationships among environmental change, economic forces, and political governance, the series explores the role of international institutions and instruments, national and sub-federal governments, private sector firms, scientists, and civil society, and provides a comprehensive body of progressive analyses on one of the world's most contentious international issues.

Africa's Health Challenges
Sovereignty, Mobility of People and Healthcare Governance

Edited by

ANDREW F. COOPER
University of Waterloo, Canada

JOHN J. KIRTON
University of Toronto, Canada

FRANKLYN LISK
University of Warwick, UK

HANY BESADA
*UN High-Level Panel Secretariat, Post-2015 Development Agenda,
New York, USA and North-South Institute, Canada*

Routledge
Taylor & Francis Group

LONDON AND NEW YORK

First published 2013 by Ashgate Publishing

Published 2016 by Routledge
2 Park Square, Milton Park, Abingdon, Oxfordshire OX14 4RN
711 Third Avenue, New York, NY 10017, USA

First issued in paperback 2016

Routledge is an imprint of the Taylor & Francis Group, an informa business

British Library Cataloguing in Publication Data
A catalogue record for this book is available from the British Library

The Library of Congress has cataloged the printed edition as follows:
Cooper, Andrew Fenton, 1950-
  Africa's health challenges : sovereignty, mobility of people and healthcare governance / by Andrew F. Cooper, John J. Kirton, Franklyn Lisk and Hany Besada.
    pages cm. -- (Global environmental governance)
  Includes bibliographical references and index.
  ISBN 978-1-4094-2832-9 (hardback)
1. Public health--Africa. 2. Medical care--Africa. 3. Health services administration--Africa. 4. Migration, Internal--Africa. I. Kirton, John J. II. Lisk, Franklyn. III. Besada, Hany. IV. Title.
  RA545.C6645 2013
  362.1096--dc23

2013009603

ISBN 13: 978-1-138-26870-8 (pbk)
ISBN 13: 978-1-4094-2832-9 (hbk)

Contents

List of Figures

List of Tables

Notes on Contributors

Jane Adar is the Technical Task Order Leader for South Africa PEPFAR Performance Assessment in the area of HIV and AIDS prevention, care, and support.

Hany Besada is a research specialist for the Secretariat of the United Nations High-Level Panel on the Post-2015 Development Agenda. He is also a theme leader at the North-South Institute, an adjunct research professor at Carleton University, and PhD candidate at the University of Warwick.

Andrew F. Cooper is a professor at the Balsillie School of International Affairs and the department of political science at the University of Waterloo.

Anita A. Davies is a public health specialist in the Migration Health Division of the International Organization for Migration.

Ibadat S. Dhillon is a health advisor with the Danish International Development Agency (Danida) in Tanzania.

John J. Kirton is the co-director of the Global Health Diplomacy Program, based at the Munk School for Global Affairs at Trinity College in the University of Toronto, and a professor of political science at the University of Toronto.

Franklyn Lisk is a visiting professorial research fellow at the Centre for the Study of Globalisation and Regionalisation at the University of Warwick and a senior associate at the Center for Research on Political Economy in Dakar, Senegal.

Rudi Robinson conducts research in the field of population health and economic development, focusing on globalization, migration, health inequality, and economic development in East and Southern Africa.

Charles Sampford is Foundation Dean and professor of law at Griffith University and is currently Director of The Institute for Ethics, Governance, and Law (a joint initiative of the United Nations University, Griffith University, Queensland University of Technology, Australia National University, Center for Asian Integrity in Manila, and O.P. Jindal Global University).

Nelson Sewankambo is the principal of Makerere University's College of Health Sciences and chair of the Medical Education for Equitable Services for All Ugandans (MESAU) consortium.

Allyn L. Taylor is a visiting professor of law at the Georgetown University Law Center. She is also an adjunct professor of international relations at the Johns Hopkins Paul H. Nitze School of Advanced International Studies.

Mengsteab Tesfayohannes is an associate professor of management at Susquehanna University's Sigmund Weis School of Business and formerly an Alexander Humboldt Fellow in Germany.

Preface

This book began as a follow-on to a project, inspired by the 2003 outbreak of severe acute respiratory syndrome (SARS), on Innovation in Global Health Governance. That project developed and tested a framework of challenge-response-innovation for analyzing global health governance, and published the results in two volumes: *Global Health Governance: Challenge, Response, Innovation,* edited by Andrew F. Cooper, John J. Kirton, and Ted Schrecker, and *Innovation in Global Health Governance: Critical Cases,* edited by Andrew F. Cooper and John J. Kirton.

These works sparked a broader reflection on how the core concepts and institutions of the state-centric Westphalian world were adapting to save human lives in the face of fast-moving, free-flowing disease that so easily penetrated national boundaries on a global scale. Nowhere were these dynamics more advanced than in sub-Saharan Africa, where people dealt with the equivalent of a SARS outbreak every day, where transborder population movements were massive, where state capacity was often slight, and where the toll of disease and death was huge. Thus this new project on Moving Health Sovereignty in Africa was launched, under the auspices of The Centre for International Governance Innovation (CIGI), the University of Toronto's Munk School of Global Affairs, and Warwick University's Centre for the Study of Globalisation and Regionalisation.

Such was the popularity of the project and the quality of the contributions produced that the editors decided to report the results in two separate volumes. This first volume, *Africa's Health Challenges,* focuses on the particular problem posted by the movements of people, as distinct from pathogens, both within and outside Africa, applying concepts of sovereignty to the migration of the healthcare workforce in particular. The second volume presents the general problématique, concepts, and applications in ways that flow from the earlier framework on challenge, response, and innovation.

Andrew F. Cooper, John J. Kirton, Franklyn Lisk, and Hany Besada
October 2011

Acknowledgements

In producing this book we have acquired an enormous debt to many individuals in many ways.

Our first debt is to The Centre for International Governance Innovation, which provided the funding to initiate the research project on which this book is based. The second is to our colleagues at our home institutions, who offered valuable encouragement and support as we worked on this book. We are also grateful to our researchers and research assistants who helped transform rough drafts into finished prose. At the University of Toronto and its Global Health Diplomacy Program, co-directed by John Kirton and James Orbinski, these are Madeline Koch, Jenilee Guebert, Caroline Bracht, Julia Kulik, Corinne Ton That, Colleen Keilty, Robin Lennox, Zaria Shaw, and Baillie McGurn.

At the University of Waterloo, these are Asif Farooq and Ryan Hilimoniuk.

At Warwick University these are Sharifah Sekalala and Penelope Muzanenhamo.

At the North-South Institute, these are Rachael Calleja, Kristen Winters, and Maria Habanikova.

At Tyndale University College and Seminary, there is Leah McMillan.

At Ashgate, Kirstin Howgate, Margaret Younger, and their colleagues were—as always—a pleasure to work with, especially as their patience was a particularly valuable asset this time.

Finally, we are most grateful to our students, for the constant inspiration they have offered as this book was being conceived, researched, written, and revised. It is dedicated to them.

Abbreviations and Acronyms

ART	antiretroviral treatment
AU	African Union
DOTS	Directly Observed Treatment—Short Course
DRC	Democratic Republic of Congo
FAIMER	Foundation for Advancement of International Medical Education and Research
GCC	Gulf Cooperation Countries
GHWA	Global Health Workforce Alliance
ICISS	International Commission on Intervention and State Sovereignty
IHR	International Health Regulations
IAVI	International AIDS Vaccine Initiative
IMF	International Monetary Fund
IMG	international medical graduate
IOM	International Organization for Migration
IPR	intellectual property right
LMICs	low- and middle-income countries
MDG	Millennium Development Goal
MDR-TB	multidrug-resistant tuberculosis
MIDA	Migration for Development in Africa
MOU	memorandum of understanding
NEPAD	New Partnership for Africa's Development
NGO	nongovernmental organization
NHS	National Health Service (in the United Kingdom)
OECD	Organisation for Economic Co-operation and Development
SARS	severe acute respiratory syndrome
SMARTER	specific, measurable, attainable, realistic, timely, effective, and resourceful
UNHCR	United Nations High Commissioner for Refugees
UNSC	United Nations Security Council
WHA	World Health Assembly
WHO	World Health Organization
WHO/AFRO	World Health Organization Regional Office for Africa
WHO/EURO	World Health Organization Regional Office for Europe
XDR-TB	extensively drug-resistant tuberculosis

PART I
Introduction

Chapter 1

The Global Health Challenge in Africa

Andrew F. Cooper and John Kirton

Globalization has generated a great upsurge in mobility on an accentuated, if highly differentiated, scale. Much of this movement of people is of an optional nature, facilitated by the rapid growth in the pattern of travel and commercial activity. Individuals connect with friends and relatives more frequently and further away. Tourists take off for vacations in distant locales, seeking relaxation, rest and recovery, and faster or cheaper health services beyond the confines of their territorial home. Professionals routinely travel on business throughout the full global marketplace. Migration and international student flows have increased and diversified enormously.

Yet, in a variety of scenarios, such movement of people is conducted not on a voluntary or benign basis with little choice. Refugees, including conflict refugees, climate refugees, and natural disaster refugees, move across penetrable borders, due to disruptions and crisis. Military personnel go abroad and come home. Individuals move across borders with and without papers to conduct legal as well as illegal activities.

As people move in proliferating fashion, so too do the pathogens they carry. Often unfamiliar diseases flow rapidly from anywhere to everywhere, to cause death and devastation behind the national borders that once kept their citizens safe inside the comfortable confines of their own sovereign state. Moreover, it is now quite possible to move around the world faster than the incubation periods for infectious diseases, as was illustrated in 2009 by the pace of advance of the H1N1 virus (European Centre for Disease Prevention and Control 2009).

In still other cases questions about the voluntary or coerced motivations for movement of people—and the results—are blurred. The movement of people is commonly linked to the transmission of diseases, especially in conflict situations as public health is severely reduced. Estimates concerning the conflicts in the Democratic Republic of the Congo located most deaths during recent wars as a consequence of the erosion of health-supporting infrastructure of society, including medical care, supply of safe food and water, sanitation and sewage systems, power generation, transportation, and communication (Coghlan et al. 2009).

Still, in some specific cases, this view is contested by a few influential practitioners. The Angolan health minister, for example, has advanced the argument the conflicts waged in southern Africa prevented the movement of people—and so curtailed the spread of HIV/AIDS (Angola Press Agency 2010). Although such assertion has not yet been demonstrated with empirical findings, the possibility cannot be discounted. Nonetheless, the movement of people can be highly disruptive and sometimes tragic. Such dynamics are often associated with social and economic development and other positive spillover effects such as remittances (United Nations Development Programme 2009).

Moreover, the pattern of the movement of people has become marked not only by its scale but also by its complexity. Africa has the largest scale of movement among populations in the world. However, not all this movement is externally transnational. A good deal of it is internal transnational in composition. As such the profile of such migration has changed from being unidirectional and permanent to being increasingly temporary, seasonal, and circular (Carballo and Mboup 2005).

It must also be mentioned that not only war and other crises bring about problems through the movement of people. Voluntary and otherwise benign patterns of mobility often increase the movement of diseases. Mobile workers such as long-distance truck drivers have very high rates of HIV infection, as do migrant workers more generally.

Trajectories Toward—and Defences Against—Globalization in the Context of Global Health Governance

In many ways the challenge facing Africa in terms of health is a subset of a larger global trajectory. At both the global and the regional levels, both positive and negative consequences emerge from the movement of people across territorial lines. Not only does the movement of people bring with it the search (and often the achievement) of better lives, but it also brings the search (and often the achievement) of better ideas and norms in terms of dealing with the health challenge.

Increasingly the tools traditionally employed by the governments of Westphalian sovereign states and by the intergovernmental institutions that they have formally ceded slight slivers of their sovereignty to are recognized as being too small, slow, and static to cope with this fast, fluid, far-reaching new world of moving people and pathogens and proliferating disease and death. Furthermore, many African states—ravaged by protracted ethnic conflicts and insurgency—have trouble exercising their sovereign right to govern parts of their own territories (Collier 2007). As a result, some states fall short of de facto sovereignty—legitimate and territorial right to rule—compared to other Westphalian sovereign states. Many African states are also influenced by former colonial powers (Clapham 1996). Some states are at the same time struggling to establish political stability and democracy while going through post-conflict reconstruction and state building (Bratton and van de Walle 1997; Ogbaharya 2008). While these states are willing to develop human resources and capacity for specialized fields, such as the health sector, their endeavours are often challenged by inadequate financial resources and donors' unreliability. On top of that, African states have often been victims of damaging policies, imposed by international financial institutions. Structural adjustment programs under the Washington Consensus restrained many

African countries from taking beneficial policies and also eroded their trusts in policies advocated by the western institutions (Chabal and Daloz 1999; Harbeson et al. 1994; Stiglitz 2002). As a result, many African countries have recently been vocal in exercising their sovereign rights to follow a development path that they deem appropriate for them. Such issue of jurisdiction has always been a contentious issue for global health governance.

Africa as a continent thus presents a unique challenge on many issues, among which the health sector is one of the most important. There is consequently an urgent need for innovation in global governance to close this great and growing gap between the new physical challenge of a world on the move and the old public policy response from governments fixed in territorial space. On top of all of this, there are challenges in ensuring the adaptation of African countries from traditional state-centric governance to multilateral governance on various health issues. This adaptation has to be led carefully without compromising countries' own institutional and cultural needs, since wrong policies can cause detrimental outcome for a society. The pros and cons of various HIV/AIDS policies in the African countries further test that assertion (Biesma et al. 2009). Therefore, innovation in health governance in Africa is imperative but challenging.

In this regard to visualize the twenty-first century as being continuous with the twentieth century, an era in which Angus Deaton (2004) suggests that health improvements in developing countries "ultimately came from the globalization of knowledge, facilitated by local political, economic, and educational outcomes."

To look forward in this manner is not to overlook the barriers. Controls in the area of health governance carry little or no stigma. Rather, they are deemed to be an acceptable part of the application of national authority through quarantines and other devices aimed to close off borders and hoard resources such as vaccines. To overcome this form of sovereign trap, innovative impulses both in term of ideational and institutional design are needed. Those impulses remain tied to the mental leap necessary to break with the traditional image of the global South as a reservoir of human diseases to be guarded against by better medicines, bigger border barriers, and more protective policies at home (Aginam 2004).

As showcased in this volume, such innovative impulses privilege solutions involving multi-actors and multilevel networking. If the exact shape of this order is unclear and contested, there is an emerging consensus that this approach must rely on a multi-centred and transformative mode of global governance. As Jeff Collin, Kelley Lee, and Karen Bissell (2005, 260) have pointed out,

> In a world where many health risks and opportunities are becoming increasingly globalised, influencing health determinants, status and outcomes cannot be achieved through actions taken at the national level alone. The intensification of transborder flows of people, ideas, goods and services necessitates a reassessment of the rules and institutions that govern health policy and practice.

The Exceptional Nature of the African Health Challenge

Notwithstanding the salient characteristic of this more generalized context, a very strong argument can be made that points to the exceptional nature of this challenge that makes it more acute in Africa, especially in its southern geographical component. There are many other issues that influence the African health challenge profoundly, i.e. political will and financial resources. However, the development of human resource capacity is one the most important issues that needs special attention. This capacity development for the African health sector is severely affected and constrained by the movement of healthcare workers, for it is in this region that the pattern of movement to escape economic and ecological deprivation and deadly conflict is at its most intense. Moreover, the challenge is not only to get overwhelmed by the various interpretations of the migration problem but also to realize the heterogeneity of the migration issue for best policy practice (De Haas 2010).

Africa hosts approximately 25 percent of all refugees (United Nations High Commissioner for Refugees 2007). Notwithstanding the impression that there is a "healthy migrant" effect, migrants—especially those under pressure or coercion— face widespread hazards and barriers to receiving health care when they move from home. Many flee dangerous environments; most increase their exposure to risks during the time they are moving, and often encounter barriers to receiving adequate health care when they stop their journey or settle in a new country.

While such conditions need to be overcome, they should not be explored in isolation. The scale of movement of people in Africa cannot be separated from voluntary dynamics, as most clearly illustrated by the movement of health professionals. Facing the exceptional burden of world leading rates of infectious and chronic diseases, and lacking the facilities required to cope, healthcare professionals in Africa flow from underfunded public systems to better endowed ones close at hand, or follow their patients and people by moving to distant developed countries where they will be better off. One study suggests that 23,000 healthcare professionals emigrate annually from Africa (International Organization for Migration 2005c). For example, between 1993 and 2002, Ghana lost 630 medical doctors, 410 pharmacists, 87 laboratory technicians, and 11,325 nurses; in 2002 alone, 70 doctors, 77 pharmacists, and 214 nurses left Ghana.

While healthcare workers move into Africa from the governments, foundations, and nongovernmental organizations (NGOs) of the developed world, there are never enough to fill the gaps from the departures and meet Africans healthcare needs. And few tourists fly from rich countries to Africa for treatment because the facilities and price tags are so much better there. In such a world there is a compelling need for far-reaching innovation in global health governance, to save the lives of so many in Africa, and everywhere else in a world that is now only plane ride away.

In attempting to assess this dilemma, this volume moves from a critical approach to a problem-solving one. Although the broad aim continues to be on a visionary multi-centred and transformative mode of global governance, space is provided for detailed remedies with a particular regional emphasis by not only leading scholars but practitioners from and beyond Africa.

The Analytic Framework

The contribution of every chapter in this volume can be synthesized in a common and evolving analytical framework. Although the authors do not necessarily follow the analytical framework per se, each nevertheless addresses its core issues in a particular fashion. This analytical framework was first devised to address contemporary global health governance and developed in application to several critical diseases on the global health agenda today (Cooper and Kirton 2009; Cooper et al. 2007; Kirton 2009). In this study, the framework is adapted for the experience of the particular region of sub-Saharan African, given the pervasive poverty and pronounced poverty that exists there.

Sovereignty: Classic, Competing, and Changing Conceptions

The first step on this innovation agenda is to consider classic, competing, and changing conceptions of sovereignty, and how they are challenged by this new world of moving health. Among the many severe health problems faced by the Africans, which are the most acute in deserving a priority place in the public policy response? Among the many changes over the centuries in the meaning of sovereignty, both in general and in application to health, which are the most promising as an ideational guide to the global health governance innovations needed to save the lives of Africans and others?

The African Health Dilemma: Movement, Migration, and Match

The second step is to examine in empirical detail the moving world of pathogens, patients, people, and health professionals. This requires charting, largely within Africa, the moving pathogens and people with disease or people moving to escape disease, tracking the migrating healthcare professionals who move for many motives, including to care and cure, and assessing how much the double movements match as healthcare professionals go where their patients shift. When healthcare professionals migrate on the same global trajectories as their new patients and pathogens, they are presumably familiar with the exotic diseases and traditional medicines, languages, and cultures that might help in the cure—if their credentials are recognized and they are integrated into the polity of their receiving healthcare system in time. Multicultural populations and patients created by global movement should be matched by healthcare professionals created by multiculturalism and movement too.

This involves exploring the migration of healthcare professionals from the perspective of the poorer places and polities they left. Do they have, along with a right to move, a responsibility to stay, protect care for, and cure their present and prospective patients in places of their departure? In practice, do their remittances, as well as the return and reciprocal transfer of knowledge and the creation of transnational communities of caring, compensate for the gap created by their departure?

The African Refugee Problem

The third step is to explore the match in the world of mobile, orbiting diasporas, focusing on the movements taking place within Africa itself in the acute case of refugees. When people travel not just in a one-way direction for long-term resettlement but temporarily or in sequential moves from country to country or in rapid reciprocal sequences of back-and-forth, who is responsible for protecting their health?

National and Regional Public Policy Response and Innovation

The fourth step is to see whether national and regional public authorities, even equipped with the proper concepts and configurations, have the capacity to cope with these new arrivals. Unknown diseases suddenly dropping in from distant locations can poorly match and quickly overwhelm the most capable, well-trained healthcare infrastructure focused on very different things. What should be the preferred policies of the countries of arrival? Should they accept their new people and patients as equals for whom they have a sovereign responsibility to protect in the health domain, whether these people have or claim an individual human right for such care? Should recipient governments recruit health professionals from poorer places and, if so, under what codes of responsible conduct, and established and managed by whom? Should they encourage the flow at home by rapidly integrating new arrivals into their healthcare systems? Should they provide reparations for their removal of healthcare workers? Should they give aid, from public and private actors, that simply moves healthcare workers within and between developing countries from indigenous systems to well-paid positions to deal with diseases with high-profile appeal in developed countries? Should the focus be not on replacing the outmigrants with like professionals but on empowering local communities and ordinary citizens to provide the needed health care instead?

Global Governance Response and Innovation

The fifth step is to examine the existing record and role of global intergovernmental institutions and transnational institutions that operate above and through this moving, mismatched world. How and how well are they coping with the long-term movements, the impacts in the polities of arrival and departure, and the fluid diasporas? How do states adapt to broader cooperation and integration, discounting the contentious issue of jurisdiction in favour of global health governance? How can states cope with various perspectives of health workers' migration for best policy practice? How are policies to be developed by the international health institutions that not only reflect the global health concerns but also include immediate and long-term national interests of the individual states? Can such policies be equally beneficial for all parties without undermining cultural and ideational sensitivities? How can health diplomacy bolster this process so that individual states can avoid historical animosity and cooperate with other states and non-state actors for regional and global solutions on health issues?

Conclusion: What's Needed, What's Moving, What's the Way Ahead?

What innovations are needed in the ever more mobile Africa that lies ahead? The answer comes, first, in the realm of ideas. Here the need is to invent and introduce new concepts of sovereignty to capture this emerging world of single, dual, and mutual citizens moving among homelands, stateless people and recent non-citizens such as refugee claimants, and to determine the rights they have in their polity of arrival or new residence (including the right to publicly funded health care), the responsibilities they have to their polity of departure, and the rights and responsibilities of the national governments of arrival and departure and the international institutions that stand above both.

A second need, in the realm of instruments, is to consider innovations in several fields, including migration policy, official development assistance, remittances, dual citizenship, and community care.

The third need, in the realm of institutions, is to examine how governance institutions can and should innovate in order to reflect these new conceptions of sovereignty and the physical world that lies behind. This includes national and sub-federal governments, intergovernmental institutions, and the NGOs of transnational civil society.

The Authors' Arguments

Part I begins with Chapter 2, "Sovereignty: Changing Conceptions and Challenges," in which Charles Sampford addresses how issues of state sovereignty affect humanitarian intervention efforts and, more specifically, the training, movement, and regulation of health professionals. This chapter addresses issues raised in the first step of the analytical framework. In Latin America and Africa, internal political strife has had damaging effects on the ability of humanitarian healthcare workers to assist populations. Sampford questions at what point the responsibility to protect supersedes sovereign state power. He insists that there is a role for both governments and the international community to play in solving this dilemma. Globalization and shifting power structures, including the increased role of transnational corporations, the United Nations, international agencies, and NGOs, have all challenged the concept of a state as the ultimate authority and power. Nonstate actors can be more beneficial to populations of failed states than their actual governments. Given this reality, a compromise must be found between individual state power and international governance norms. With respect to health governance, Sampford raises the question of how best to recruit healthcare workers ethically, without leaving poorer states with fewer healthcare resources. The solutions here, he says, are within the power of sovereign states to exercise and the international community to establish. With the participation of the World Health Organization (WHO), states can work together to solidify global standards for the healthcare profession and balance the migration of South–North workers more equitably. Here national, domestic action leads to an international "integrity" system for the international health workforce. In this way sovereign states can pursue national goals while being part of an international governance system and, in so doing, respond better to the challenges of the twenty-first century.

Part III examines "The African Health Problem." In Chapter 3, "Globalization and Health Systems in Sub-Saharan Africa: A Labour Market Perspective," Rudi Robinson focuses on both the negative and positive impacts of globalization on the healthcare workforce in sub-Saharan Africa, and addresses the second step of the analytical framework. Robinson notes that well-resourced healthcare workers are the best asset of any health system because of the technical skills, management abilities, and institutional capacity they are able to use to help populations effectively. These efforts in turn lead to healthier populations that are better able to produce economic wealth, thereby reducing poverty. The healthcare workforce of each country is therefore fundamental, not only for the betterment of health systems, but also ultimately for society as a whole. Robinson argues, however, that the "trickle down" effect of a properly resourced healthcare workforce is hampered as well as helped in sub-Saharan Africa by the effects of globalization. In a positive way, globalization has allowed for more career opportunities for healthcare workers and greater integration of healthcare services, which have facilitated resource flows to poor countries. On the negative side, the international mobility of healthcare workers, usually from poor countries to rich countries, has resulted in a deficit in the healthcare labour force in poor countries. Robinson maintains that the internationalization of healthcare workforces has had a particularly harmful effect on sub-Saharan Africa, an area that needs to increase its number of health workers by 140 percent to deliver essential health services. Instead, the area is losing healthcare workers at an unsustainable rate. Robinson concludes that it is necessary to address the structure and dynamics of the international labour market for physicians and nurses specifically in order to minimize the costs and maximize the benefits of migrating healthcare workers. This is particularly important for the poorest countries of the world.

In Chapter 4, "Managing the Mobility of Health Professionals," Robinson discusses the importance of the effective management of international healthcare professionals in order to have the least negative impact on the poorest countries, specifically in the region of sub-Saharan Africa. This chapter reflects the issues mentioned in the second step of the analytical framework. International labour mobility has created great opportunities for healthcare professionals from sub-Saharan Africa to work in countries that are members of the Organisation for Economic Co-operation and Development (OECD). However, too often international migration has created greater economic and social gains for destination countries than for countries of origin. Countries of origin may benefit from remittances, knowledge, skills, and investments of migrant workers, but, as Robinson asserts, the overall net result is an unequal distribution of economic and social costs and benefits in origin and destination countries. This inequality needs to be better managed in order to reward all stakeholders more equitably. For example, more effective policies through policy coherence in OECD countries could be achieved by taking into account potential negative effects on the country of origin of a migrant healthcare professional. Robinson advocates taking this management style approach to integrate the main stakeholders—origin countries, destination countries, and healthcare professionals—in a way that maximizes results and minimizes costs for the system as a whole. This co-development framework, as opposed to a "stay-at-home" strategy (that entices healthcare professionals to stay in their country of origin), is a more strategic way to turn what had been a zero-sum game of greater losses overall for countries of origin into a "triple win" solution for the destination country, country of origin, and the healthcare professional. In this way, it produces a more equitably managed international healthcare workforce.

In Chapter 5, "International Migration, the Health of Migrants, and Global Health Governance," Anita Davies contends that global health governance has a direct impact on the mobility of populations. This chapter addresses both the refugee issues of the third step of the analytical framework as well as the core issues of the fourth step. With the rise in international migration, particularly in Africa, expanded health governance is necessary in order to deliver health services effectively and deal adequately with the increased possibility of the spread of disease by migrating populations. Davies contends that multi-sectoral, regional, subregional, national, and international approaches are required to address the challenges of migrant health and health governance. Internationally, the International Code of Human Rights and the Convention of the Rights of the Child are examples of such collaborative efforts. Another such effort is the Migration for Development in Africa (MIDA) initiative where country of origin, country of destination, migrants, and international organizations work together to strengthen human resource capacity in developing countries through knowledge and skills transfer of migrant workers. This strengthening often involves the migrant worker returning to the country of origin to assist with development. Davies says that all countries across all sectors in Africa must work together to coordinate health governance better in the region, and seek to respect, protect, and facilitate life for migrant workers, who are important for their economies. The African Charter on Human and Peoples' Rights and the African Charter on the Rights and Welfare of the Child were important steps in this direction. Davies suggests these innovative initiatives and an "integrated and globally focused" approach are required to deal with migration health issues and recommends that MIDA, the New Partnership for Africa's Development (NEPAD), the African Union (AU), the UN, governments, civil society, academia, and research institutions must work together to coordinate migration, health, and development issues in order to build capacity in Africa.

Part IV, "National and Regional Policy Responses and Innovation," begins with Chapter 6, entitled "Integrating Science and Community Development: The Practice of Traditional Medicine in Fighting HIV and AIDS." Jane Adar asks, hypothetically, what would be the main reasons for millions of Africans still being affected by HIV/AIDS in 2025. She argues that such a scenario would be due to a lack of political will to change behaviour and stop the key drivers of the epidemic. Globalization has imposed more structural adjustments and debt in poor countries. This has forced healthcare professionals to leave their country of origin as governments decrease healthcare funding and privatize the sector. In 2008, a special session of the UN General Assembly reported that access to treatment had decreased because of weak local health systems, insufficient funding for treatment, and a neglect to integrate HIV/AIDS care within a country's overall health system infrastructure. Adar offers one solution that highlights the very important role of traditional medicine in Africa and incorporates it into the region's health system architecture. Traditional medicine has not always been accepted by conventional medical practitioners, but remains the most widely used medical treatment in Africa—80 percent of the population uses traditional medicine. This pluralism of medical practices is the reality in Africa, where traditional healers offer HIV/ AIDS patients affordable treatments. Adar contends that there are challenges in integrating traditional with conventional practices but, done properly with sufficient funding, research, and regulation, the benefits could alleviate the healthcare burden in the continent and provide enhanced treatment. Traditional medicine has been successfully integrated into mainstream health care in China and Japan: Africa can learn from these examples. Researchers, biomedical scientists, and traditional medicine practitioners can work together to test the safety, efficacy, and limitations of traditional medicine with the goal of bettering African health systems overall. This chapter highlights possible local solutions as public policy response and innovation, which is the fourth step of the analytical framework.

In Chapter 7, "Health Professionals and Sustainable Economic Development in the Horn of Africa," Mengsteab Tesfayohannes writes about the gravity of the healthcare situation in the Horn of Africa, and the relationship between health and economic growth. This chapter provides the economic effects of issues mentioned in the second step of the analytical framework. Tesfayohannes maintains that the region's healthcare sector, mostly available to wealthier urban populations than to poorer rural ones, has suffered years of neglect and underfunding. In addition, local healthcare workers are recruited for work outside the country, which diminishes capacity. This brain drain has had dire consequences on the region and must be reversed. Tesfayohannes insists that tailored support from the international community is needed in order for the region to meet the Millennium Development Goals in the Horn of Africa and to retain skilled healthcare workers in the region.

In Chapter 8, "Strengthening Health Capacity in Sub-Saharan Africa: A Millennium Development Challenge," Nelson Sewankambo discusses how to achieve better healthcare services in sub-Saharan Africa, that is related to the policy issues raised in the fourth step of the analytical framework. Sewankambo identifies health as a crucial determinant of economic growth, labour force productivity, and poverty reduction. Health is also the focus of the eight Millennium Development Goals (MDGs) for the very reason that it is the central tenet of the well-being of populations, productivity of labour forces, and wealth of a country and its citizens. However, in sub-Saharan Africa health outcomes are often not progressing and, in some areas, are even regressing. Sewankambo asks how it is possible to move forward with health goals in the region more effectively and quickly. He notes that the MDGs represent "a welcome agenda for action" and, coupled with vertical and horizontal programs, should continue to work to deliver effective, equitable, and affordable health services. With a population of more than 660 million, sub-Saharan Africa would require approximately 1 million healthcare workers (including 700,000 physicians) to meet the MDGs and deliver basic healthcare services. The current lack of capacity has been unfortunately neglected by governments, donor agencies, and global health initiatives. Sewankambo observes that, in addition to the MDGs, the hope in the mandate and goals of relevant organizations (donor, international, government) has galvanized action. This momentum needs to continue. Here, the best way to proceed lies in innovative ideas that focus on solutions that states themselves can implement, assisted by the international community. The emphasis is on the need to build health systems using this nationally defined approach that combines all interdependent sectors of the economy to achieve optimal results in health care, creating a complex adaptive system able to achieve higher economic growth rates, labour productivity, and a reduction in poverty due to increased individual wealth and well-being.

In Chapter 9, "The WHO Global Code of Practice on the International Recruitment of Health Personnel: The Evolution of Global Health Diplomacy," Allyn L. Taylor and Ibadat S. Dhillon offer some imaginative and practical solutions to the problem of the migration of health workers to middle- and high-income countries. Such policy-oriented analysis falls within the content of the fourth step of the analytical framework. Taylor and Dhillon point out that at the hub of the problem lies a gap between the development agenda related to global health and the domestic health workforce policies of many donor countries. The way forward is provided through the vehicle of the WHO's Global Code of Practice on the International Recruitment of Health Personnel, which puts in place a global architecture to guide international cooperation on the issue of health worker migration and serves as a platform for continuing dialogue. Although cognizant that the WHO's Global Code is neither a perfect text nor a solution to the challenges associated with health worker migration, Taylor and Dhillon maintain that the code, particularly the key legal and institutional arrangements, provides a robust instrument for ongoing global cooperation that may lead to a deepening of commitment over time.

References

Aginam, Obijifor (2004). "Salvaging Our Global Neighbourhood: Critical Reflections on the G8 Summit and Global Health Governance in an Interdependent World." *Law, Social Justice, and Global Development* 1. Available online: www2.warwick.ac.uk/fac/soc/law/elj/lgd/2004_1/aginam (October 2012).

Angola Press Agency (2010). "Health Minister Says War Hindered HIV/Aids Spread in Nation." March 19.

Biesma, Regien G., Ruairí Brugha, Andrew Harmer et al. (2009). "The Effects of Global Health Initiatives on Country Health Systems: A Review of the Evidence from HIV/AIDS Control." *Health Policy and Planning* 24: 239–52.

Bratton, Michael and Nicholas van de Walle (1997). *Democratic Experiments in Africa: Regime Transitions in Comparative Perspective.* Cambridge: Cambridge University Press.

Carballo, Manuel and Mourtala Mboup (2005). "International Migration and Health." Paper prepared for the Policy Analysis and Research Programme, September, Global Commission on International Migration. Available online: www.iom.int/jahia/webdav/site/myjahiasite/shared/shared/mainsite/policy_ and_research/gcim/tp/TP13.pdf (October 2012).

Chabal, Patrick and Jean-Pascal Daloz (1999). *Africa Works: Disorder as Political Instrument.* Bloomington, IN: Indiana University Press.

Clapham, Christopher (1996). *Africa and the International System: The Politics of State Survival.* Cambridge: Cambridge University Press.

Coghlan, Benjamin, Pascal Ngoy, Flavien Mulumba et al. (2009). "Update on Mortality in the Democratic Republic of Congo: Results from a Third Nationwide Survey." *Disaster Medicine and Public Health Preparedness* 3: 88–96.

Collier, Paul (2007). *The Bottom Billion: Why the Poorest Countries Are Failing and What Can Be Done About It.* Oxford: Oxford University Press.

Collin, Jeff, Kelley Lee, and Karen Bissell (2005). "Negotiating the Framework Convention on Tobacco Control: An Updated Politics of Global Health Governance." In *The Global Governance Reader*, Rorden Wilkinson (ed.) New York: Routledge.

Cooper, Andrew F. and John J. Kirton (eds) (2009). *Innovation in Global Health Governance: Critical Cases.* Farnham: Ashgate.

Cooper, Andrew F., John J. Kirton, and Ted Schrecker (eds) (2007). *Governing Global Health: Challenge, Response, Innovation.* Aldershot: Ashgate.

De Haas, Hein (2010). "Migration and Development: A Theoretical Perspective." *International Migration Review* 44(1): 227–64.

Deaton, Angus (2004). "Health in an Age of Globalization." Working Paper 10669, National Bureau of Economic Research, Cambridge, MA. Available online: www.nber.org/papers/w10669 (October 2012).

European Centre for Disease Prevention and Control (2009). "ECDC Interim Guidance: Uses of Specific Pandemic Influenza Vaccines During the H1N1 2009 Pandemic." August, Stockholm. Available online: ecdc.europa. eu/en/publications/publications/0908_gui_pandemic_influenza_vaccines_ during_the_h1n1_2009_pandemic.pdf (October 2012).

Harbeson, John W., Raymond F. Hopkins, and David Smith (eds) (1994). *Responsible Governance: The Global Challenge.* Lanham, MD: University Press of America.

International Organization for Migration (2005). "World Migration Report 2005: Costs and Benefits of International Migration." Geneva. Available online: publications.iom.int/bookstore/free/wmr_2005.pdf (October 2012).

Kirton, John J. (ed.) (2009). *Global Health.* Farnham: Ashgate.

Ogbaharya, Daniel G. (2008). "(Re-)Building Governance in Post-Conflict Africa: The Role of the State and Informal Institutions." *Development in Practice* 18(3): 395–402.

Stiglitz, Joseph (2002). *Globalization and Its Discontents.* New York: W.W. Norton.

United Nations Development Programme (2009). "Overcoming Barriers: Human Mobility and Development." United Nations, New York. Available online: hdr. undp.org/en/reports/global/hdr2009/ (October 2012).

United Nations High Commissioner for Refugees (2007). "2006 Global Trends: Refugees, Asylum-Seekers, Returnees, Internally Displaced and Stateless Persons." Geneva. Available online: www.unhcr.org/4676a71d4.html (October 2012).

PART II
Sovereignty

Chapter 2

Sovereignty:
Changing Conceptions and Challenges

Charles Sampford

This chapter seeks to locate some of the discussions within this volume in the context of more general debates about the nature of sovereignty and the current challenges that it faces. In so doing, it draws on some of the thinking behind and within a major Australian–Canadian project on "Re-conceiving Sovereignty" involving the Institute for Ethics, Governance, and Law at the United Nations University and The Centre for International Governance Innovation.[1] Within that context, it considers one particular challenge arising from health issues—the training, movement, and regulation of health professionals.

Sovereign Debate

"Sovereignty" is a central concept in international relations and international law. Indeed, it predates the separation of those disciplines and arose in a time when the disciplines of law, politics, and political philosophy were not differentiated, and writers from Bodin to Bentham would not have found that this disconnection made much sense (Sampford 2010a). However, any historical or philosophical examination will show that its meaning and effect are unstable and hotly contested within and between disciplines. One source of growing tension has been between long-standing conceptions of state sovereignty based on the effective control of territory—dubbed the "prior successful use of force" by Charles Sampford—and popular sovereignty (on the concept of state sovereignty, see Kelsen 2005; Sampford 1999). While the former still dominates international relations and international law, the latter dominates domestic political and legal theory in all democracies—generating an increasing gap between the national and international

---

1 "Reconceiving Sovereignty" is one of two projects funded by the Australian Research Council with support from The Centre for International Governance Innovation. It involved Howard Adelman, Ramesh Thakur, and the author. The other, "Building the Rule of Law in International Affairs," involved Simon Chesterman, Ramesh Thakur, and the author.

conceptions of sovereignty and some significant challenges to the latter.[2] Two of these challenges were acknowledged and articulated by Kofi Annan (2000b). In his Millennium address, he challenged the international community to devise principles governing the exercise of sovereignty and the conditions under which humanitarian intervention would be justified. At the inaugural Ministerial Conference of the Community of Democracies, Annan (2000a) proposed that "wherever democracy has taken root, it will not be reversed." The International Commission on Intervention and State Sovereignty (ICISS) responded to the first challenge in 2001 (ICISS 2001). A Council on Foreign Relations task force co-chaired by Bronisław Geremek (former Polish foreign minister) and Madeleine Albright (former US Secretary of State) responded to the second challenge in 2002.[3]

---

2   Since 1988, the author has held the view that this tension is ultimately unsustainable, making the unabashedly rash prediction then that, within 50 years of that date, it will be as unacceptable to base international sovereignty on the prior successful use of force as it is for domestic sovereignty within a democracy (see Sampford 1989). At the time, it was considered hopelessly optimistic. When this same suggestion was made in 2009, some thought it was pessimistic. The response to both was that "history is a long game," rarely unidirectional and frequently disappointing. Moreover, it was not a prediction of what would happen unaided but something that might be brought about. The prediction is much more likely to be realized if the United States leads the world in building an institutionally supported rules-based international system while it remains the leading economic power and remains so until China becomes a democracy. If China secures pre-eminence before it is a democracy and before a rules-based system is developed, the outcomes are likely to be far less pleasant.

3   Some might see potential irony in the fact that one of the task force co-chairs was a major player in ICISS. As a member of the expert panel and the writing group of the task force, the author thought it more constructive not to give his views on the former expressed elsewhere (see Sampford 2002, 2005). To Albright's credit, she twice raised the question of whether she was a war criminal when meeting small groups of the task force. The author did not take up the opportunity to respond on either occasion partly for diplomatic reasons but largely because the way to determine guilt or innocence is not through canvassing the views of law professors but by testing the relevant points in a court of competent jurisdiction. If the US really believed its claims that the wars in Kosovo (and later Iraq) were legal, it should have been prepared to allow the International Court of Justice to adjudicate the matter. If the US had done so and abided by the court's decision, no issue of criminality under the crime of waging aggressive war would ever have been raised. (Note that the crime of waging aggressive war was acknowledged but not, at that time, defined by the Rome Statute. This means that, while the crime could not be prosecuted under the International Criminal Court until the crime was defined, the existence of the crime could not be reasonably doubted, and certainly not by a state that was a signatory to the Kellogg-Briand Pact. Now that the crime of aggression has been defined by the statute's parties, it would be an important source of law as to the meaning of the crime of aggression—along with the United Nations General Assembly Resolution 3314, April 1974).

Neither of these issues has been resolved, although there is movement in both directions with multiple endorsements of the responsibility to protect (R2P) but as yet no authorization by the United Nations Security Council (UNSC) for an intervention based on R2P. There has been more action on the protection of democracies from coups—including the agreement of members of the African Union (AU) for the mutual protection of their own democracies by providing for, and actually engaging in, AU interventions to reverse coups. In Latin America, the attempted Venezuelan coup in 2002 was reversed through internal action, but the support of other Latin American states was critical in that reversal—particularly in forcing the United States to withdraw its initial words of support. These regional rejections of coups and decisive action to reverse them reflects the recognition that coups d'état (a side effect of modern sovereign states) have been the curse of Latin American for two centuries and an even greater curse for Africa over the last half century.

These responses have stimulated rather than resolved debate between traditional state sovereignty based on power and popular sovereignty based on the active choice of the governed. Indeed, they now compete with a cosmopolitan vision that aspires to supersede both and an imperial vision of sovereign power assumed by the government of George W. Bush. However, it would be wrong to focus only on the challenges to sovereignty posed by the understandable urge to protect peoples from sovereign states or non-state actors that tyrannize them.[4] Sovereignty in all its variations is constantly and increasingly tested as a result of the globalization of trade and commerce, communications, and the rapid interstate transfer of people, ideas, and capital. New diseases, environmental degradation, international terrorism, concern for and threat of refugee flows, illicit drugs, human smuggling, and laundered money by international criminal syndicates raise questions about the ability of sovereign states to control these problems.

These conceptual and real challenges are so significant that they cannot be answered by piece-meal tinkering with the concept. Such efforts weaken the sense of state sovereignty even more and raise the possibility that it may go the way of the sovereign divinity and His ostensible earthly monarchical representative—a conception that seemed fixed and immutable even as it unravelled in the West during the seventeenth to nineteenth centuries. What is needed is a systematic effort to re-envision sovereignty through conceptual analysis and cross-disciplinary theorizing, through historical comparisons of the demise of the old regal sense of the sovereign, through the rise of the variety of different conceptions of sovereignty in modernity, and by applied functionalist empirical studies in relationship to specific cases and specific challenges. The goal is to examine emerging conceptions of sovereignty and to craft a coherent conception that can respond to the multiple challenges, and then to consider the institutional structures that would realize such a reconceived sovereignty.

---

4 Those challenges include criminal elements within the military that stage coups against particular communities or against their representatives.

Multiple and Confusing Conceptions of Sovereignty

Sovereignty is a central concept in national histories, international relations, international law, political theory, and political philosophy. Most historical accounts focused on the histories of "independent" sovereign states, not recognizing that the very conception of state sovereignty was not a vehicle to overthrow empires but a product of their disintegration. Jeremy Adelman's (2006) research has shown that modern conceptions of sovereignty developed out of regal sovereignty and the dissolution of empires with three versions in contention—republican, popular, and social credit conceptions of sovereignty. The last fell into desuetude and republican sovereignty metamorphosed into state sovereignty. The dominant trend in international relations focused on inter-state relations between sovereign states that recognized each other's independence in the domestic sphere as the ultimate source of law and as the exclusive repository of coercion in determining when and where to use the state's instruments of might in governing and protecting its citizens and a defined land mass (Sampford 1989). Effective domestic control became the primary basis for international recognition of sovereign legitimacy and the right to take part in the international order (Krasner 2005; Tilly 1990). With states varying so radically in power, international relations focused on trying to establish an equilibrium to avoid inter-state wars to protect incumbent elites or republican sovereignty that evidently worked, according to a recent comparative case study, when local elites provided strong leadership (Bayly 2003; Chesterman et al. 2005). Without that enlightened leadership, the effective sovereignty of less powerful states is frequently compromised and occasionally extinguished (Krisch 2003). In contrast, ignoring inequalities in power, international law is based on a model of an international community composed of legally equal sovereign states, so that the classical sources of international law are inter-state activity such as treaties and state custom and practice. So there are at least two competing conceptions of the sovereign state, an absolute state based on power enjoying unequal relations with other states, and a state enjoying equal legal and economic relations with other states.

The approach taken to domestic sovereignty has varied over time and been affected by domestic political theory. In absolutist states, the sovereign entity enjoyed absolute power in which the lack of international checks was matched by a lack of internal checks. The twentieth-century successors were totalitarian states devoted to a secular ideology or religious radicalism. In liberal states, state sovereign power was initially seen as limited by conditions of an imagined social contract and later a real constitution (Russett 1995). With the rise of democracy, state sovereignty was challenged by popular sovereignty, first conceived of as the consent, and then active choice, of the governed. Internal power relations suffered a Feuerbachian reversal—subjects were no longer accountable to sovereigns but states were accountable to citizens. This 180-degree turn has previously been characterized as the "great leap forward" of enlightenment political theory—an irreversible inversion of authority which was and is instantly attractive to any peoples (Sampford 1999). Some challenged this with a version of republican sovereignty rooted in Montesquieu and Edmund Burke, in which the people are those who have inherited common traditions and possess the virtues to be self-legislators in a homogeneous nation-state (Appleby 1992). These new sovereignties generated secessionist versions in multi-ethnic, multi-religious, and multi-lingual states and demands by dispossessed indigenous peoples for sovereign recognition (Larson 2004). Those demands were based on new conceptions of societal security (the Copenhagen School), which challenged state-centric assumptions of international relations theory (Keal 2003). The scope of self-determination remains controversial in international law (Cárdenas and Cañás 2002; Crawford 1979; McCorquodale 2000). Its potential width has not been widely recognized except during the period of European decolonization.[5]

While the limitations of domestic sovereignty have been long recognized, it is only recently that limitations have been suggested for international sovereignty (i.e. the international recognition of sovereign power within its own territory. This has with discussion of suspended sovereignty, interrupted sovereignty (e.g. trusteeships), and, most significantly, conditional sovereignty (Helman and Ratner 1992–93; Yannis 2002) (ICISS 2001). ICISS argued that states had a responsibility to protect the rights of their citizens. The best solution to disintegrating states "was to strengthen and legitimize states rather than overthrow the system of states" (Chesterman et al. 2005). However, the gross failure of a state to meet that responsibility triggered a broader international responsibility to protect those rights via UN-sanctioned intervention. *A More Secure World: Our Shared Responsibility* (2004), the report prepared by the UN's High-Level Panel on Threats, Challenges, and Change (2004) emphasized the connection between the responsibility to protect and the responsibilities associated with being a signatory to the UN Charter (High-Level Panel on Threats 2004; Slaughter 2005). Locke had asserted that domestic sovereignty was held in trust, conditional on meeting subsequently asserted duties and revocable by popular revolution. The ICISS was making a similar claim for international state sovereignty—with the trust revocable by the UNSC. Even more controversial is the American claim that this function could be taken on by coalitions of democracies, with the claimed right to invade states either for a smorgasbord of reasons including the elimination of an asserted future threat to security or non-democratic rule. By declaring a "war" on terrorism, others' sovereignty is necessarily compromised, as warring parties do not recognize the sovereign rights of "enemies" (an approach placed by Stephen Krasner in a long tradition of states insisting on their own absolute sovereignty while violating others; see Krasner 2003–2004, 2005). At the international level, justice and internal public order are continually contested concepts that reflect the pluralistic nature of the international system itself (Roth 1999, 2004).

---

5 An example of that width is the 1970 Declaration of Principles of International Law Concerning Friendly Relations and Co-operation Among States in Accordance with the Charter of the United Nations, known as the Friendly Relations Declaration.

Concrete Challenges

It would be a major mistake, however, to treat sovereignty as mainly a function of the law and practice of state intervention. The concept of a state as the ultimate authority and power is also challenged by the realities of the twenty-first century. Certainly, one set of challenges relates to recognizing the power dynamics of the international system where the only superpower, the US, had considerable power that it was able to exercise, virtually unchecked, for 20 years. The relationship between the distribution of power—in particular, unipolarity—and sovereignty demands attention. The war against Iraq in 2003 and the willingness of some countries to use preventive and pre-emptive force against asymmetrical threats represented a significant challenge to the post-war international order based upon deterrence, stability, and sovereignty. As the world moves back to either bipolarity or multipolarity and possibly to Chinese pre-eminence, these challenges may recede or be exacerbated if China comes too quickly to power with the precedents of the last 20 years too fresh in memories. Ideally, the US will recommit to a rules-based multilateral system that respects international law and supports the extension of that law to fill gaps and meet challenges as well as accepts the authoritative interpretation of that law by courts of competent jurisdiction. If this leads other likeminded countries in doing so, and does that before China surpasses it in economic and military power, there is a good chance that China would be willing to stay within such a system—and that it would be a democratic China that does so. If the United States is not capable of either providing that leadership or making that leadership effective, the scenario is much less happy.

More fundamental is the set of challenges that come from the rise and recognition of new actors playing significant roles and wielding significant power, including transnational corporations (a hundred of which are wealthier than all but eight states), the UN itself, international agencies that impose aid conditionality (such as the World Bank and International Monetary Fund), indigenous peoples, international nongovernmental organizations, "government networks," and powerful individuals (on aid conditionality, see Cosnard 2003; on networks, see Slaughter 2004; on powerful individuals, see Josselin and Wallace 2001). Indeed, individuals have become subjects of international law as bearers of duties (since the Nuremberg trials) and holders of rights under human rights instruments and some treaties (Brand 2008). The prominence of new actors is evident in notions of shared sovereignty created by agreements established between an internationally recognized sovereignty and an external entity aimed at promoting governance based on democratic principles (Krasner 2003–2004, 2005).

A third set of challenges comes from the apparent inability of some states to maintain the internal order and control that are central to sovereignty. Accordingly, state breakups and state failure may mean the end of viable central public authority and control so that the rights of citizens cannot be met and inter-state relationships cannot be meaningfully pursued. Non-state arrangements, including international trusteeships and affiliations with external bodies and states, have been suggested as possible mechanisms that may benefit the populations of failed states more than responses that focus primarily on restoration (Brooks 2005).

A fourth set of challenges lies in the formal end of professed indifference to the internal governance of other states and the attempts to formulate norms for such internal governance that are intended to be enforced. Some argue for an emerging right of democratic governance—at least where democracy has been established (Franck 1992; High-Level Panel on Threats 2004). This highlights the disjunction already noted between international relations and international law conceptions of sovereignty as the prior successful use of force and the internal conceptions of popular sovereignty that now dominate a majority of nations. Of course, the consequences of transferring domestic and internal approaches to sovereign legitimacy to international relations would be so profound that there is a natural hesitation in linking international legitimacy to domestic democratic legitimacy. Nevertheless, there is clear movement in this direction with some states joining bodies that impose obligations concerning internal governance (e.g. the European Union and the AU). While armed intervention is still relatively rarely used to enforce internal standards of governance and respect for human rights, there are increasing attempts to generate formal mechanisms for protecting human rights, such as the UN Committee on Human Rights and the European Court of Human Rights, which can give binding orders to sovereign states as well as tie aid and trade to what is considered to be acceptable internal behaviour of states.

A fifth set of challenges is based on the fact that many issues cannot be dealt with within traditional boundaries (the global financial crisis, climate change and the spread of disease including AIDS, severe acute respiratory syndrome, avian influenza, and swine influenza). Indeed, many of the most intractable governance problems occur when inadequacies at one level of governance are reinforced and exacerbated by inadequacies at other levels. This has always been the case, for instance, in issues of peace and security where the inadequacies of global governance are exposed by governance failures within states. It is paradigmatically the case in the response to climate change, where governance issues at global, national, and corporate levels contribute to the problem and make finding solutions difficult. It is also most certainly the case with the 2008 global financial crisis, where problems of global, regional, national, corporate, and professional governance produced the greatest set of interlocking governance failures since the 1930s with its threatened but prevented implosion that may yet eventuate if there is a second round. The risk is certainly there in health issues. Attempts to deal with the movement of disease may be exacerbated by

- failures by governments to identify the emergence of a new disease, and their inability to deal with (and sometimes refusal to acknowledge) it;
- failures to reach agreement at the international level on action and insufficient resources to deal with the issue;
- failures in hospital systems that may be run by either the profit or non-profit sector; and

- failures by health professionals to understand their role in such a complex situation.

The adequacy of training and availability of health professionals may result from a number of factors, such as

- lack of international standards for health professionals—with or without variations for local needs and practices (e.g. the relative role of nurses and doctors in primary and preventive health care—especially whether the former can be the first point of contact for patients);
- professional bodies that restrict entry because of different ways of training and testing or to protect their economic position;
- governments in developed countries seeking to cap rising health costs by reducing the number of health professionals being educated; and
- hospital systems (provincial/state, commercial, or not-for-profit) filling their staffing needs with professionals from developing countries.

The most pervasive set of challenges arises from the movement of people, ideas, money, goods, and disease. International communications weaken a state's control over its own people (Addis 2004). More people are on the move, which reduces loyalty to the state. Economics, not coercive power or legal authority, can become the primary source of identity. Commerce is boundary-less, while the state's authority and ability to use its laws and coercive power stop at its borders and one of the most lucrative businesses of all—the $400 billion trade in illicit drugs and human smuggling—grows exponentially. Transnational criminals use weak or failed states as bases and safe havens as well as sources to fund their operations (Galeotti 1995; Stern 1999). Just when police officials in pursuit of a suspect must halt at a border, money launderers cross with ease and transfer millions of dollars all over the globe instantaneously. As the state weakens economically, so does any real threat to use its coercive power and its system of the rule of law to coerce other states to follow its pattern. Instead, chimerical wars on drugs are launched at the same time as anti-terrorist wars unleash new sources for those same illicit drugs. Many of these challenges are reinforcing and produce contradictory behaviour. Countries that provide legal protection to refugees in flight from persecution also interdict refugees and prevent them from arriving on their shores. The threats to sovereign states themselves heighten the debate over the conception of sovereignty. Accordingly, the sovereignty of states unwilling or unable to fulfil certain basic standards of human rights may be jeopardized, while their actions (for example, in generating refugees) may threaten the security of other states (Adelman 2008; Chesterman 2001; Chesterman et al. 2005; Loescher 1992; Newman and van Selm 2004). These challenges have an impact on public authority by influencing the structure of governance in terms of internal state structures, and at the regional and international levels (Grande and Pauly 2005).

Of course, the transnational trade in paper—loans, currencies, and ever more complex derivatives—is even more lucrative and potentially even more damaging. No war on global financial manipulation has yet been launched to match that on terror or drugs. This is likely because the futility of such wars on activities and substances rather than campaigns to recognize and reduce risks, catch the relevant criminals, and protect the victims. However, it more likely to be because the perpetrators are too like the "us" represented by leaders of western governments to be defined as "other" for the launch of a new war. This is despite the fact that the creators and traders in paper are more remote from, more alien to, and seen as less deserving of support by the majority of those they lead.

Erosion or Reconception?

The concept of sovereignty is the primary tenet of international law and international relations and a mainstay in historical writing and political theory. It is central to any understanding how nation-states are distinct from, yet part of, a region and a world composed of sovereign states. Yet this concept is an amalgam of conflicting and confusing interpretations even in the history of international law (Benton 2002). Although the strong version of state sovereignty associated with the Treaty of Westphalia has rarely been a reality for the majority of states, some fear that this dominant conception of state sovereignty is being so eroded by a range of forces that it is coming to an end. Historically, conceptions of sovereignty operate according to the specific contextual circumstances of the time and fluctuate according to a variety of domestic and external forces: "lawmakers improvised syncretic models shaped by circumstances and principles they derived from particular interpretations of their own histories" (Adelman 2006, 365; see also Bayly 2003; Chesterman et al. 2005).

Accordingly, it is a mistake to talk about the erosion of sovereignty (Camilleri and Falk 1992; Giddens 2000; Omae 1990; Strange 1996). The "Re-conceiving Sovereignty" project places the current challenges in a historical and conceptual context and considers how sovereignty might be re-envisioned for the twenty-first century. This approach is overdue and of great practical importance. Governments are jealous of the sovereignty of the states they govern and resist responding creatively to challenges. They frequently use Westphalian concepts to insist that compliance with international norms is voluntary to avoid collective action on common problems. The international community must consider the extent to which sovereignty should either be bolstered against these challenges or modified to deal with them. The ability of international law and international relations as well as political and philosophical theory to respond to the reality of change has been limited. Tackling the issues of conception, historical dynamics, international law, and international relations in the context of rich textual comparative case studies (without using hard and soft variables and patterns of co-variation given the limited number of cases) is more likely to produce genuine results than ardent defences of one conception or another (Ragin 1987).

"It is time to … examine, analyze, reconceive the concept [of sovereignty], cut it down to size, break out its normative content, repackage it, perhaps even rename it" (Henkin 1993). Although views differ on whether an entirely new model or only some revisions are required, a new methodology is long overdue (Bilder 1994; Linklater 1998). Positivists cannot accommodate instances of humanitarian intervention that have broad support as morally justified exceptions to the non-intervention norm (Independent International Commission on Kosovo 2000). Ignoring the disparate views of UN member states, the policy-oriented jurisprudence school risks legitimizing the unilateral use of force by the most powerful in contravention of the UN Charter, based on a view of universal values and the requirements of justice (McDougal et al. 1967; Wiessner and Willard 1999). So scholars simply talk past one another, pushing their respective univocal notions of sovereignty.

From Government through Sovereign States to Governance through Integrity Systems

Strong sovereign states involved an internal sovereign power that claimed the sole right to make laws within their territory and the sole right to represent it externally—each backed by the claim to the monopoly of legitimate violence through which it could enforce its will throughout that territory. While that claim was either a matter of theory or definition and states were not the "only game in town," they were certainly the principal game in town containing the most powerful institutions with the widest reach. The study of government was the central concern of that group who studied a largely undifferentiated field that gave rise to law, political science, economics, and legal/social philosophy. Even with the Feuerbachian reversal, the study of government was how a people exercised control over what was now their government. The principal concern was how a sovereign people could ensure, as far as possible, that the power that was conferred on government to be used for their benefit really was devoted to serving them rather than oppressing them.[6] The answers suggested involved:

- embracing constitutionalism;
- respecting civil and political rights—especially freedom of speech, association, and assembly, and a vigorously free press:
- entrenching a strong division between judicial and legislative/executive power and a division of varying strength and substance between the legislature and the executive.

In addition, there were several institutions that did not fit easily within the tripartite separation of powers such as ombudsmen and auditors general.

---

6   That is to ensure that the Feuerbachian shift really was irreversible.

Of course, the sovereign state was never the only game in town. Some of the other pre-Westphalian institutions remained important in Europe, such as churches and universities. Some withered (like military bands and feudal ties) and others were transformed as guilds became professions and unions and armed collections of merchants like the British and Dutch East India companies gave way to joint stock companies.[7] In recognition of the importance of these other institutions, the governance of these bodies was studied for the same purpose—to ensure that these institutions served the community rather than use their power to extract benefits for themselves. Indeed, it could be said that institutions are created to concentrate power, people, and resources because it is believed that more can be achieved collectively than can be achieved individually.[8] The essential governance problem is that the concentration of power, people, and resources can be used by institutional leaders for other purposes (and hence, according a common definition, corruptly).[9] While it is not true that all power corrupts, there is no doubt that the concentration of power creates the risk of abuse and that anyone designing or redesigning such institutions who fails to take that fact into account is grossly negligent.

This problem emerges during scandals involving the abuse of power by states, corporations, religious institutions, unions, professions, and the armed forces— sometimes independently and sometimes simultaneously when corrupt business executives team up with corrupt officials. The scandals in the 1980s led to a new approach to dealing with the above problem. First, the problem is not just one of preventing government corruption (something that could be easily achieved by getting rid of government). The point is to try to ensure that institutions are clear about the purposes for which they seek power and are structured to ensure, as far as possible, that their powers are used for those purposes rather than diverted into other (corrupt) uses. Second, the way to achieve this end is not simply through democracy, the tripartite separation of powers or an independent commission against corruption. What is needed is an "integrity system" in which several institutions, agencies, laws, and codes simultaneously seek to promote integrity (the use of entrusted powers for publicly justified and democratically endorsed ends) and reduce the likelihood that those powers are abused. The concept of an integrity system can be applied to a corporation, a nation-state, or a larger global set of institutions—such as those designed to preserve financial integrity or to provide health outcomes. As is the case in many countries, the integrity system may be weak and in much need of enhancement and even redesign. However, it is a useful approach that recognizes the fact that many institutions other than sovereign states are involved in generating the major global problems facing the

---

7   The use of violence by the British and Dutch East India companies in pursuit of profit would make the much maligned "Private Military Companies" blush.

8   See Sampford (1991, 2010a) and various works in between.

9   Transparency International defines corruption as "the abuse of entrusted power for private gain."

world and that must be involved in the solution. This fact is as true of health as it is in finance and climate change.

One of the main challenges to sovereignty is the fact that sovereign states are only part of the problem and part of the solution. This does not mean that they ought to be ignored, but that they should be considered key parts of national and global integrity systems by which ends are articulated and implemented.

Health Governance

Various "health rights" are recognized in international instruments such as the 1948 Universal Declaration of Human Rights (article 12: "Everyone has the right to a standard of living adequate for the health and well-being of himself and of his family"), the preamble to the constitution of World Health Organization (WHO), the 1966 International Covenant in Economic, Social, and Cultural Rights (article 28: "right of everyone to the enjoyment of the highest attainable standard of physical and mental health" and the "provision for the reduction of … infant mortality and for the healthy development of the child; the improvement of all aspects of environmental and industrial hygiene; the prevention, treatment and control of epidemic, endemic, occupational and other diseases; the creation of conditions which would assure to all medical service and medical attention in the event of sickness") (UN 1948; UN Office of the High Commission for Human Rights 1966). Two of the eight Millennium Development Goals (MDGs) relate to health (HIV/AIDS and child health).

The 1948 declaration and the 1966 covenant were signed at a time when it was assumed that the way in which such rights would be achieved would be in and through strong sovereign states. This could be seen as part of a "UN project" in which all communities would be part of strong sovereign states and each sovereign state would be a respecter and deliverer of human rights. International agencies such as WHO would assist states to do so. Some states actually wrote the right to health into their constitutions (such as Indonesia), although those that did so were among the least likely to have the capacity to do so and those that were most effective in delivering health rights did so through legislation and some of the institutions of the "welfare state" or a mixture of provision and insurance (as in Australia). As is recognized in the MDGs, the realization of health rights will not be through sovereign states alone but by a mixture of sovereign states, regional governments, global institutions, bilateral arrangements, professions, corporations, not-for-profits, regulators, and ethical standard setters. The integrity systems approach might be particularly useful in considering how these may interact. The goal of improving global health outcomes becomes the key goal whose pursuit constitutes the criterion for integrity. Diverting resources concentrated for that purpose is a particularly ugly form of corruption.

Only one issue within global health governance will be addressed here without any effort to offer either a solution or an integrity system that would deliver that solution. However, this discussion should illustrate the themes addressed above and the rise and decline of the role of the sovereign state and its claim to control all that passes within the territory it claims to control.

The Training and Movement of Health Professionals

The medical profession is one of the oldest and is almost certainly the most respected.[10] It predates the sovereign state by at least two millennia and will long outlive sovereign states. In pre-Westphalian Europe it was certainly a cosmopolitan profession in which physicians trained in one institution could practise anywhere. Indeed, those trained in the Islamic world (first in the Middle East and later in Moorish Spain) were particularly prized, as Arabic medical texts incorporated the work of Greek, Roman, Persian, and Indian traditions. The first school of medicine in medieval Europe was in Salerno, established around a century before the University of Bologna and based on Arabic learning. Other medical schools followed, but the largest source of knowledge and practice of medicine lay in some of the hospitals established by religious orders (the term was not initially limited to places to care for the sick). Because medical schools and hospitals were, or were affiliated to, religious institutions and generally staffed by those in religious orders, a division emerged between physicians and barber-surgeons by the thirteenth century because of a papal decree and the 1215 Lateran Council decision that priests could not practise surgery because it involved the shedding of blood. This left the way open to the rise of barber-surgeons and their guild. This too was a highly cosmopolitan profession, where entry depended on education according to the standards and precepts of the guild, which issued licences to practise rather than depending on the edicts of sovereigns or the state-based regulatory agencies that are now familiar. Of course, the guilds would often have charters or even legislative backing (as was the case when, in 1540 under Henry VIII of England, the barbers' and surgeons' guilds were united into the Company of Barber-Surgeons).

The rise of the sovereign state had a profound effect on other cosmopolitan professions—an effect that is slowly being reversed (especially in the professions of law and arms; see Sampford 2010b). This was initially less pronounced in medical education. However, from the mid nineteenth century national or sub-

---

10 Whether it has deserved such respect for much of its history is uncertain. Western doctors probably killed more patients than they cured until they started washing their hands, using anaesthetics, sterilizing their equipment, and realizing that sick people needed their blood. The author has frequently asked doctors, in a teasing manner, when the profession finally emerged into positive territory and could confidently claim that it had, at last, saved more than it had killed. Some epidemiologists have not been offended and have suggested some time in the last 20 years of the nineteenth century. Over the last century, complaints have tended to concentrate on venality rather than incompetence.

national governments took on the licensing of institutions that trained doctors and their practice. While nurses were initially trained in hospitals, they too were professionalized and both educators and practitioners were licensed by national or sub-national governments.

The essential transferability of medical (as opposed to legal) skills and freer movement of peoples meant that many practitioners sought to move. However, as licensing was now a state-based matter, foreign qualifications were not always recognized. Australian, Canadian, and English qualifications were generally recognized by each other, yet those countries did not recognize Indian qualifications.

However, the rising cost of both medical training and health care, and the fact that the rising healthcare costs were driven largely by the number of doctors, led some jurisdictions such as Australia to limit access to medical education. This opened up demand for foreign-trained doctors and nurses who were increasingly recruited from the countries of the global South, who had previously been unwelcome. There were concerns about training, accreditation, and language skills. Some of those concerns were dramatically realized when an Indian trained doctor (Jayant Patel), whose permission to practise in the United States had been restricted, became head of surgery at the Bundaberg Hospital in Queensland and was subsequently linked to 87 deaths. A commission of inquiry under Geoff Davies found that Patel's negligence caused between 13 and 17 of those deaths. Of greater concern is the fact that already inadequate health workforces of countries of the South are being denuded by the demands of the North.

With regard to nursing professionals, there is a global shortage (Buchan 2008b). Australia, like other English-speaking western countries, increasingly depends on the import of health professionals educated abroad (exceeding 6,500 nurses per year). Queensland Health estimates that it needs to recruit, retrain, and retain at least 1,500 registered nurses by 2016 to staff its expanding number of hospitals. It faces an acute problem of how to recruit overseas qualified nurses in an ethical manner.

The Philippines is the largest exporter of nurses in the world. Of all the nurses educated in the Philippines, 85 percent work outside the country (Lorenzo et al. 2007). In the past, many Philippine-educated nurses went to the United States and the United Kingdom, but the US ceased recruiting nurses from the Philippines following 9/11 and the UK now gives priority to nurses from the European Union. Therefore, a great number have been going to Canada and, to a lesser extent, Australia (frequently via two or three other countries). While the best higher education institutions and hospitals in the Philippines have high standards and train well, the general standard means that nurses are unable to pass the English language test and examinations required to register for practise in Australia. Until 2007, qualified nurses from the Philippines obtained visas to work in Australia as nursing assistants. They then spent one or two years studying and preparing for English, theory, and practical tests. This pathway for recruits was subsequently closed off by changes in immigration regulations and policy. So a new approach is required.

The potential damage that the North can do in recruiting the scarce health professionals—the so-called South–North brain drain—is now well recognized. Health professionals, particularly nurses, are migrating in larger and larger numbers (Pittman et al. 2007; Stilwell et al. 2003). This comes usually at the expense of the South, which pays for their education and training, and at the expense of their domestic health systems in lost and badly needed health human resources (Diallo 2004). Recognition of this brain-drain problem has led to the development of ethical norms and codes to guide the recruitment of health professionals (Alliance for Ethical International Recruitment Practices 2011; Australian Nursing and Midwifery Council 2007; Australian Health Workforce Advisory Committee and Australian Medical Workforce Advisory Committee 2005; Commonwealth Health Ministers 2003). These ethical guidelines are generally seen to be abstract, inadequate, unfair, and unsustainable (Buchan and McPake 2007). They are certainly not grounded and supported within any sustainable governance regime. The problem is how to recruit overseas-trained medical professionals ethically, especially as the most able and mobile will be recruited and thus lost to the healthcare systems in which they trained. Under these circumstances, the rights to health care in the South are not being delivered and indeed are being undermined by the North.

Nevertheless, solutions are possible. One economic driver is the fact that education at the highest standards costs much less in the South than in the North (possibly by as much as 10 times). It is theoretically possible to train three times as many professionals in a developing country as are needed in the North, leaving more professionals in the South, saving money for Northern countries, and leaving money to spare for the provision of health services. To achieve this one would need:

1. a recognition of the health rights of citizens of the countries of the South;
2. global educational standards for education, admission to the professions, and continuing education;
3. global standards for renewal, review, discipline, and de-licensing of health practitioners;
4. linking of the above to immigration and transfer of professionals;
5. transfers of some of the savings by Northern countries to Southern countries to ensure a win-win outcome—either in cash or in the form of expertise; and
6. active participation by WHO.

Delivering these elements cannot be achieved by any sovereign state acting alone. It requires an international integrity system for the international health workforce. In health as in security, the global financial crisis, and the potential global carbon crisis, sovereign states have a role within integrity systems (Sampford 2010a).

References

Addis, Adeno (2004). "The Thin State in Thick Globalism: Sovereignty in the Information Age." *Vanderbilt Journal of Transnational Law* 37(1): 1–107.

Adelman, Howard (ed.) (2008). *Protracted Displacement in Asia: No Place to Call Home.* Aldershot: Ashgate.

Adelman, Jeremy (2006). *Sovereignty and Revolution in the Iberian Atlantic.* Princeton, NJ: Princeton University Press.

Alliance for Ethical International Recruitment Practices (2011). "Voluntary Code of Ethical Conduct for the Recruitment of Foreign-Educated Health Professionals to the United States." April, Washington, DC. Available online: www.fairinternationalrecruitment.org/images/uploads/THE%20CODE%281%29.pdf (October 2012).

Annan, Kofi (2000a). "UN Secretary General Kofi Annan's Closing Remarks to the Ministerial." June 27, Council for a Community of Democracies, Warsaw. Available online: www.ccd21.org/pdf/annan_warsaw_closing_remarks.pdf (October 2012).

Annan, Kofi (2000b). "'We the Peoples': The Role of the United Nations in the 21st Century." United Nations, New York. Available online: www.un.org/millennium/sg/report/ (October 2012).

Appleby, Joyce (1992). *Liberalism and Republicanism in the Historical Imagination.* Cambridge, MA: Harvard University Press.

Australian Health Workforce Advisory Committee and Australian Medical Workforce Advisory Committee (2005). "A Models of Care Approach to Health Workforce Planning." Health Workforce Information Paper No. 1, March, Sydney. Available online: www.ahwo.gov.au/documents/Publications/2005/A%20models%20of%20care%20approach%20to%20health%20workforce%20planning.pdf (October 2012).

Australian Nursing and Midwifery Council (2007). "Position Statement: Ethical Recruitment of Internationally Qualified and Registered Nurses and Midwives." August, Canberra. Available online: www.anmc.org.au/userfiles/file/guidelines_and_position_statements/Ethical%20Recruitment%20of%20Internationally%20Qualified%20and%20Registered%20Nurses%20and%20Midwives.pdf (October 2012).

Bayly, C.A. (2003). *The Birth of the Modern World, 1780–1914: Global Connections and Comparisons.* Malden, MA: Blackwell Publishing.

Benton, Lauren (2002). *Law and Colonial Cultures: Legal Regimes in World History, 1400–1900.* Cambridge: Cambridge University Press.

Bilder, Richard (1994). "Perspectives on Sovereignty in the Current Context: An American Viewpoint." *Canada-United States Law Journal* 20: 9–17. Available online: ssrn.com/abstract=1551964 (October 2012).

Brand, Ronald A. (2008). "Sovereignty: The State, the Individual, and the International Legal System in the Twenty First Century." *Hastings International and Comparative Law Review* 25: 279–95. Available online: ssrn.com/ abstract=1214210 (October 2012).

Brooks, Rosa Ehrenreich (2005). "Failed States, or the State as Failure?" *University of Chicago Law Review* 72(4): 1159–96.

Buchan, James (2008). "New Opportunities: United Kingdom Recruitment of Filipino Nurses." In *The International Migration of Health Workers: A Global Health System?*, John Connell (ed.). New York: Routledge, pp. 47–61.

Buchan, James and Barbara McPake (2007). "The Impact of the Department of Health, England, Code of Practice on International Recruitment of Health Professionals." June. Available online: www.aspeninstitute.org/sites/default/ files/content/images/Impact%20of%20the%20Department%20of%20 Health%20England%20Code%20of%20Practice%20on%20International%20 Recruitment.pdf (October 2012).

Camilleri, Joseph A. and Jim Falk (1992). *End of Sovereignty? The Politics of a Shrinking and Fragmenting World*. Aldershot: Elgar.

Cárdenas, Emilio J. and María Fernanda Cañás (2002). "The Limits of Self-Determination." In *The Self-Determination of Peoples: Community, Nation, and State in an Interdependent World*, Wolfgang Danspeckgruber (ed.). Boulder, CO: Lynne Rienner Publishers, pp. 101–18.

Chesterman, Simon (2001). *Just War or Just Peace? Humanitarian Intervention and International Law*. Oxford: Oxford University Press.

Chesterman, Simon, Michael Ignatieff, and Ramesh Thakur (eds) (2005). *Making States Work: State Failure and the Crisis of Governance*. Tokyo: United Nations University Press.

Commonwealth Health Ministers (2003). "Commonwealth Code of Practice for the International Recruitment of Health Workers." May 18, Geneva. Available online: www.thecommonwealth.org/ shared_asp_files/uploadedfiles/%7B7BDD970B-53AE-441D-81DB-1B64C37E992A%7D_CommonwealthCodeofPractice.pdf (October 2012).

Cosnard, Michel (2003). "Sovereign Equality—'The *Wimbledon* Sails On.'" In *United States Hegemony and the Foundations of International Law*, Michael Byers and George Nolte (eds). Cambridge: Cambridge University Press.

Crawford, James (1979). *The Creation of States in International Law*. New York: Clarendon Press.

Diallo, Khassoum (2004). "Data on the Migration of Health-Care Workers: Sources, Uses, and Challenges." *Bulletin of the World Health Organization* 82(8): 601–7. Available online: www.who.int/bulletin/volumes/82/8/601.pdf (October 2012).

Franck, Thomas (1992). "The Emerging Right to Democratic Governance." *American Journal of International Law* 86: 46–91.

Galeotti, Mark (1995). "Cross-Border Crime in the Former Soviet Union." Boundary and Territory Briefing, vol. 1, no. 5, International Boundaries Research Unit, University of Durham.

Giddens, Anthony (2000). *The Third Way and Its Critics*. Cambridge: Polity Press.

Grande, Edgar and Louis W. Pauly (eds) (2005). *Complex Sovereignty: Reconstituting Political Authority in the Twenty-First Century*. Toronto: University of Toronto Press.

Helman, Gerald B. and Steven R. Ratner (1992–93). "Serving Failed States." *Foreign Policy* 89 (Winter): 3–20.

Henkin, Louis (1993). "The Mythology of Sovereignty." *American Society of International Law Newsletter*, March.

High-Level Panel on Threats, Challenges, and Change (2004). "A More Secure World: Our Shared Responsibility." United Nations, New York. Available online: www.un.org/secureworld/ (October 2012).

Independent International Commission on Kosovo (2000). *The Kosovo Report: Conflict, International Response, Lessons Learned*. doi: 10.1093/0199243093.001.0001. Available online: www.oxfordscholarship.com/view/10.1093/0199243093.001.0001/acprof-9780199243099 (October 2012).

International Commission on Intervention and State Sovereignty (2001). "The Responsibility to Protect: Report of the International Commission on Intervention and State Sovereignty." December. Available online: responsibilitytoprotect.org/ICISS%20Report.pdf (October 2012).

Josselin, Daphné and William Wallace (eds) (2001). *Non-State Actors in World Politics*. Houndmills: Palgrave Macmillan.

Keal, Paul (2003). *European Conquest and the Rights of Indigenous Peoples: The Moral Backwardness of International Society*. Cambridge: Cambridge University Press.

Kelsen, Hans (2005). *Pure Theory of Law*. Clark, NJ: Lawbook Exchange.

Krasner, Stephen (2003–2004). "The Hole in the Whole: Sovereignty, Shared Sovereignty, and International Law." *Michigan Journal of International Law* 25(4): 1075–101.

Krasner, Stephen (2005). "The Case for Shared Sovereignty." *Journal of Democracy* 16(1): 69–83.

Krisch, Nico (2003). "More Equal Than the Rest? Hierarchy, Equality, and US Predominance in International Law." In *United States Hegemony and the Foundations of International Law*, Michael Byers and George Nolte (eds). Cambridge: Cambridge University Press.

Larson, Brooke (2004). *Trials of National Making: Liberalism, Race, and Ethnicity in the Andes, 1810–1910*. Cambridge: Cambridge University Press.

Linklater, Andrew (1998). *The Transformation of Political Community: Ethical Foundations of the Post-Westphalian Era*. London: Polity Press.

Loescher, Gil (1992). "Refugee Movements and International Security." *Adelphi Papers* 32(268): 3–8. doi: 10.1080/05679329208449097.

Lorenzo, Fely Marilyn E., Jaime Galvez-Tan, Kriselle Icamina et al. (2007, July). "Nurse Migration from a Source Country Perspective: Philippine Country Case Study." *Health Services Research* 42(3): 1406–18. doi: 10.1111/j.1475-6773.2007.00716.x.

McCorquodale, Robert (2000). "Concepts: Self-Determination." In *Self-Determination in International Law*, Robert McCorquodale (ed.). Aldershot: Ashgate.

McDougal, Myres S., Harold D. Lasswell, and W. Michael Reisman (1967). "The World Constitutive Process of Authoritative Decision." *Faculty Scholarship Series,* Paper 675. Available online: digitalcommons.law.yale.edu/fss_papers/675/

Newman, Edward and Joanne van Selm (eds) (2004). *Refugees and Forced Displacement: International Security, Human Vulnerability, and the State.* Tokyo: United Nations University Press.

Omae, Kenichi (1990). *The Borderless World: Power and Strategy in the Interlinked Economy.* New York: HarperBusiness.

Pittman, Patricia, Amanda Folsom, Emily Bass et al. (2007). "US-Based International Nurse Recruitment: Structure and Practices of a Burgeoning Industry." Report on Year I of the Project International Recruitment of Nurses to the United States: Toward a Consensus on Ethical Standards of Practice, November. Available online: www.intlnursemigration.org/assets/pdfs/Report-on-Year-I.pdf (October 2012).

Ragin, Charles C. (1987). *The Comparative Method: Moving Beyond Qualitative and Quantitative Strategies.* Berkeley, CA: University of California Press.

Roth, Brad R. (1999). *Governmental Illegitimacy in International Law.* Oxford: Clarendon Press.

Roth, Brad R. (2004). "The Enduring Significance of State Sovereignty." *Florida Law Review* 56(12): 1017–51.

Russett, Bruce M. (1995). *Grasping the Democratic Peace: Principles for a Post-Cold War World.* Princeton, NJ: Princeton University Press.

Sampford, Charles (1989). "Coups d'États and Law." *Bulletin of the Australian Society of Legal Philosophy* 13(3): 253–86.

Sampford, Charles (1991). "Law, Institutions and the Public/Private Divide." *Federal Law Review* 20(2): 185–222.

Sampford, Charles (1999). "Sovereignty and Intervention." 19th World Congress on Philosophy of Law and Social Philosophy, 29 June, New York.

Sampford, Charles (2002). "Get New Lawyers." *Legal Ethics* 6(1): 85.

Sampford, Charles (2005). "More and More Lawyers But Still No Judges." *Legal Ethics* 8(1): 16.

Sampford, Charles (2010a). "Adam Smith's Dinner." In *The Future of Financial Regulation*, Ian MacNeil and Justin O'Brien (eds). Oxford: Hart, pp. 23–40.

Sampford, Charles (2010b). "Legal Ethics in a Post-Westphalian World: Building the International Rule of Law and Other Tasks." In *Reaffirming Legal Ethics: Taking Stock and New Ideas*, Kieran Tranter, Francesca Bartlett, Lillian Corbin et al. (eds). London: Routledge.

Slaughter, Anne-Marie (2004). "Sovereignty and Power in a Networked World Order." *Stanford Journal of International Law* 40(7): 283–387.

Slaughter, Anne-Marie (2005). "Security, Solidarity, and Sovereignty: The Grand Themes of UN Reform." *American Journal of International Law* 99(7): 619–31.

Stern, Jessica (1999). *The Ultimate Terrorists*. Cambridge, MA: Harvard University Press.

Stilwell, Barbara, Khassoum Diallo, Pascal Zurn et al. (2003). "Developing Evidence-Based Ethical Policies on the Migration of Health Workers: Conceptual and Practical Challenges." *Human Resources for Health* 1(8). doi: 10.1186/1478-4491-1-8. Available online: www.human-resources-health. com/content/1/1/8 (October 2012).

Strange, Susan (1996). *The Retreat of the State: The Diffusion of Power in the World Economy*. Cambridge: Cambridge University Press.

Tilly, Charles (1990). *Coercion, Capital, and European States, AD 990–1990*. Cambridge, MA: Blackwell.

United Nations (1948). "Universal Declaration of Human Rights." Available online: www.un.org/en/documents/udhr (October 2012).

United Nations Office of the High Commission for Human Rights (1966). "International Covenant on Economic, Social, and Cultural Rights." Available online: www2.ohchr.org/english/law/cescr.htm (October 2012).

Wiessner, Siegfried and Andrew R. Willard (1999). "Policy-Oriented Jurisprudence and Human Rights Abuses in Internal Conflict: Toward a World Public Order of Human Dignity." *American Journal of International Law* 93(2): 316–34.

Yannis, Alexandros (2002). "The Concept of Suspended Sovereignty in International Law and Its Implications in International Politics." *European Journal of International Law* 13(5): 1037–52.

PART III
The African Health Problem

Chapter 3

Globalization and Health Systems in Sub-Saharan Africa: A Labour Market Perspective

Rudi Robinson

Improving and maintaining health depend on the production and delivery of health care. In turn, the production and delivery of health care depend on health systems, and health systems depend on the capacity of the healthcare workforce to function. It follows, then, that healthcare systems with sufficient human resources are critical in producing and delivering health care and, consequently, in reducing poverty and spurring economic growth in poor countries. Health care is defined here as the prevention, treatment, and management of illness, the preservation and promotion of health through the production and delivery of medical goods, services, and information of a diagnostic, preventive, curative, and palliative nature to all those who need them, when and where needed. The organized provision of such services constitutes a healthcare system.

The crucial role of health systems makes the healthcare workforce its single most important asset (Homedes and Ugalde 2005; World Health Organization [WHO] 2000). Finance, infrastructure, technology, information, policy, and commodities are important inputs in the production and delivery of health care; but it is the healthcare workforce that gives health systems the technical, management, and institutional capacity to combine all these inputs consistently and to effectively absorb new inputs, scale up proven interventions, and ensure that health systems function to achieve healthcare outcomes. Moreover, health worker–population densities are strongly correlated with indicators of overall positive healthcare outcomes such as maternal, child, and infant survival rates (WHO 2006). As well, healthcare interventions are rooted in population health knowledge, which health workers are uniquely endowed with. Consequently, healthcare labour markets that balance the quantity, quality, mix, and placement of skills with the demand for those skills are central to the capacity of health systems and the way they function to achieve healthcare outcomes at all levels of society.

Problèmatique

Globalization is the foremost driver of change in the world today, with consequences both beneficial and contradictory, for all sectors of an economy. The health sector—a sector that has been traditionally closed, non-commercial in nature, and nationally focused—is one such sector in which globalization has driven change with beneficial and contradictory consequences for health systems, particularly in poor countries. These consequences are mediated through trade and healthcare labour market channels (Chanda 2002; Wibulpolprasert et al. 2004; Woodward 2003). The trade effects are transmitted to the health system through the cross-border delivery of services (e.g. electronic delivery of health shipment of cheap generic drugs, diagnosis), consumption of health services (e.g. patients travelling abroad to obtain advanced health care), and commercial presence (e.g. foreign investment in hospitals, clinics, diagnostic centres, nursing homes). Health services are also traded internationally via the cross-border movement of health professionals. Movement is both temporary and permanent from South to North, North to South, and South to South. Permanent movements are mainly from poor countries in the South to rich countries in the North and are driven by relatively better employment opportunities and working conditions in the healthcare labour markets. These developments have facilitated the international integration of healthcare labour markets and transformed migration into a global labour allocation mechanism, which has different implications for health systems in both poor and rich countries.

Greater integration of healthcare markets is one outcome of increasingly globalized health services. On the one hand, the global integration of healthcare labour markets provides rich countries with access to ready-made pools of health professionals in poor countries to meet their own supply shortages. On the other hand, while globalization of health services is expected to produce health gains for poor countries through resource flows, the integration of healthcare labour markets has increased the international mobility of their health professionals, further aggravating supply–demand imbalances in the workforce in those poor countries. The movement of health professionals from poor to rich countries is not a new phenomenon. High-level health experts from poor countries have always been internationally mobile. What is new, however, is the emergence of an international healthcare labour market providing increased opportunities for a growing number of health professionals from poor countries to seek international mobility in response to "pull" factors on the demand side and "push" factors on the supply side. This type of international labour mobility is here to stay and will increase as health services become even more globalized (WHO 2003).

This chapter focuses on the internationalization of healthcare markets and the consequences for health systems in sub-Saharan African countries. Although the internationalization of healthcare labour markets presents challenges to health systems in all developing countries, sub-Saharan Africa faces the greatest challenges. According to the World Heath Organization (2006), of the 57 countries worldwide where health worker densities are well below the absolute minimum of 2.3 per 10,000, 36 are in sub-Saharan Africa.[1] These countries would need to increase (not lose) their healthcare workforce numbers by 140 percent in order to equip their health systems with the capacity to place the right numbers of health workers in the right places to achieve enough coverage in the delivery of essential healthcare services (Anyangwe and Mtonga 2007; WHO 2006).

This chapter considers the global labour market for physicians and nurses—healthcare professionals who are the main focus of the ongoing policy discussion on globalization and healthcare labour markets. Three main questions are addressed: What are the structure and dynamics of international labour markets for physicians and nurses? Has the international mobility of sub-Saharan African physicians and nurses weakened or eroded the human resource capacity of healthcare system in its countries? What are the costs and benefits associated with the increasingly globalized labour market for health professionals?

The Structure of the International Labour Markets for Healthcare Professionals

Demand Side

The composition of the stocks of foreign-born and -trained professionals in the healthcare workforce of developed countries has changed over the past few decades. In 2004, foreign-born and -trained physicians made up between 23 percent and 28 percent of the workforce in the United States, the United Kingdom, Canada, and Australia (Mullan 2005). Of these, 40 percent in Australia and 75 percent in the UK came from low- and middle-income countries (see Table 3.1). In 2000, in the UK, US, Canada, France, Australia, Portugal, Spain, and Belgium—all members of the Organisation for Economic Co-operation and Development (OECD)—there were approximately 63,500 physicians and 69,000 nurses who had been born and trained in Africa (Clemens and Pettersson 2007). Of this total, approximately 35,000 (55 percent) physicians and 53,000 (76 percent) nurses were born and trained in sub-Saharan Africa.[2]

---

1   In comparison, health worker population density in North America is 25 per 1,000 and in Europe 19 per 1,000.

2   According to the Center for Global Development these eight countries alone—which are all members of the Organisation for Economic Co-operation and Development (OECD)—account for 94.2 percent of all African-born university graduates residing in all OECD members in 2000 (Clemens and Pettersson 2007). They therefore constitute a

Table 3.1   **Characteristics of international medical graduates trained in low- and middle-income countries in Canada, United Kingdom, United States, and Australia, 2004**

Country	Physicians per 100,000 population	# of IMGs	% of IMGs	% of IMGs from low- and middle-income countries	% of IMGs from United Kingdom, United States, and Australia
Canada	220	15,701	23.1	43.4	22.3
United Kingdom	231	39,266	28.3	75.2	2.5
United States	293	208,733	25.0	60.2	6.5
Australia	271	14,346	26.5	40.0	33.5

Note: IMG = international medical graduate.
Source: Adapted from Mullan (2005).

An important structural feature of the market is the number of countries that offer the greatest employment draw for health professionals from sub-Saharan Africa. The above-mentioned stocks of physicians and nurses in the eight OECD destination countries were heavily concentrated in the UK and US (see Table 3.2) (Clemens and Pettersson 2007). Together, these two destinations combined commanded 60 percent and 75 percent of the flows of physicians and nurses from sub-Saharan Africa respectively into developed countries' healthcare labour markets.

The dominance of the UK and US in the international labour market is not limited to health professionals from sub-Saharan Africa; it is global in scope (Hagopian et al. 2004; Mensah et al. 2005; Mullan 2005). Undoubtedly, this market dominance is due to the economic and career opportunity structures in the destinations (e.g. large health systems, financial resources, expenditure on research and development and infrastructure, medical education infrastructure, science and technology infrastructure, and accomplishments in medical science), their growing need for English-speaking health professionals, as well as the manner in which they actively promote international recruitment of health professionals (Aiken et al. 2004; Bach 2006; Clemens and Pettersson 2007).

highly representative sample of the most important destinations for physicians born in sub-Saharan African.

Table 3.2   Proportion of physicians and nurses trained in sub-Saharan Africa in the top nine destinations, 2000

Destination	Physicians	Rank	Nurses	Rank
United Kingdom	36.4	1	38.2	1
United States	23.3	2	36.7	2
France	11.5	3	8.1	3
Portugal	10.5	4	5.6	4
Canada	7.6	5	3.2	6
Australia	4.4	6	3.2	7
South Africa	3.9	7	0.4	8
Belgium	1.9	8	4.3	5
Spain	0.5	9	0.3	9
Total	100.0		100.0	

Source: Adapted from Clemens and Pettersson (2007).

The relative proportions of sub-Saharan African physicians and nurses in France, Portugal, and Canada suggest that these countries' healthcare labour markets are second-tier choices for physicians and nurses migrating from the region. South Africa, Australia, Belgium, and Spain complete the list of favoured destinations for internationally mobile sub-Saharan African physicians and nurses. Other factors that explain destination choices are historical, cultural, and language links; the presence of active migrant networks; and the ease or difficulty in obtaining professional recognition of medical education and training acquired in the source country or obtaining a license to practise in a particular OECD destination.

Supply Side

On the side of the source country, a handful of sub-Saharan African countries supplies the majority of health professionals to rich countries. According to the Center for Global Development, in 2000 the largest sub-Saharan African suppliers of physicians to the UK were South Africa (3,509), Kenya (2,733), Nigeria (1,997), and Uganda (1,136) (Clemens and Pettersson 2007). Together these four countries accounted for 9,375 or 70 percent of the stock of sub-Saharan African-trained and -born physicians in the UK healthcare workforce. In terms of nurses, Mauritius (4,042), Nigeria (3,415), South Africa (2,884), Zimbabwe (2,834), Ghana, (2,381) and Kenya (1,336) were the UK's largest sub-Saharan African suppliers, accounting for 16,892 or 83 percent of the stock of nurses from sub-Saharan Africa. The structural pattern that emerges is that the international market for nurses between the UK and sub-Saharan Africa is not only more active than for physicians but also more active between some sub-Saharan African countries and the UK than others.

A similar structural pattern emerges for the international markets for physicians and nurses between the US and sub-Saharan Africa (Clemens and Pettersson 2007). In 2000, the largest sources of physicians from the region were Nigeria (2,510), South Africa (1,950), Kenya (865), and Ghana (850), which supplied a total of 6,175 or 72 percent of the total stock of physicians from sub-Saharan Africa in the US healthcare labour market. Nigeria (8,954), Ghana (2,101), Ethiopia (888), South Africa (877), Liberia (773), Kenya (765), and Sierra Leone (747) supplied the largest numbers of nurses to the US workforce in 2000, totalling 15,054 or 77 percent of the stock of sub-Saharan African nurses.

The structural patterns of the supply of physicians and nurses from sub-Saharan Africa to Canada and France differ from those of either the UK or the US, with higher flows of nurses than of physicians (Clemens and Pettersson 2007). In 2000, South Africa, Tanzania, Kenya, Uganda, Nigeria, and Mauritius accounted for 84 percent of the stock of sub-Saharan African physicians in Canada, whereas Ghana, South Africa, Tanzania, Nigeria, and Kenya together accounted for 64 percent of the stock of sub-Saharan African nurses. In France in the same year, Madagascar, Senegal, Republic of Congo, Cameroon, Mauritius, Côte d'Ivoire, Benin, Togo, Democratic Republic of the Congo, and Mali accounted for 83 percent of the physicians from sub-Saharan Africa, and Madagascar, Senegal, Republic of Congo, Cameroon, Côte d'Ivoire, Mali, and Democratic Republic of Congo accounted for 72 percent of the sub-Saharan African nurses.

The general picture is thus that healthcare markets in the UK and the US import a higher proportion of nurses than physicians from sub-Saharan Africa to meet their human resource needs. In contrast, healthcare labour markets in Canada and France import a higher proportion of physicians than nurses from sub-Saharan African countries. In 2000, compared to the UK, the US had a higher proportion of sub-Saharan African nurses and a lower proportion of sub-Saharan African physicians. This suggests differential impacts of these destinations' policies on immigration and workforce integration in sub-Saharan African countries. More sub-Saharan African nurses than physicians migrate to the US possibly because it is easier for them to integrate into the US health system than into the UK's. The same could be said for the higher number of physicians than nurses who migrate to the UK.

Country-specific differences exist, however. Ghanaian-trained physicians find it easier to integrate into the US healthcare labour market than in the UK, whereas Ghanaian-trained nurses find it easier to integrate into the UK healthcare labour market than in the US (Quartey et al. 2008).

Medical and nursing schools constitute another dimension of the supply-side structure of the international markets for physicians and nurses. The medical schools most often cited in surveys as producing the highest number of physicians who migrated to OECD countries include the universities of Witwatersrand, Pretoria, Cape Town (South Africa); the universities of Ibadan, Lagos, Nigeria, Benin, Ife (Nigeria); the University of Ghana, Kwame Nkruma University, Kwame Nkrumah University of Science and Technology (Ghana), and Addis

Ababa University (Ethiopia) (Hagopian et al. 2004). Nearly 80 percent of the sub-Saharan African–trained physicians practising in the US graduated from only 10 of these medical schools. In Ghana, 50 percent of every graduating class from the country's three medical schools emigrated in their second year; cumulatively, 80 percent emigrated by the fifth year after graduation (Quartey et al. 2008).

The Dynamics of the Healthcare Labour Market

Interaction between Demand and Supply

For any receiving country, the demand for foreign healthcare professionals can be defined as some measure of the number of these professionals from the source country that the receiving country is willing to accept. For any source country, the supply of healthcare professionals can be defined as some measure of the number of these professionals who wish to migrate temporarily or permanently. The interaction between receiving country demand and sending country supply will determine the level of immigration of healthcare professionals at any time. The dynamics of the international labour market for immigrant physicians and nurses revolves around the interaction between the receiving country's demand for immigrant physicians and nurses, the source country's supply, and the various mechanisms (e.g. immigration regulation and policy, recruitment, social networks) through which the source country's supply interacts with the receiving country's demand (Vujicic et al. 2004).[3]

The Demand for Migrant Physicians and Nurses

A receiving country's demand for immigrant physicians and nurses is based on needs and driven by demand (Stilwell et al. 2003). It is derived from the actual and potential growth in demand for the type of healthcare services that physicians and nurses are trained to provide. The receiving country's derived demand over and above its current domestic stocks is reflected in factors such as absolute shortages of physicians and nurses, geographical misdistribution of the existing stocks, changing demographic trends, changing patient/consumer needs and expectations, and above-average wait times for medical care (Canadian Institute for Health Information 2007). This has particularly been the case in most OECD countries since the 1990s (Simoens and Hurst 2006). After a period of retrenchment in medical education investments in the first half of the 1990s predicated on the assumption of an oversupply of physicians, healthcare workforce planners in OECD countries are now confronted with the challenge of physician demand outstripping supply. In the US, for example, the physician shortfall has been

---

3   These definitions make no assumptions about whether the forces of supply and demand for health workers operate freely in the international healthcare labour market.

estimated to be 75,000 and could rise as high as 200,000 by 2020 (Rockey 2006; Talbott 2007). Registered nurses comprise the single largest occupation group in health care. Nursing shortfalls in the UK and US were predicted to be 53,000 and 275,000 nurses respectively in 2010 and 78,000 in Canada in 2011 (Aiken et al. 2004). This situation is related to expected growth in the elderly population, the aging healthcare workforce, the feminization of the physician workforce, the reluctance of medical students to choose specialties and locations where they are most needed, new practice patterns (e.g. balancing of work and family life, lifestyle goals), and difficulties in recruiting physicians to practice in rural areas (Dumont et al. 2008; Simoens and Hurst 2006; WHO 2003).

The Supply of Migrant Physicians and Nurses

In an increasingly globalized healthcare labour market, domestic and international factors converge to influence physicians and nurses in poor countries to seek international mobility. The literature describes these as push and pull factors (see, for example, Awases et al. 2004; Bach 2006; Clark et al. 2006; McCoy et al. 2008; Pillay and Mahlati 2008; Vujicic et al. 2004; WHO 2003). Push factors in a source country include low pay and working conditions, and broad management and governance factors that encourage health professionals to seek employment in a receiving country. Pull factors include higher pay, more career opportunities, and better working conditions that encourage health professionals to migrate to the receiving country. In the individual's decision-making model, push factors tend to place low market valuation on the human capital assets of the health professional, whereas pull factors tend to place a market premium on them.

Mechanisms that Mediate Demand and Supply

Several OECD countries (e.g. the UK, the US, and Canada) either actively or passively recruit physicians and nurses from developing countries. For these countries, recruiting, clinical re-training, licensing, and employing physicians and nurses from poor countries are more cost-effective strategies for workforce management than domestic investments in medical education and training. One advantage is that increasing the number of healthcare professionals from developing countries offers a quick fix to supply shortages because it provides policy scope for expanding the human resource capacity of the health system quickly without the full resource costs implied in the "grow your own option" (Buchan 2006; Dovlo and Martineau 2004). Second, overseas recruitment provides policy scope to improve the distribution of healthcare professionals in rural, remote, and other underserved areas, particularly in family medicine (Dumont et al. 2008; Kondro 2006). A third advantage is that importing physicians and nurses from poor countries provides OECD countries with a least-cost approach to maintaining and improving their dense health worker population compared to the countries from which they recruit these professionals.

International recruitment is carried out by employers, government-affiliated or independent recruitment agencies using either active or passive strategies, or a combination of both. In the UK, the National Health Service (NHS) has among the most active recruitment programs of any OECD country. Its method for overseas recruitment for physicians follows an individualized and targeted approach. The Department of Health coordinates physician recruitment activities and supports them with several initiatives and entry routes (Buchan and Dovlo 2004; Buchan and O'May 1999). For nurses, however, the NHS uses agencies to recruit groups of 10, 20, 50, or more nurses at a time from one country (Buchan and Dovlo 2004). The UK was the first country to adopt a code of practice for overseas recruitment of health professionals.

Passive recruitment may take place in different ways. Individual physicians or nurses may apply acting on information obtained through professional networks or friends already employed in the developed country. Health professionals may obtain actionable employment information through formal institutional channels such as a private agency or government department. One example of the latter approach is the practice by organizations in some OECD countries of advertising using websites, medical journals, and magazines frequently accessed in developing countries. Another example is the use of immigration policy criteria in OECD countries (e.g. Canada and the US) to appeal to the best and brightest physicians and nurses from poor countries. While it can be argued that these approaches merely make information available to individuals to help them make their own decisions, they blur the distinction between active and passive recruitment strategies (Labonté, Packer, and Klassen 2006).

Challenges for the Capacity and Quality of Health Systems in Sub-Saharan Africa

Globalization has direct consequences for health systems in poor countries thanks to the global marketplace for health professionals. On the one hand, the globalization of healthcare labour markets has significantly expanded overseas economic and career opportunities for health professionals from poor countries. These professionals have the right to take advantage of these opportunities to better themselves and their families. On the other hand, the resulting expansion of global labour mobility has exacerbated shortages and mal-distribution of health professionals in poor countries. This, in turn, has significantly weakened the human resource capacity of health systems in those countries to deliver healthcare services equitably. The outcome is undermining the right to health of populations in poor countries (Bueno de Mesquita and Gordon 2005; Mensah et al. 2005; Ogilvie et al. 2007; WHO 2004b). To what extent has the international mobility of sub-Saharan African physicians and nurses weakened the human resource capacity of healthcare systems in that region?

The Impact of the International Mobility of Physicians and Nurses

No single statistic can adequately capture the consequences of the international mobility of healthcare workers for health systems in poor countries. However, the emigration rate, a concept and measurement developed by Frederic Docquier and Abdeslam Marfouk (2004) and Fitzhugh Mullan (2005), is one statistical approach. Docquier and Marfouk use the emigration rate to measure the scale and intensity of the skilled workers in order to assess the economic impact of emigration on developing countries. Mullan (2005), along with Michael Clemens and Gunilla Pettersson (2007), uses it to estimate the fraction of immigrant health professionals from a source country practising in a receiving country.

The emigration rate incorporates properties that are useful for analysing whether international mobility has eroded the human resource capacity of healthcare systems. First, it measures the proportion of a source country's total healthcare workforce working abroad relative to the proportion remaining at home. Second, for any source country, the emigration rate is a tool for evaluating the scale and severity of the human resource impacts of health worker migration on health systems (Docquier and Marfouk 2004). An emigration rate of 10 percent or higher indicates the scale and severity of the impacts on the human resource capacity of health systems in poor countries (Adams Jr. 2003). The emigration rate for a particular country thus provides information on the scale and intensity of the health professionals' brain drain, or of the fraction of the healthcare workforce working outside that country, while also providing information on the capacity level of the healthcare professional workforce remaining at home to service the health system.

As might be expected, the proportion of the health workforce working overseas in relation to the proportion remaining at home to service the health system varies considerably across sub-Saharan African countries and within sub-regions. Physician workforce emigration rates vary from a low of 8.7 percent in Niger, a country with a small physician workforce and one medical school (listed in the International Medical Education Directory published by the Foundation for Advancement of International Medical Education and Research [FAIMER]) to a high of 75.4 percent in Mozambique, a country with a marginally larger physician workforce but only one FAIMER-listed medical school (see Table 3.3). There is also considerable variation in emigration rates between these two extremes. Nigeria (a country with 18 FAIMER-listed medical schools) and South Africa (with at least 10 FAIMER-listed medical schools) had the two largest physician workforces in 2000: 35,741 and 34,914, respectively. But South Africa's emigration rate was 21.1 percent compared to Nigeria's 13.6 percent. In contrast, Gambia (which does not have a FAIMER-listed medical school) and Liberia (which boasts only one such school) have the smallest physician workforces—86 and 199 respectively—but both have very high physician emigration rates: 53.5 percent and 63.3 percent respectively.

Table 3.3   Physicians at home versus abroad, emigration rates, and domestic workforce capacity in selected sub-Saharan African countries, 2000

Country	Practising at home (1)	Practising abroad (2)	Emigration rate (%) 2/(1+2) × 100	Capacity level of workforce at home (%)
Angola	881	2,102	70.5	29.6
Benin	405	224	35.6	64.4
Botswana	530	68	11.4	88.6
Burkina Faso	314	78	19.9	80.1
Cape Verde	202	211	51.1	48.9
Côte d'Ivoire	1,763	284	13.9	86.1
Democratic Republic of Congo	5,647	552	8.9	91.1
Gambia	40	46	53.5	46.5
Ghana	1,294	1,639	55.9	44.1
Guinea	898	115	11.4	88.6
Guinea Bissau	103	251	70.9	29.1
Kenya	3,855	3,975	50.8	49.2
Lesotho	114	57	33.3	66.7
Liberia	73	126	63.3	36.7
Madagascar	1,428	920	39.2	60.08
Malawi	200	293	59.4	40.6
Mali	529	157	22.9	77.1
Mauritius	960	822	46.1	53.9
Mozambique	435	1,334	75.4	24.6
Namibia	466	382	45.0	55.0
Niger	386	37	8.7	91.3
Nigeria	30,885	4,856	13.6	86.4
Senegal	640	678	51.4	48.6
Seychelles	120	50	29.4	70.6
Sierra Leone	338	249	42.4	57.6
South Africa	27,551	7,363	21.1	78.9
Swaziland	133	53	28.5	71.5
Tanzania	1,264	1,356	51.8	48.2
Togo	265	180	40.4	59.6
Uganda	2,429	1,837	43.1	56.9
Zambia	670	883	56.9	43.1
Zimbabwe	1,530	1,602	51.1	48.9
All Africa	280,808	64,941	18.8	81.2
All Sub-Sahara Africa	96,405	36,679	27.5	72.5

Note: Based upon emigration rates for physicians born and trained in sub-Saharan Africa and employed in Australia, Belgium, Canada, France, Portugal, South Africa, Spain, United Kingdom, and United States.
Source: Based on Clemens and Pettersson (2007).

The emigration rates for nurses also vary considerably across sub-Saharan African countries and within sub-regions. They range from a very low of 2.2 percent in Botswana to the astonishingly high of 81.4 in Liberia (see Table 3.4). However, 12 of the countries listed in Table 3.4 had nurse workforce emigration rates below 10 percent in 2000, 6 marginally above the 10 percent threshold, and 14 significantly above the 10 percent threshold. The general picture that emerges is that the scale, intensity, and pervasiveness of cost pressures in human resources imposed by the international mobility of nurses on sub-Saharan African health systems are lower than the cost pressures from the international mobility of physicians. The 2,000 nurse workforce remaining at home was more than four times the size of the physician workforce remaining at home (414,605 versus 96,405). One possible reason is that the larger the domestic healthcare workforce, the lower the scale, intensity, and severity of migration-induced cost pressures on health human resources.

Healthcare Workforce Capacity and the Functions of Health Systems

The performance of health systems "centres on three main goals: improving health; enhancing responsiveness to the expectations of the population; and assuring fairness in the level and distribution of financial contributions" (WHO 2002a). Each system functions in relation to the key system functions of financing, provision of healthcare services, resource generation, and stewardship. The capacity of a health system to organize its key functions, perform its tasks, and achieve its main goals depends on the ability of the health workforce to function in "ways that are responsive, fair and efficient to achieve the best health outcomes possible, given available resources and circumstances" (WHO 2007a). That is, "there are sufficient staff, fairly distributed; they are competent, responsive and productive." The emigration rate is also a useful tool for assessing the impact of international mobility on the capacity of the healthcare workforce in relation to the capacity of health systems to deliver on their goals.

There is a very strong correlation between the emigration rates of physicians and nurses and the capacity of the domestic healthcare workforce to enable the health system to perform its tasks and achieve its goals (see figures 3.1 and 3.2). The higher the emigration rate is, the lower the capacity of the healthcare workforce at home, and the more fragile the health system becomes in delivering on its goals. The impact of the erosion of human resources as a result of international mobility is likely to be felt most severely in rural and underserved communities in most sub-Saharan African countries, where the need for health systems to deliver on their goals is the greatest.

Table 3.4   Nurses at home versus abroad, emigration rates, and domestic workforce capacity in selected sub-Saharan African countries, 2000

Country	Practising at home (1)	Practising abroad (2)	Emigration rate (%) 2/(1+2) × 100	Capacity level of workforce at home (%)
Angola	13,155	1,841	12.3	87.7
Benin	1,315	187	12.5	87.5
Botswana	3,556	80	2.2	97.8
Burkina Faso	3,097	76	2.4	97.6
Cape Verde	355	244	40.7	59.3
Côte d'Ivoire	7,233	509	6.6	93.4
Democratic Republic of Congo	16,969	2,288	11.9	88.1
Gambia	144	282	66.2	33.8
Ghana	14,972	4,766	24.1	75.9
Guinea	3,847	267	6.5	93.5
Guinea Bissau	799	262	24.7	75.3
Kenya	26,267	2,372	8.3	91.7
Lesotho	1,266	36	2.8	97.2
Liberia	185	807	81.4	18.6
Madagascar	3,088	1,171	27.5	72.5
Malawi	1,871	377	16.8	83.2
Mali	1,501	265	15.0	85.0
Mauritius	2,629	4,531	63.3	36.7
Mozambique	3,664	853	18.9	81.1
Namibia	2,654	152	5.4	94.6
Niger	2,668	66	2.4	97.6
Nigeria	94,747	12,579	11.7	88.3
Senegal	1,887	695	26.9	73.1
Seychelles	422	175	29.3	70.7
Sierra Leone	1,524	1,457	48.9	51.1
South Africa	90,986	4,844	5.1	94.9
Swaziland	3,345	96	2.8	97.2
Tanzania	26,023	953	3.5	96.5
Togo	782	186	19.2	80.8
Uganda	9,851	1,122	10.2	89.8
Zambia	10,987	1,110	9.2	90.08
Zimbabwe	11,640	3,723	24.2	75.8
All Africa	758,698	69,589	8.4	91.5
All Sub-Saharan Africa	414,605	53,365	11.4	88.6

Source: Based on Clemens and Pettersson (2007).

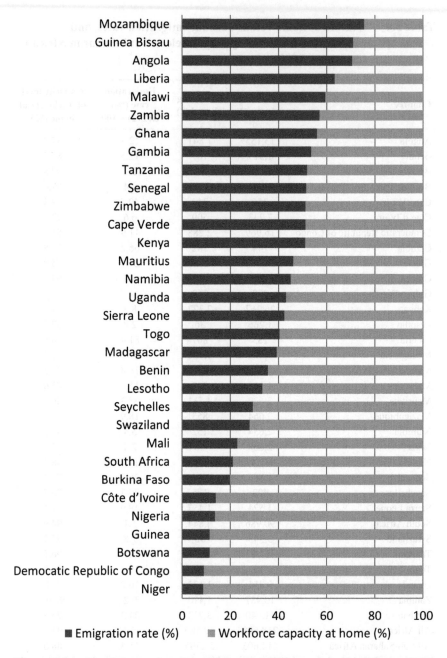

Figure 3.1   Physician emigration rate and workforce capacity at home, 2000

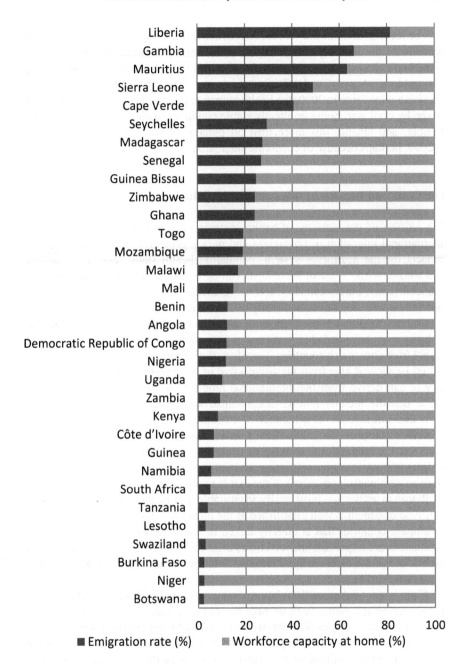

Figure 3.2   Nurse emigration rate and workforce capacity at home, 2000

The level of such migration-related erosion varies from country to country and depends on the intensity of the impact of the multiple forces that influence the individual's decision to seek international mobility. In countries such as Liberia, Mozambique, Angola, and Liberia, which lost more than 60 percent of their physician workforce in 2000, the health human resources are eroded by migration driven by civil war. Some politically stable countries, such as Malawi, Tanzania, Zambia, and Ghana, lost more than 50 percent of their physician workforce in 2000, perhaps because of economic stagnation.

The Costs and Benefits of International Mobility

The erosion of the capacity of health systems in poor countries as a result of international migration of physicians and nurses generates a wide range of cost impacts for the healthcare system, population health status, and the economy as a whole. While some of these costs can be easily identified and quantified in financial terms, others cannot. Table 3.5 presents some of the cost impacts and indicates where they fall both directly and indirectly.

One of the direct consequences of globalization is that falling international mobility costs have ended migration as a permanent one-way flow of intellectual capital from poor to rich countries. Therefore, the information presented in Table 3.5 should be viewed also from the perspective of the benefits that source countries may or can derive from the international mobility of their health professionals. These benefits include remittances, medical knowledge exchange, transfer of skills and information, and transfer of standards of practice from rich to poor, as well as the provision of medical products, trade, and investments. Properly managed, the international mobility of health professionals can strengthen health systems in poor countries, offsetting some of the costs associated with the exit of these professionals, particularly if the exit is permanent.

Remittances are the most easily identifiable and quantifiable of the benefits. This type of benefit is well established as the most important source of finance for developing countries that is directly linked to international migration. Recorded remittances are important financial flows after foreign investment, and more than double foreign aid received by developing countries (United Nations Development Programme 2011).

There is some debate on the relation of remittances to health system development in poor countries. Some analysts take the negative view that since remittances are personal flows channelled directly into households for consumption purposes, they "do very little to offset the public health investment losses incurred by source countries upon the emigration of health care professionals" (Labonté, Packer, and Klassen 2006; see also Stilwell et al. 2003).

Others take the view that at the household and community level of the health system, remittances have a positive impact in ways that those who study migration outside that context would not recognize. Erica Usher (2005) has argued that

Table 3.5   Direct and indirect costs of health professional migration to sub-Saharan Africa

Cost	Health system	Population health status	Economy as a whole
Opportunity costs of medical educational investment	•	•	•
Fiscal loss from foregone tax revenues	•	•	•
Economic loss from foregone income	•	•	•
Suboptimal physician-patient ratio	•	•	•
Suboptimal nurse-patient ratio	•	•	•
Replacement costs (family physician)	•	•	•
Replacement costs (specialist physician)	•	•	•
Replacement costs (general nurse)	•	•	•
Replacement costs (specialist)	•	•	•
Sharp rise in wages, salaries, etc.	•	–	•
Medical research capacity constraints	•	•	•
Education and training capacity constraints	•	•	•
Reduction in collaborative advantage	•	•	•
Reduction in network advantage	•	•	•
Lives lost due to non-emergency care	•	•	•
Lives lost due to lack of specialist care	•	•	•
Incapacity to maximize health funding	•	•	•
Incapacity to develop new programs	•	•	•
Incapacity for medical innovations	•	•	•
Imperfect substitutability of staff	•	•	•
Expatriate personnel costs	•	–	–
Longer average working hours	•	•	•
Deepening healthcare inequities	•	•	•
Decrease quality of health care	–	•	•
Increases in morbidity and mortality	–	•	•
Impairment of supervisory capacity	•	•	•
Impairment of managerial capacity	•	•	•
Increase in poverty and inequality	–	•	•
Out-of-country health costs	–	•	•
Closure of clinics and hospital wards	•	•	•
Implicit income redistribution	–	•	•
Lower labour market productivity	–	–	•

Source: Awases, Gbary, Nyoni et al. (2004), Chikanda (2004, 2005), Forcier, Simoens, and Giuffrida (2004), Labonté and Packer (2006), Martineau, Drecker, and Bundred (2002), Mejia and Pizurki (2005), Meyer (2001), Ntuli (2003), and Stilwell, Diallo, Zurn et al. (2003).

remittances in the hands of the poor families function essentially as a health safety net and in some cases are also used to finance community projects such as hospitals and clinics. In a study of the relationship between US migration, remittances, and health care in Mexican households, Reanne Frank (2008) found that remittances are used as a form of health insurance, providing access to health care for individuals who would otherwise be shut out of the Mexican health system due to poverty. In their study of the relationship between migration and child health in Mexican households, Nicole Hildebrant and David McKenzie (2005) found that migration positively affects child health through income effects, because increased flows of remittances allow recipient households to purchase more medical care or health-improving goods, and health knowledge facilitates the transfer of health information from migrants to family members, which, in turn, improves the efficiency of household health. In their study of low birthweight among infants of migrant and non-migrant households in Mexico, Reanne Frank and Robert Hummer (2002) found evidence that in receiving households, remittance flows protect children from the risk of low birthweight. These household-level research findings support the argument that remittances can play a positive role in reducing the effects of the constraints imposed by the international mobility of physicians and nurses on health systems in poor countries.

Conclusion

A well-functioning health system is both the backbone of a country's population health and a social determinant of global public health. Healthcare workforce is essential to the health system. The global integration of healthcare labour markets has expanded economic and career opportunities for more and more sub-Saharan African health professionals seeking international mobility. However, the international mobility of physicians and nurses weakens the human resource capacity of health systems in sub-Saharan African countries. The emigration rates among physicians and nurses can be used to evaluate the impact of the international mobility of health professionals from sub-Saharan African countries on the capacity of their health systems. On this measure, the majority of sub-Saharan African countries are those with very high rates of physician and nurse international mobility, and are consequently countries with weaker health system capacity. That weakened capacity manifests itself in a wide range of direct and indirect costs for the health system, population health, and the economy as a whole.

The global integration of healthcare labour markets has generated costs as well as benefits for sub-Saharan African countries. Therefore, the reduction in human resource capacity of health systems in sub-Saharan African countries that can be attributed to the international mobility of their physicians and nurses should also be looked at from this perspective. It is impractical in terms of both human rights and political terms to prevent health professionals from emigrating to pursue their income and career goals. Therefore, the best strategic option is to manage the international mobility of health professionals in a way that maximizes the benefits while minimizing the costs.

References

Adams Jr., Richard H. (2003). "International Migration, Remittances and the Brain Drain: A Study of 24 Labor Exporting Countries." World Bank, Washington, DC. go.worldbank.org/FOFTG7F4V0 (October 2012).
Aiken, Linda H., James Buchan, Julie Sochalski et al. (2004). "Trends in International Nurse Migration." *Health Affairs* 23(3): 69–77. Available online: content.healthaffairs.org/content/23/3/69.full (October 2012).
Anyangwe, Stella C. and Chipayeni Mtonga (2007). "Inequities in the Global Health Workforce: The Greatest Impediment to Health in Sub-Saharan Africa." *International Journal of Environmental Research and Health* 4(2): 93–100. Available online: www.mdpi.org/ijerph/papers/ijerph2007040002.pdf (October 2012).
Awases, Magda, Akpa R. Gbary, Jennifer Nyoni et al. (2004). "Migration of Health Professionals in Six Countries: A Synthesis Report." World Health Organization Regional Office for Africa. Available online: info.worldbank.org/etools/docs/library/206860/Migration%20study%20AFRO.pdf (October 2012).
Bach, Stephen (2006). "International Mobility of Health Professionals: Brain Drain or Brain Exchange?" United Nations University World Institute for Development Economics Research. Available online: www.wider.unu.edu/publications/working-papers/research-papers/2006/en_GB/rp2006-82/_files/78091786133112658/default/rp2006-82.pdf (October 2012).
Buchan, James (2006, 27 January). "International Recruitment of Health Professionals." *British Medical Journal.* doi: 10.1136/bmj.330.7485.210.
Buchan, James and Delanyo Dovlo (2004). "International Recruitment of Health Workers to the UK: A Report for DFID." Department for International Development Health Systems Resource Centre, London. Available online: www.equinetafrica.org/bibl/docs/BUChres310108.pdf (October 2012).
Buchan, James and Fiona O'May (1999). "Globalisation and Healthcare Labour Markets: A Case Study from the United Kingdom." *Human Resources for Health Development Journal* 3(3): 199–209. Available online: www.who.int/hrh/en/HRDJ_3_3_04.pdf (October 2012).
Bueno de Mesquita, Judith and Matt Gordon (2005). "The International Migration of Health Workers: A Human Rights Analysis." Medact, London. Available online: www.medact.org/content/Skills%20drain/Bueno%20de%20Mesquita%20and%20Gordon.pdf (October 2012).
Canadian Institute for Health Information (2007). "Health Care in Canada 2007." Ottawa. Available online: secure.cihi.ca/free_products/hcic2007_e.pdf (October 2012).

Chanda, Rupa (2002). "Trade in Health Services." *Bulletin of the World Health Organization* 80(2): 158–63. Available online: www.who.int/bulletin/archives/80(2)158.pdf (October 2012).

Chikanda, Abel (2004). "Skilled Health Professionals' Migration and Its Impact on Health Delivery in Zimbabwe." Policy and Society Working Paper No. 4, Centre on Migration, University of Oxford. Available online: hdl.handle.net/10646/48 (October 2012).

Chikanda, Abel (2005). "Nurse Migration from Zimbabwe: Analysis of Recent Trends and Impacts." *Nursing Inquiry* 12(3): 162–75.

Clark, Paul F., James B. Stewart, and Darlene A. Clark (2006). "The Globalization of the Labour Market for Health-Care Professionals." *International Labour Review* 145(1/2): 37–64.

Clemens, Michael A. and Gunilla Pettersson (2007). "A New Database of Health Professional Emigration from Africa." Working Paper No. 95, August, Center for Global Development. Available online: www.cgdev.org/files/9267_file_CGDWP95_Feb_2007.pdf (October 2012).

Docquier, Frederic and Abdeslam Marfouk (2004). "Measuring the International Mobility of Skilled Workers (1990–2000): Release 1.0." World Bank, Washington, DC. doi: 10.1596/1813-9450-3381. Available online: elibrary.worldbank.org/content/workingpaper/10.1596/1813-9450-3381 (October 2012).

Dovlo, Delanyo and Tim Martineau (2004). "A Review of the Migration of Africa's Health Professionals." JLI Working Paper 4–4, Ministry of Health, Ghana.

Dumont, Jean-Christophe, Pascal Zurn, Jody Church et al. (2008). "International Mobility of Health Professionals and Health Workforce Management in Canada: Myths and Realties." Working Paper No. 40, Organisation for Economic Co-operation and Development, Paris. Available online: www.oecd.org/canada/41590427.pdf (October 2012).

Forcier, Mélanie B., Steven Simoens, and Antonio Giuffrida (2004). "Impact, Regulation, and Health Policy Implications of Physician Migration in OECD Countries." Human Resources for Health 2(12). doi: 10.1186/1478-4491-2-12. Available online: www.human-resources-health.com/content/2/1/12 (October 2012).

Frank, Reanne (2008). "Migradollars as a Form of Health Insurance? The Relationship between U.S. Migration, Remittances, and Health Care in Mexico." Paper presented at the annual meeting of the American Sociological Association, 31 July, Boston. Available online: www.allacademic.com/meta/p242491_index.html (October 2012).

Frank, Reanne and Robert A. Hummer (2002). "The Other Side of the Paradox: The Risk of Low Birth Weight among Infants of Migrant and Nonmigrant Households within Mexico." *International Migration Review* 36(3): 746–65. doi: 10.1111/j.1747-7379.2002.tb00103.x.

Hagopian, Amy, Matthew J. Thompson, Meredith Fordyce et al. (2004). "The Migration of Physicians from Sub-Saharan Africa to the United States of America: Measures of the African Brain Drain." *Human Resources for*

Health 2(17). doi: 10.1186/1478-4491-2-17. Available online: www.human-resources-health.com/content/2/1/17 (October 2012).

Hildebrandt, Nicole and David J. McKenzie (2005). "The Effects of Migration on Child Health in Mexico." Policy Research Working Paper No. 3573, World Bank, Washington, DC. doi: 10.1596/1813-9450-3573. Available online: elibrary.worldbank.org/content/workingpaper/10.1596/1813-9450-3573 (October 2012).

Homedes, Núria and Antonio Ugalde (2005). "Human Resources: The Cinderella of Health Sector Reform in Latin America." *Human Resources for Health* 3(1). doi: 10.1186/1478-4491-3-1. Available online: www.human-resources-health.com/content/3/1/1 (October 2012).

Kondro, Wayne (2006, 21 November). "Pulse: Trends in Physician Supply." *Canadian Medical Association Journal* 175(11): 1362. doi: 10.1503/cmaj.061434.

Labonté, Ronald and Corinne Packer (2006). "Globalisation and the Health Worker Migration Crisis." Draft, Institute for Population Health, University of Ottawa, Ottawa.

Labonté, Ronald, Corinne Packer, and Nathan Klassen (2006). "Managing Health Professional Migration from Sub-Saharan Africa to Canada: A Stakeholder Inquiry into Public Options." *Human Resources for Health* 4(22). doi: 10.1186/1478-4491-4-22. Available online: www.human-resources-health.com/content/4/1/22 (October 2012).

Martineau, Tim, Karola Drecker, and Peter Bundred (2002). "Briefing Note on International Migration of Health Professionals: Levelling the Playing Field for Developing Country Health Systems." Liverpool School of Tropical Medicine, Liverpool.

McCoy, David, Sara Bennett, Sophie Witter et al. (2008). "Salaries and Incomes of Health Workers in Sub-Saharan Africa." *Lancet* 371(9613): 675–81. Available online: www.thelancet.com/journals/lancet/article/PIIS0140-6736%2808%2960306-2/abstract (October 2012).

Mejia, Alfonso and Helena Pizurki (2005). "Migration of Health Personnel." World Health Organization Regional Office for the Western Pacific, Manila.

Mensah, Kwadwo, Maureen Mackintosh, and Leroi Henry (2005). "The 'Skills Drain' of Health Professionals from the Developing World: A Framework for Policy Formulation." Medact, London. Available online: www.medact.org/content//Skills%20drain/Mensah%20et%20al.%202005.pdf (October 2012).

Meyer, Jean-Baptiste (2001). "The Brain Drain: New Aspects of the South/North Exodus." *ACP-EU Courier* 187 (July/August).

Mullan, Fitzhugh (2005). "The Metrics of the Physician Brain Drain." *New England Journal of Medicine* 353: 1810–18. Available online: www.nejm.org/doi/full/10.1056/NEJMsa050004 (October 2012).

Ntuli, Antoinette (2003). "Equity in the Distribution of Health Personnel." Equinet, Harare. Available online: www.equinetafrica.org/bibl/docs/HRHdiscussiondoc.pdf (October 2012).

Ogilvie, Linda, Judy E. Mill, Barbara Astle et al. (2007). "The Exodus of Health Professionals from Sub-Saharan Africa: Balancing Human Rights and Societal Needs in the Twenty-First Century." *Nursing Inquiry* 14(2): 114–24.

Pillay, Yogan and Percy Mahlati (2008). "Health-Worker Salaries and Incomes in Sub-Saharan Africa." *Lancet* 371(9613): 632–34. Available online: www.thelancet.com/journals/lancet/article/PIIS0140-6736%2808%2960283-4/fulltext (October 2012).

Quartey, Peter, Evelyn Kwakye, and Gifty Merdiemah (2008). "The Impact of Rich Countries' Policies on Poverty in LDCs: The Case of Migrant Nurses from Ghana." *Research Monitor* 5: 19–21. Available online: cloud2.gdnet.org/CMS/getFile.php?id=rm_issue5 (October 2012).

Rockey, Paul H. (2006). "Fixing the U.S. Physician Shortage Requires Many More Slots for Resident Physicians in Training." *Medscape General Medicine* 8(2): 52. Available online: www.ncbi.nlm.nih.gov/pmc/articles/PMC1785175/ (October 2012).

Simoens, Steven and Jeremy Hurst (2006). "The Supply of Physician Services in OECD Countries." OECD Health Working Paper No. 21, Organisation for Economic Co-operation and Development, Paris. Available online: www.oecd.org/health/healthpoliciesanddata/35987490.pdf (October 2012).

Stilwell, Barbara, Khassoum Diallo, Pascal Zurn et al. (2003). "Developing Evidence-Based Ethical Policies on the Migration of Health Workers: Conceptual and Practical Challenges." *Human Resources for Health* 1(8). doi: 10.1186/1478-4491-1-8. Available online: www.human-resources-health.com/content/1/1/8 (October 2012).

Talbott, Chris (2007). "Shortage of Doctors Affects Rural U.S." *Washington Post*, July 22. Available online: www.washingtonpost.com/wp-dyn/content/article/2007/07/21/AR2007072100432.html (October 2012).

United Nations Development Programme (2011). "Towards Human Resilience: Sustaining MDG Progress in an Age of Economic Uncertainty." United Nations, New York. Available online: www.undp.org/content/dam/undp/library/Poverty%20Reduction/Towards_SustainingMDG_Web1005.pdf (October 2012).

Usher, Erica (2005). "The Millennium Development Goals and Migration." International Organization for Migration, Geneva. Available online: www.iom.int/jahia/webdav/site/myjahiasite/shared/shared/mainsite/published_docs/serial_publications/mrs20.pdf (October 2012).

Vujicic, Marko, Pascal Zurn, Khassoum Diallo et al. (2004). "The Role of Wages in the Migration of Health Care Professionals from Developing Countries." *Human Resources for Health* 2(3). doi: 10.1186/1478-4491-2-3. Available online: www.human-resources-health.com/content/2/1/3 (October 2012).

Wibulpolprasert, Suwit, Cha-aim Pachanee, Siriwan Pitayarangsarit et al. (2004). "International Service Trade and Its Implications for Resources for Health: A Case Study of Thailand." *Human Resources for Health* 2(10). doi: 10.1186/1478-

4491-2-10. Available online: www.human-resources-health.com/content/2/1/10 (October 2012).

Woodward, David (2003). "Trading Health for Profit: The Implications of the GATS and Trade in Health Services for Health in Developing Countries." UK Partnership for Global Health. Available online: web.archive.org/web/20031201074316/ www.ukglobalhealth.org/content/Text/GATS_Woodward.pdf (October 2012).

World Health Organization (2000). "The World Health Report 2000—Health Systems: Improving Performance." World Health Organization, Geneva. Available online: www.who.int/whr/2000/en (October 2012).

World Health Organization (2002). "Human Resources for Health: Developing Policy Options for Change." Draft discussion paper, November, Geneva. Available online: www.who.int/hrh/documents/en/Developing_policy_ options.pdf (October 2012).

World Health Organization (2003). "The World Health Report 2003: Shaping the Future." World Health Organization, Geneva. Available online: www.who.int/ whr/2003/en/ (October 2012).

World Health Organization (2004). "World Report on Knowledge for Better Health: Strengthening Health Systems." World Health Organization, Geneva. Available online: www.who.int/rpc/meetings/pub1/en/ (October 2012).

World Health Organization (2006). "The World Health Report 2006: Working Together for Health." World Health Organization, Geneva. Available online: www.who.int/whr/2006/en/ (October 2012).

World Health Organization (2007). "Everybody's Business: Strengthening Health Systems to Improve Health Outcomes—WHO's Framework for Action." World Health Organization, Geneva. Available online: www.who.int/healthsystems/ strategy/everybodys_business.pdf (October 2012).

Chapter 4

Managing the Mobility of Health Professionals

Rudi Robinson

The consensus at the national, regional, and international levels is that migration of health professionals contributes significantly to the inadequate supply of health workers in sub-Saharan Africa. Sub-Saharan Africa bears 25 percent of the global disease burden and only 1.3 percent of the world's trained health workforce. The impacts of the health worker crisis on the region's health systems and the implications for progress toward the Millennium Development Goals (MDGs) have made the mobility of sub-Saharan African health professionals a priority issue in health human resource policy. This chapter focuses on the migration of physicians and nurses from sub-Saharan Africa, arguably the two most strategically important occupational groups in the health workforce and the most active participants in international mobility, and whose mobility dominates the discourse on the international migration of health workers.

The term "mobility" is used here specifically to mean the permanent migration of physicians and nurses born and trained in sub-Saharan Africa from their country of origin to a member of the Organisation for Economic Co-operation and Development (OECD) to provide healthcare services in that destination country. This migration is not the only pattern of mobility in which health professionals engage, however. There are also rural-to-urban, inter-sectoral, and inter-regional patterns. In addition there is also the mobility of healthcare workers to non-healthcare occupations. These other patterns of mobility also have consequences for health system performance and the attainment of the health MDGs, and, therefore, need to be effectively managed.

International Mobility Management

The international mobility of health workers is part of an increasingly globalized labour market and is here to stay. In general, internationally mobile sub-Saharan African health professionals gain more in net terms from their mobility, relative to staying in their country of origin. If their employment in OECD countries represents a subsidy to these countries' health systems, their destination countries also gain in net terms from their mobility. But their countries of origin may gain or lose in net terms from the return flow of resources in the form of remittances, knowledge, and skills, and even investments. This is because, as with all aspects of globalization, in net terms international migration generates economic and social gains for some countries and economic and social losses for others. For example, dynamic migrant-origin countries may gain more from their health professionals working in OECD countries, whereas the less dynamic ones may lose out, while OECD countries effectively meet their healthcare labour demands from the supply of foreign health professionals at greatly reduced supply costs. Consequently, due to differences in objective conditions both between destination and origin countries as well as among origin countries, the international mobility of health professionals may have greater net positive impacts on destination than on origin countries. However, the net positive impact may be greater in some origin countries than in others. The overall result is an unequal distribution of social and economic costs and benefits between destination and origin countries.

This chapter makes two assumptions. First, the three main stakeholders affected by the international mobility of health professionals are destination countries, origin countries, and migrant health professionals themselves. Second, as a permanent feature of contemporary globalization, the main goal is to manage the international mobility of health professionals in a manner that maximizes the social and economic benefits and reduces the negative social and economic outcomes for all three stakeholders. The chapter addresses the following three questions based upon these assumptions: What is the scale of mobility of sub-Saharan African health professionals to OECD countries, and what are the main impacts of that mobility on health systems? What are some of the key management issues? In what conceptual terms might a balanced and comprehensive approach to managing the international mobility of health professionals be formulated if the goal is to maximize the benefits of that mobility while reducing the negative impacts on the supply remaining at home?

The main underlying argument is that in an increasingly globalized healthcare labour market and given the persistent differences in income and career opportunities for health professionals that exist between developed and developing countries, stay-at-home strategies for managing the international mobility of health professionals will be ineffective. In contrast, a management approach that seeks to maximize the benefits from that mobility for the three stakeholders and minimize the negative effects is a "triple-win" solution that turns what is traditionally thought to be a zero-sum game into a non-zero-sum game. Based upon this argument, the chapter proposes co-development as an alternative approach to stay-at-home strategies for managing the international mobility of health professionals from sub-Saharan Africa to OECD countries.

The Scale, Characteristics, and Effects of the Mobility of Health Professionals

In terms of managing human resources, the strategic importance of the healthcare workforce to health system performance has sharpened the focus on the increasing international mobility of health professionals over the past decade. The healthcare workforce is perceived as the most important of the capital resource inputs to any health system, the others being physical and financial capital. It is also the most costly to develop, manage, motivate, maintain, and retain (Fritzen 2007; Kabene et al. 2006; World Health Organization [WHO] 2002a). In general, African governments spend a high percentage of their educational budgets on tertiary education, relative to the rest of the world (see Table 4.1). Given that there are more publicly funded than privately funded medical and nursing schools, government expenditures largely determine the supply of medically certified health workers in most sub-Saharan African countries (Easterly and Nyarko 2008). Consequently, the growth in the number of health professionals from sub-Saharan Africa migrating to OECD countries should become a central issue for managing the healthcare workforce.

Table 4.1   Public expenditure on education in selected sub-Saharan African countries, 2010

	Expenditure per student as % of GDP per capita: Tertiary	% of GDP	% total government expenditure
Burundi	477.4	9.2	25.1
Cameroon	28.0	3.5	17.9
Central African Republic	96.0	1.2	12.0
Chad	279.1	2.8	10.1
Ethiopia	31.0	4.7	25.4
Gambia	94.4	5.0	22.8
Ghana	171.7	5.5	24.4
Madagascar	144.8	3.2	13.4
Malawi	1,937.6	5.7	14.7
Mali	135.3	4.5	22.0
Mauritius	16.1	3.1	11.4
Niger	438.8	3.8	16.9
Rwanda	186.8	4.7	16.9
Senegal	186.9	5.6	24.0
Tanzania	873.3	6.2	18.3
Uganda	104.3	3.2	15.0

Note: GDP = gross domestic product.
Source: World Bank (2012c).

As seen in Table 4.2, the levels and rates of mobility among professionals who emigrate is much higher for physicians born and trained in sub-Saharan Africa, while the reverse is true for nurses from many sub-Saharan Africa countries.

Table 4.2   Emigration rates of physicians and nurses versus all professionals from selected sub-Saharan African countries, 2000

Sub-Saharan Africa countries	All professionals	Physicians	Nurses
Angola	25.6	70.5	12.3
Botswana	2.1	11.4	2.2
Burkina Faso	3.3	19.9	2.4
Côte d'Ivoire	7.8	13.9	6.6
Democratic Republic of Congo	7.9	8.9	11.9
Ghana	42.9	55.9	24.1
Guinea-Bissau	29.4	70.9	24.7
Kenya	26.3	50.8	8.3
Lesotho	2.4	33.3	2.8
Madagascar	36.0	39.2	27.5
Malawi	9.4	59.4	16.8
Mali	11.5	22.9	15.0
Mauritius	48.0	46.1	63.3
Mozambique	42.0	75.4	18.9
Nigeria	36.1	13.6	11.7
Namibia	3.4	45.0	5.4
Senegal	24.1	51.4	26.9
Sierra Leone	41.0	42.4	48.9
South Africa	5.4	21.1	5.1
Swaziland	5.8	28.5	2.8
Tanzania	15.8	51.8	3.5
Uganda	21.6	43.1	10.2
Zambia	10.0	56.9	9.2
Zimbabwe	7.6	51.1	24.2

Source: Adapted from Docquier and Marfouk (2004) and Clemens and Pettersson (2007).

In addition to being about service delivery and health outcomes, health systems are about broader development outcomes such as school performance and educational achievement of children as well as adults, labour force participation, attendance at work, and, consequently, labour productivity, economic growth, and poverty reduction. Therefore, the effects of the international mobility of health professionals both directly and indirectly go beyond the direct health system to growth and development in the economy as a whole. Moreover, both the net health system effects and the consequent economic impacts can be either negative or positive, and depend on factors including the stock of health professionals remaining at home and the economic and financial contribution of those abroad to health system and broader economic development in their country of origin (see also Chapter 3).

In a comparison of the effects of international mobility on the human resource capacity of health systems in selected sub-Saharan African countries, two general features stand out (see tables 3.3 and 3.4 in Chapter 3). First, among both physicians and nurses, in terms of reduced domestic capacity the impact is less dramatic for countries such as South Africa and Nigeria, with relatively large stocks of physicians and nurses remaining at home and a strong medical and nursing education infrastructure, than it is for countries with smaller stocks of physicians and nurses at home and no medical education infrastructure. For example, the 4,856 Nigerian physicians working in OECD countries in 2000 represented 13.6 percent of the physician workforce in Nigeria (Clemens and Pettersson 2007). In contrast, the 293 physicians from Malawi working in OECD countries in 2000 represented 59.4 percent of its physician workforce. Second, the international mobility of nurses seems to have less dramatic effects on the health system at home than the international mobility of physicians. Although the health system effects vary widely from country to country, whereas the international mobility of nurses reduces the supply of nurses in sub-Saharan Africa by 11.4 percent, the international mobility of physicians reduces the supply by 27.5 percent.

Like most highly skilled migrants, health professionals seek international mobility in response to economic and professional career opportunities abroad that they perceive to be better than those available at home. These opportunities arise from a convergence of the misalignment between the demand for and supply of health professionals in foreign healthcare labour markets and precarious health labour market and work environments at home. Other factors on both the demand and supply sides influence the decision to migrate and in the choice of destination, such as the liberalization of labour market access and targeted health worker recruitment policies (Cerna 2007; Newland 2004; Quartey et al. 2008). On the supply side, domestic politics, war, deteriorating economic conditions, and religious persecution are key factors.

Issues in the International Mobility of Health Professionals

Managing the international mobility of health professionals is fundamentally complex, because of the global scope and multidimensionality of the process. The multiplicity of stakeholders and actors involved in the process must be considered, as well as the multiple domains of actions, and the multiple effects and impacts of the process in both destination and origin countries. These characteristics make formulating a strategy to manage the international mobility of health professionals a formidable challenge. One approach is to develop a workable understanding of some key management issues that affect the three major stakeholders.

Economic Issues

Economic considerations alone do not drive migration flows. But economic arguments, most notably about the costs and benefits associated with these flows, dominate the debate on policy and management in terms of both demand and supply. Information and knowledge about the economic costs and benefits associated with the international mobility of health professionals remain spotty, largely qualitative, anecdotal, and confusing in some quarters and accusatory and emotional in others.

Pessimist models stress the actual and potential economic costs to origin countries while downplaying the actual and potential economic gains that may offset some of those costs (for a survey of the literature see Robinson 2007). Such costs include

- the loss of the knowledge and skills embodied in the physician or nurse;
- the loss of the financial investments in medical education and training;
- the loss of fiscal revenues from the income of those who emigrate;
- the erosion of the national capacity to care for the local population;
- reduced productivity of the health system and the economy as a whole; and
- increased opportunity costs of medical education resulting from replacement costs.

Although pessimist models concede that remittances may mitigate some of these costs, they argue that unless these resources are channelled directly into the health systems of poor countries, they offset none of the direct losses to the system resulting from the emigration of their health professionals. The obvious conclusion is that the economic impact in the country of origin is overwhelmingly negative. Supply-side policy responses arising from these models stress stay-at-home management strategies (e.g. restrictive and incentive policies designed to make international mobility more difficult or less attractive). Demand-side policy responses stress compensatory strategies (designed to make destination countries compensate origin countries for reaping the returns on their investments in their stock of internationally mobile human capital).

Optimist models, in contrast, stress that the international mobility of health professionals is driven by globalization that improves welfare globally. Everyone gains when health professionals migrate from resource-poor environments, where their productivity is low, to resource-rich environments, where their productivity is high. Destination countries benefit to the extent that the international mobility of health professionals is a response to the relative scarcity value of these professionals. Migrant health professionals benefit through the acquisition of more up-to-date and in-depth healthcare and medical knowledge, skills, experience and expertise, career advancement, and increased professional incomes. Origin countries also gain through remittances, transfers of advanced healthcare technologies (through tacit and explicit knowledge) from destination to origin countries, growth in the stock of highly skilled workforce at home (the "beneficial brain drain effect"), and, in the more dynamic countries, trade, and investments in medical tourism.

Optimist models admit, however, that the international mobility of health professionals generates welfare losses. But the welfare gains in the aggregate, they argue, offset the welfare losses. Demand-side policy responses include more liberal immigration regimes that permit the free international flow of human capital. Supply-side policy responses include institutionalization of diaspora networks as development resources and improved economic, administrative, legal, and political governance to permit brain circulation among health professionals (that is, the opposite of brain drain), their temporary return as well as the frictionless reintegration of any who wish to return permanently.

Non-economic Issues

Health equity

Commitment to health equity is one of the core principles of primary healthcare as outlined at the Alma-Ata Declaration in 1978 (International Conference on Primary Health Care 1978). The WHO Commission on Social Determinants of Health (2008) reaffirmed this principle in 2008 by concluding that reducing health inequities is an ethical imperative. Therefore, it would be a mistake to base management decisions on the international mobility of health professionals solely on the analysis of economic costs and benefits, important as they may be, when that mobility is linked to health equity and a range of other significant non-economic issues.

Equity in health implies addressing differences in health status or outcomes that are avoidable, unfair, and systematically related to social inequality and disadvantage (Gardner 2008; Johnson 2007). The argument is that international mobility compromises the capacity of health systems to deliver health care equitably in a number of ways. First, the emigration of highly skilled health professionals reduces the domestic supply of highly skilled health personnel available to provide basic health services to the poor and most marginalized, which raises the cost of providing basic healthcare and consequently aggravates income inequality. Second, such emigration diminishes the capacity of health systems to provide adequate services and coverage to the most vulnerable and marginalized population groups (WHO 2004a). Third, it diminishes the quality of care offered in public health institutions with the result of falling standards of care provided to the poor (Chikanda 2004). Fourth, emigration adversely affects distribution of health professional in rural versus urban areas and between the public and private sectors (Padarath et al. 2003).

The basic proposition of the economic argument is that in a globalizing economy, the international migration of health professionals is a mechanism for reallocating scarce human resources from economies with low labour productivity to those with high labour productivity, which benefits both sides. This argument seems admissible, given the widely acknowledged push factors that characterize low-productivity economies and the equally widely acknowledged pull factors that characterize high-productivity ones. However, sub-Saharan Africa has an estimated 750,000 health workers serving 682 million people. By comparison, the ratio is as much as 15 times higher in OECD countries. Therefore, it is useful to also examine this proposition within the framework of primary health care to develop an understanding of the other side of globalization with respect to health equity. As a general proposition, the international mobility of health professionals from poor to OECD countries could be argued to weaken health provision and the right to health in poor countries at the same time as it strengthens health provision and the right to health in OECD countries. This further widens the already growing divide in coverage and universal access to cost-effective and time-efficient quality healthcare services between rich and poor countries. This argument brings to the forefront the human rights perspective on the international mobility of health professionals from poor to OECD countries.

Human rights
Human rights are nationally and internationally guaranteed legal protection for individuals and groups against actions that interfere with their fundamental freedoms and human dignity. These rights encompass a range of civil, cultural, economic, political, and social rights and apply universally. International frameworks and instruments (e.g. Universal Declaration of Human Rights, WHO constitution) explicitly recognize that human rights, including specific health-related rights, apply to all persons including migrants, refugees, and other non-nationals (Bueno de Mesquita and Gordon 2005).

The international mobility of health professionals encompasses the human rights of three population groups: the right of health professionals to leave their country of origin to seek a better life in the destination of their choice, the right to health of the population left behind in the country of origin, and the right to health of the population in the destination country population (Ogilvie et al. 2007).[1] Policy proposals have either implicitly or explicitly accepted hierarchies among different groups based on these competing sets of human rights (Mensah et al. 2005). At one end of the spectrum are economic policy proposals that defend the right of health professionals to emigrate. At the other end are policy proposals that place higher priority on the right to health of the population left behind by the health professionals in their country of origin (Alkire and Chen 2002; Bueno de Mesquita and Gordon 2005).

---

1   It also includes labour rights and the right to nondiscrimination and equality.

Healthcare Workforce Management

Demand side: Destination countries

Most OECD countries are grappling with the challenge of chronic shortages of health professionals. This problem is a result of the deficit in the domestic supply of health professionals arising from poor planning, underinvestment in medical education, and an aging workforce. One response is targeted immigration designed to secure a supply of health professionals from low-income countries as well as from other OECD members (Gerlinger and Schmucker 2007; Girardin 2006). In 2005, for example, foreign-trained physicians comprised between 23 percent and 28 percent of the physician workforce in each of the four OECD countries that import the most health workers: the United States, the United Kingdom, Canada, and Australia (Mullan 2005). Low-income countries provided between 40 percent and 75 percent of the total overseas supply in these four countries. In Canada alone, permanent migration of doctors tripled and temporary migration increased by more than 10 percent, while permanent migration of nurses increased by almost 40 percent (Dumont et al. 2008).

Immigrant health professionals are recruited on demand and admitted to OECD countries primarily on the basis of their human capital credentials. Paradoxically, in spite of their recruitment demand and human capital credentials, upon arrival these health professionals face a lack of correspondence among the demand for their recruitment, the admission criteria for immigrating, and their integration into the destination's healthcare labour market in the occupation in which they were trained and practised before emigrating (Boyd and Schellenberg 2005). Two main factors seem to explain this non-correspondence. One is the "country of origin effect" of their prior professional education, training, and work experience, which in turn defines what Clarence Lochhead (2003) has described as the "transition penalty," a period of adjustment as immigrant health professionals establish themselves in their new country. During this period they experience underemployment and unemployment associated with their initial status as new members of another country—a status characterized by unfamiliarity with the structure and culture of the healthcare system, language skills, and work experience in the destination country. The transition penalty undermines the country's capacity to expeditiously and fully integrate health professionals born and trained in low-income countries into its health system. The second is that the demands and costs of reaccreditation constitute barriers to entering the healthcare labour market, particularly for health professionals born and trained in developing countries.[2] The purpose of accreditation demands (e.g. clinical retraining, licensing, certification, and registration) is to assure public health safety, "although it also is true that these practices are the defining characteristics of occupational internal labour markets which create

---

2 Other scholars (for example, Teelucksingh and Galabuzi 2005) have argued that racism as also a determinant of non-correspondence.

monopolies on products and/or services by controlling labour supply" (Boyd and Schellenberg 2005).[3]

Supply side: Origin countries
The economic and non-economic consequences of the international health worker mobility on sub-Saharan Africa have led to policy responses that see the emigration of physicians and nurses essentially as a human resource loss. These responses are primarily designed to counteract this loss through stay-at-home strategies to manage human resources, such as bonding or compulsory service, financial and non-financial incentives, ethical recruitment, restitution, and skills substitution.

Evaluations indicate that stay-at-home management strategies do not generally reduce the negative effects of the international mobility of health workers on supply. Bonding, perhaps the most widely used strategy in sub-Saharan Africa, has not worked well for a number of reasons, including the poor administrative efficiency of human resource management systems and inadequate coordination between the education and health sectors (Dovlo 2003). Other measures, rather than creating incentives, often encourage health workers to emigrate because salary differentials are so great and working conditions so bad that there is little reason to honour the bond (Bueno de Mesquita and Gordon 2005; Mensah et al. 2005). Although there are some success stories (particularly regarding funding by aid agencies), financial incentive schemes—another widely used strategy—often work poorly because of inadequate domestic financial sustainability when foreign aid comes to an end, bureaucratic centralization, arbitrary local decision making, and non-inclusiveness (Munga and Mbilinyi 2008). Ethical recruitment has been criticized for its ineffectiveness because it is essentially voluntary and often ignored. Restitution schemes by which destination countries compensate origin countries have been described as another form of taxation, difficult to implement, and an infringement on the right of health professionals to emigrate. Skills substitution through the use of quasi-health professionals whose qualifications would not be internationally recognized has been denounced as creating a two-tiered health workforce, one comprising unqualified health professionals—for the poor—and the other qualified health professionals—for the rich (People's Health Movement et al. 2005).

Stay-at-home strategies will not always be effective, especially given the increasing globalization of labour markets and persistent disparities in wages and opportunity. Therefore, a management approach to maximize the benefits of

---

3   Canada, however, has had some success with the Internationally Educated Health Professionals Initiatives (IEHPI) in integrating immigrant health professionals into the healthcare system. Nonetheless, some argue that because of the highly decentralized nature of its healthcare system, Canada still fails to integrate the majority of some of the very immigrants it has gone out of its way to attract. See, for example, Chicha and Charest (2008), Baldacchino, Chandrasekere, and Saunders (2007), and von Zweck (2006).

migration of these professionals and minimize its negative effects for countries of origin is necessary.

Co-development: Turning a Zero-Sum Game into a Non-Zero-Sum Game

The international community and developing countries are faced with developing a balanced and comprehensive strategy to manage the international mobility of health workers. It should be an approach that creates triple-win solutions that turn what is usually perceived to be a zero-sum game into a non-zero-sum game by linking integration and development and by creating coherence among different policy domains, partnerships, and cooperation strategies. It should create synergy between integration at destination and development at origin. The concept of co-development has come to dominate the discussion on migration policy and management within the European Union. The United Nations endorses the concept because it offers both destination and origin countries the opportunity to examine how to manage international migration effectively to respond to the labour market needs of the former while fostering the potential for brain circulation, circular migration, and the positive effects of remittances in the latter. Co-development can provide the essential building blocks of a balanced and comprehensive approach to managing the international mobility of health workers.

Co-development highlights the need to conceptualize development cooperation as a two-way process between developed and developing countries. It was only when migration became a major public policy issue in Western European countries—France especially—that the term was introduced into policy discussions on migration and development (Chou 2006). In order to conceptualize the relationship between immigrants' integration in their destination country and development in their country of origin, the concept was redefined as a way to combine immigration and development so that migration flows benefit both (Nair 1997). This is a consensual relationship between two countries that ensures that migration flows to the destination country do not entail a net loss for the country of origin.

Co-development Propositions

Integration at destination and development at origin

The international mobility of health professionals revolves around two interrelated axes: integration at destination and development at origin. Consequently, there is a direct correlation between the integration of health professionals in destination countries and their contribution to development in their country of origin. Migrant health professionals who are well integrated in their destination country acquire the capacities and capabilities to engage in the development of their country of origin effectively.

Migrants as agents of development
Migrant professionals are transnational actors and partners in development for both destination and origin countries. They are both an addition to the destination country's workforce and an extension of the workforce of their country of origin. In the case of health professionals, they are simultaneously connected to two health systems and two health environments, making them stakeholders in both simultaneously. They are thus uniquely positioned to bring about policy changes in the health sector of their country of origin. This is because they have the advantage of being able to draw on the human, financial, and social capital acquired by their destination country and combine it with their knowledge of their country of origin and their networks there. They can contribute to formulating and implementing health-sector development projects at home (Østergaard-Nielsen 2005). Migrant health professionals whose human rights are respected are best equipped to contribute to the economies of both their destination and origin countries.

Balancing stakeholders' interests
In contrast to stay-at-home and other coercive policies, co-development takes into consideration the needs of all three stakeholders in international migration— the destination country, the country of origin, and the migrant—and attempts to balance the distribution of risks and benefits to create win-win outcomes for all three (Chou 2006; Laganà 2007).

Brain gain, not brain drain
Practising migrant health professionals are an active part of the brain drain for one country that represents a successful part of the brain gain of another. International mobility from poor to rich countries should not necessarily be considered a loss of skills, ideas, and innovation, or of investments in education or tax revenues, but as a potential gain for increasing the medical skills, knowledge, and other human resources available for developing health systems in their countries of origin.

Breaking the monopoly over integration policy
The concept of economic self-interest dominates immigration and integration policies in the destination countries. This makes human resource managers in some of these countries unaware of the links between the international mobility of health professionals and country-of-origin development; if they are not unaware, they may ignore the linkages. Co-development breaks the predominance of the domestic agenda that is so influential in policy making for immigration and labour market integration in some OECD countries, particularly in North America.

Enhancing policy/institutional coherence and promoting partnerships
The dynamics of the international mobility of health professionals are shaped in multiple policy domains involving complex relationships between multiple stakeholders and actors, including the migrant professionals in countries of destination and origin. Effective management of this process and the relationships

involved requires coherence in action, cooperation, and partnerships involving all the stakeholders and actors, including governments, international organizations, civil society, employers, and migrant and diaspora associations.

Dimensions of a Co-development Approach

Integration at Destination

Traditional approaches: Inclusion and exclusion
Migration and development policy regimes that emphasize stay-at-home strategies fail to address the issue of integration of health professionals in their destination country. Successful integration of these professionals is the critical determinant of their capacity to engage in development in their country of origin and, therefore, a critical component of a comprehensive mobility management system. Consequently, effective integration of health professionals is an important component of co-development.

It is useful to differentiate the co-development approach to integration from traditional approaches. Assimilation, multiculturalism, and even segregation are the traditional policy approaches in destination countries. Each reflects these countries' normative vision of themselves that underpins immigration and integration policies in the context of managing ethnic and racial diversity. One version of assimilation, for example, envisions a mono-cultural society in which immigrants are expected to reject the cultural values and practices of their country of origin and acquire the cultural values and practices of their destination society. On the other hand, multiculturalism, which is derided by mono-culturalists, sees integration as a "two-way" process of accommodation by immigrants and the native born and emphasizes coexistence among different cultural values and practices within society.

Labour market assimilation—the economic version of immigrant integration—is the dominant paradigm that provides the theoretical and empirical underpinnings for current immigrant integration policy and practice, particularly in North America. According to this paradigm integration is the process by which immigrants become "more like" the native born along some specified dimension, usually annual real wage convergence (Grant 1999).[4] The key assumption here is that successful integration of new immigrants is directly related to their labour market characteristics, mainly their human capital endowments. Immigrants whose labour market performance fails the annual real-wage convergence "test"

---

4   Immigrant economic assimilation models provide the theoretical and empirical underpinnings for the domestic agenda on immigration and integration in other OECD countries as well. In North America, these models take an inward-looking approach to immigration by emphasizing only the demand side of the international migration equation in the integration process while ignoring the supply side.

are those with labour market characteristics acquired in their country of origin but not internationally transferable or those who lack human capital specific to the destination country. Labour market assimilation models are exclusionary in their integration policy orientation, because the "best" immigrants, and by extension prospective citizens, are perceived to be those whose skills enhance the destination country's competitive position in the global economy (Abu-Laban and Gabriel 2002). Conversely, the so-called best are countered with those less desired because, by virtue of their labour market handicaps arising from a "country of origin" effect, they are deemed not to contribute to the destination country's economy.

Shifting the integration paradigm from exclusion to inclusion
Integration is a multi-dimensional "two-way process involving adaptation of migrants to the host community and the host community welcoming and adapting to migrants, respecting basic values and institutions that are part of the common societal framework [of the host society] while promoting policies of cohesion in diversity" (International Organization for Migration [IOM] 2005a). This definition suggests that while the integrative power of labour market assimilation opens channels to other dimensions of integration, it is still only one dimension and it is not independent of the social, political, legal, cultural, and civic dimensions of the overall integration process. The European Commission conceives of integration as a "balancing of rights and obligations" at all levels of the host society between immigrants and citizens of their destination countries. It defines integration as "a two-way process based on mutual rights and corresponding obligations of legally resident third country nationals and the host society which provides for full participation of the immigrant" (Commission of the European Communities 2003). This definition targets all dimensions of integration for policy attention: economic, social and political rights, cultural and religious diversity rights, and citizenship and participation rights.

    Co-development incorporates this holistic approach to immigrant integration. First, it emphasizes that effective integration provides immigrants with the capacity to contribute simultaneously and successfully to economic, social, cultural, political, and civic life in their new society and to economic development in their country of origin. Second, it emphasizes the protection of the human rights of all immigrants, including the right to secure and hold employment commensurate with their qualifications and experience. Third, with an emphasis on human rights and capacity building, co-development decisively shifts the integration paradigm from exclusion to inclusion. It thus makes the capacity of immigrants to contribute to their destination society and to their country of origin contingent on their early inclusion into existing economic and non-economic opportunity structures, which are available to the native born on the same terms and conditions irrespective of ethnicity, religion, or social class. Fourth, co-development recognizes that integration is an inclusive process that "flows from the totality of policies and practices that allow societies to close the gap between the rights, status, and opportunities (including their descendants) [whether] in the realm of education, the job market, housing, health, social services, or political and civic participation" (Dayton-Johnson et al. 2007).

Development at Origin

The diaspora option

The second objective of co-development is to promote diaspora-led initiatives aimed at helping to achieve sustainable development in the migrants' country of origin and engaging them as partners for development there. The diaspora option emerged in the late 1990s in response to limitations of stay-at-home and return management strategies. In contrast to these traditional strategies, it represents a fundamentally different management response to the international mobility of health professionals from poor to OECD countries. The diaspora option has two main features (Brown 2000; Tettey 2003).

First, highly-trained diaspora professionals, in the health sector or elsewhere, thrive in an environment that enables them to develop their technical capabilities further through collaborative activities, knowledge sharing, research, and strategic alliances. Industrialized countries tend to provide such an environment, thereby adding value to the human capital of diaspora professionals' in ways that their country of origin could not.

Diaspora transnational networks are today the most important development resource associated with international migration. These networks link highly skilled immigrants and their country-of-origin counterparts, allowing for the transfer of their expertise, skills, knowledge, and information to the country of origin, without necessarily the migrants returning home permanently. In this way, the country of origin gains access to the human and financial resources of its diaspora community, as well as to the knowledge networks in which the professional participates in the destination country (Brown 2000; Newland 2003).

Co-development incorporates the diaspora option as a human resource tool for managing the international mobility of health professionals. However, several associations of health professionals from the African diaspora actively engage in developing health systems at home.[5] This is accomplished through four main channels: community-based health projects, healthcare workforce training through virtual return programs, financial and in-kind remittances, research, information technology, and telemedicine (Robinson 2009). So there is nothing really new about the diaspora option. What is new from the co-development perspective is

---

5   Examples: the Association of South African Nurses in the United Kingdom, the South African Network of Skills Abroad, the Medical Association of Nigerian Specialists and General Practitioners, the Ethiopian North American Health Professionals Association, the Oxford House Somali Diaspora Association in the UK, Kenyan Diaspora Health Professionals in the United States, and the Association of Somali Health Professionals in the Nordic Countries.

the radical shift from the brain-drain concept to the brain-circulation concept of managing the international mobility of health professionals, and this is as a direct result of diasporas' initiatives themselves.

Institutionalization of the diaspora option
The feasibility of the diaspora option depends on a number of underlying challenges in some African countries. First, the domestic economic, political, or social circumstances that motivated health professionals to seek international mobility in the first place may not change enough to motivate some of them with the capacity to engage or re-engage in the healthcare system of their country of origin, even though they may have the desire to do so. Second, the diaspora option depends on collaboration and partnerships between diaspora health professionals and their counterparts at home. Such collaborative efforts may be challenged by a plethora of factors from a variety of political, social, academic, professional, inter-generational, infrastructural, economic, and cultural platforms (Teferra 2000; Tettey 2003). Recognizing these challenges, some African countries (e.g. Ghana, Nigeria, Kenya, Ethiopia) have moved beyond rhetoric and devised new laws, policies, and tools to "institutionalize" their diaspora communities so that they can tap into their network resources for development at home (IOM 2005b). The African Union's African Diaspora Health Initiative is a sector-based approach in furtherance of this institutionalization process.

Healthcare Workforce Management

The co-development concept as originally formulated by Nair does not explicitly address the issue of human resource management. Nevertheless, the deficits in health human resource management—on both the demand and supply sides—produce healthcare labour market outcomes, which in combination pull and push health professionals to seek international mobility. Therefore, workforce planning and management are also essential components of effective management of the mobility of health professionals. The discussion that follows here, however, will be limited primarily to the supply side of this issue.

The World Health Organization's Health Workforce Advocacy Initiative defines the goal of healthcare workforce planning as ensuring that all persons, particularly the poor and most vulnerable, in all places, have access to a skilled health worker who is equipped, motivated, and supported. Furthermore, planning should be oriented toward achieving national health goals, commitments, and obligations, including the health-related MDGs and universal access to HIV/AIDS treatment, care, and support.[6] A healthcare workforce in which the demand for and supply of

---

6   The Health Workforce Advocacy Initiative is the civil society-led network of the Global Health Workforce Alliance. See www.healthworkforce.info.

health services are balanced with regard to function, geography, and facilities is a strategic imperative if the health system is to deliver on its planning goals.

Strategic management of the healthcare workforce has been defined as a "coordinated, systematic policy approach to the workforce based on a clear situation analysis and linked to at least a medium-term vision of desired outcomes for the health sector as a whole" (Fritzen 2007). The literature on health human resources has identified workforce imbalances, the changing nature of the healthcare workforce, and workforce capacity and performance motivation as key challenges of strategic management (Fritzen 2007; Zurn et al. 2002).

- Workforce imbalances include:
  - supply/demand imbalances arising from the rate of new entrants relative to the rate of exits;
  - profession/specialty imbalances across and within health professions;
  - geographic imbalances relating to the "urban bias" in the distribution of health personnel, which reinforces disparities in access to health services and in health outcomes;
  - institutional imbalances relating to differences in health workforce endowments among health system facilities and between the urban and rural sectors of the health system;
  - public/private imbalances associated with differences in human resources allocation between the public and private healthcare systems; and
  - linkages of overall health sector plan, health workforce strategy, and national development policy.
- Changes that the healthcare workforce is undergoing include:
  - the growing increase of migration among health professionals;
  - retirements, deaths, and the departure of professionals to other occupations;
  - redesigned mix of skills and roles, which break down professional boundaries; and
  - new forms of interdisciplinary team work and clinical governance.
- Workforce capacity and performance motivation include:
  - investment in medical education;
  - training and career development;
  - improvement in working conditions;
  - recruitment, retention, and promotion;
  - compensation and other incentive structures;
  - workforce redesign; and
  - leadership, policy, governance, transparency, and accountability.

The High-Level Forum on the Health MDGs proposed a number of specific measures and instruments to address these challenges. However, while all health systems may have the same goals, they operate in specific contexts and under different constraints. For example, deploying a cadre of trained auxiliary health workers may work well in one country, but health services consumer attitudes could make doing so problematic measure to implement. These challenges make a global approach to workforce planning and management unsatisfactory. Tailoring the proposed measures and instruments to specific contexts might be more effective.

Coherence of Action

The international mobility of health professionals involves institutional interaction between two sets of demand and supply side factors. The first set relates to the existence of multiple groups of stakeholders at the national, regional, international, and global levels. The second set of factors relates to the multiple policy domains (immigration, foreign, development cooperation, labour market, education and training, health, trade, and security) that migration incorporates. Migration generates costs and benefits on both the demand and supply sides at both the macro and micro levels in both the destination and origin countries. The existence of multiple policy domains implies multiple actors and multiple stakeholders with competing and sometimes conflicting interests, values, claims, and perspectives with respect to the distribution of costs and benefits. Co-development takes into consideration these contesting factors in both destination countries and countries of origin, and attempts to balance the distribution of the costs and benefits among all parties by promoting coherence of actions through cooperation and partnerships at the national, regional, and international levels.

The domestic economic and foreign policy agendas of OECD governments overwhelmingly drive policy making in the domain of international migration and development. Coherence of policy action means that in making those agendas, OECD countries should consider the interaction between their immigration and integration policies and their other domestic as well as foreign policies, and how such interaction determines the distribution of migration-related benefits and costs among the three main affected stakeholders. It follows that coherence of action implies that OECD countries, in pursuing their domestic and foreign policy objectives and strategies in immigration, integration, health, trade, labour market, security, foreign aid, and so on, should avoid negative consequences and spillovers that would adversely affect the health and development prospects of origin countries (OECD 2003).

Co-development recognizes that coherence of action is difficult to achieve because of competing and conflicting interests and priorities. Nevertheless, coherence is important in order to avoid conflicting policy approaches. An example of such conflicting approaches would be when an OECD country's ministry of health recruits doctors and nurses from a developing country to fill supply gaps in its own healthcare system—thus engaging in "asset stripping"— at the same time as its development cooperation ministry finances projects and programs to improve the human resource capacity of health system in that developing country. This illustrates the problem of incoherent policy making at two levels. At the development level, while the OECD development cooperation ministry's policies strengthen the human resource capacity of the developing country, the health ministry's policies weaken it. At the level of human rights, OECD countries diminish the provision of health and the right to health of the population in those developing countries while simultaneously bolstering both the provision of health and the right to health of their own populations. As another example, OECD countries continue to attract numerous health professionals away from poor countries under their skilled-migration programs while at the same time maintaining barriers to integration in the healthcare workforce. Both these examples illustrate the importance of policy coherence in order to maximize the benefits of health professionals' mobility and reduce the negative impacts on countries of origin.

To achieve coherence of policy and action, several aspects of policy coherence must be addressed (IOM 2005b; Picciotto 2004; Robinson 2007).

- *Political coherence* focuses on achieving trade-offs among different policies, among different levels of government, among different stakeholders and among different competing interests, claims, and perspectives that are an inevitable part of the politics of immigration and integration.
- *Internal policy coherence* focuses on achieving consistency among goals, objectives, modalities, and protocols between immigration and integration of health professionals in OECD healthcare systems.
- *Intra-governmental coherence* assumes that the mobility of health professionals covers a wide range of policy and program issues that fall within the competence of different government ministries and agencies and focuses on achieving consistency and synergy among the activities of the different ministries and agencies in order that actions in one domain do not undermine those in another.
- *Intergovernmental coherence* assumes that intra-governmental coherence is a necessary but insufficient condition for achieving consistency and synergy of actions among OECD destination countries on the one hand and, on the other, between destination and origin countries through bilateral cooperation, coordination, and consultation. Such coherence would facilitate maximizing the benefits and reducing the costs associated with the international mobility of health professionals. A good example of this is compliance with ethical recruitment codes of practice by all OECD countries to ensure that the health workforce gains reaped by a country of origin from the compliance of one OECD country are not wiped out by the non-compliance of another.
- *Coherence among governments and other stakeholders* assumes that while the international mobility of health professionals is principally the domain of sovereign states, there is also a multiplicity of non-state actors with

different interests, claims, and perspectives. Deepening cooperation and partnerships among the state and non-state actors promises better capacity to maximize gains and reduce losses associated with the international mobility of health professionals (IOM, 2005; Picciotto, 2004; Robinson, 2007).

Priority Areas for Coherence of Action

Enhanced Knowledge Base for Effective Management

Priorities for the evidence-based management of the international movement of health workers are the collection, availability, timeliness, and accessibility of statistics. There is widespread agreement on the current state of statistics available to support evidence-based policy making and management. The most frequently cited challenge is the incompleteness of data in five basic areas: quantity and quality, reliability, international non-comparability, currency, and accessibility (Bach 2006; Buchan 2008a; Diallo 2004).

This challenge continues to inhibit effective management of the international mobility of health professionals in several key areas including the following:

- measuring the flows of doctors and nurses;
- monitoring and assessing trends in the flows;
- measuring the inter-temporal effects and impacts of the flows on the human resource capacity of health systems;
- assessing the cost-effectiveness of different management strategies; and
- performing a quantitative analysis of the economic costs and benefits for origin countries.

Because the knowledge base for effective management cannot be enhanced without first enhancing the data collection infrastructure in origin countries, the International Organization for Migration (IOM) has proposed a data collection and sharing program comprising the following elements:

- establishing a national network of core institutions to handle migration data;
- mapping out existing statistical infrastructures including the types of data in demand;
- identifying the national demand for migration data at different levels;
- establishing a data-sharing and exchange mechanism among countries;
- publishing a website for the exchange of statistical information;
- holding regional workshops for countries to share or exchange best practices;

- design training models that satisfy regional and national data demands; and
- develop national projects in data collection in response to needs and priorities.

Socioeconomic Integration of Immigrant Health Professionals

In addition, the integration of immigrant health professionals into the socioeconomic fabric of their destination countries can be facilitated by:

- ensuring early access to the healthcare labour market;
- ensuring that employers utilize the multiple skills of immigrant health professionals;
- reducing the level of professional underemployment and marginalization; and
- protecting the human rights of immigrant health professionals and their families.

Involvement of Diaspora Health and Other Professionals

Engaging the diaspora, which is equally important, can be achieved in various ways, such as building the capacity of diaspora associations and migrant organizations through providing technical and financial support to strengthen the organizations and their program delivery.

In addition, diaspora associations can be mainstreamed by involving diaspora health and other professionals as equals in the policy-making processes of setting principles and priorities in their destination countries, particularly in policies and programming for integrating immigrant healthcare labour market and health sector development cooperation.

Moreover, diasporas can be more deeply engaged in development cooperation. This deepening can be achieved by developing and implementing co-development projects, particularly if those projects use diaspora health professionals to develop and deliver short- and long-term technical assistance programs to the health sector in their country of origin, promote the virtual return form of development engagement, facilitate the channelling of remittances into the health sector, and reintegrate returning healthcare professionals into the health system of their country of origin.

Conclusion

The increased mobility of health professionals—in particular, doctors and nurses from sub-Saharan Africa seeking to improve their income and career fortunes in OECD countries—is part of an increasingly globalized labour market and is here to stay. However, like all aspects of globalization, such international mobility generates costs and benefits. The costs are primarily borne by the population remaining in the country of origin and by its economy and society as a result of the reduced human resource capacity of its health system. These costs can be managed within a well-designed co-development framework that uses the diaspora option as a tool for workforce planning and management.

In terms of benefits, destination countries acquire access to a supply of health professionals at lower cost than they would have had to incur to help reduce the supply–demand gaps in their healthcare workforce. At the same time, internationally mobile health professionals from developing countries fill the supply-demand gaps in destination countries and gain more in net terms from their mobility than if they stayed at home. Origin countries, especially the more dynamic and enterprising sub-Saharan African ones, gain from the knowledge, skills, experience, expertise and money of their health professionals who have settled abroad. So the process need not be portrayed as a zero-sum game in which resources are considered fixed, in which the gain for the OECD destination countries is perceived as a loss for origin countries in sub-Saharan Africa—a portrayal that results in "stay-at-home" strategies to counter such losses.

Co-development offers an effective alternative to stay-at-home management approaches. Its approach to managing the international mobility of health professionals can result in triple-win outcomes that turn what is usually thought to be a zero-sum game into a non-zero-sum game.

However, Giulia Laganà's (2007) three caveats are important to remember. First, co-development is not a magic wand for healthcare workforce policy makers, planners, and managers in sub-Saharan Africa, who struggle with developing strategies for managing the international mobility of health workers that maximize benefits and minimize costs. It only provides a framework and tools to re-engage the diaspora health professional workforce as part of part of their healthcare workforce in the countries of origin and tap into their augmented human and financial resources to develop those health systems. Second, the co-development framework and tools provide diaspora health professionals with the opportunity to harness their augmented skills and knowledge for the benefit of their country of origin without necessarily returning home permanently. Third, co-development offers destination countries the opportunity to take a fresh look at integrating migrant health professionals in a way that more effectively increases their capacity to make a greater contribution to the country they choose to live and to the country they leave behind.

References

Abu-Laban, Yasmeen and Christina Gabriel (2002). *Selling Diversity: Immigration, Multiculturalism, Employment Equity, and Globalization*. Peterborough: Broadview Press.

Alkire, Sabina and Lincoln Chen (2002). "'Medical Exceptionalism' in International Migration: Should Doctors and Nurses Be Treated Differently?" In *Globalizing Migration Regimes: New Challenges to Transnational Cooperation*, Kristof Tamas and Joakim Palme, eds. Aldershot: Ashgate, pp. 100–117.

Bach, Stephen (2006). "International Mobility of Health Professionals: Brain Drain or Brain Exchange?," United Nations University World Institute for Development Economics Research. Available online: www.wider.unu.edu/publications/working-papers/research-papers/2006/en_GB/rp2006-82/_files/78091786133112658/default/rp2006-82.pdf (October 2012).

Baldacchino, Godfrey, Sarath Chandrasekere, and Pat Saunders (2007). "Internationally Educated Health Professions in Atlantic Canada." *Canadian Issues: Foreign Credential Recognition* (Spring): 104–7. Available online: canada.metropolis.net/pdfs/cdn_issues_CITC_spring07.pdf (October 2012).

Boyd, Monica and Grant Schellenberg (2005). "Re-accreditation Demands and Skilled Labor Flows: The Paradoxes of Professional Migration." Paper presented at the International Population Conference of the International Union for the Scientific Study of Population, 18–23 July, Tours, France. Available online: iussp2005.princeton.edu/papers/50333 (October 2012).

Brown, Mercy (2000). "Using Intellectual Diaspora to Reverse the Brain Drain: Some Useful Examples." In *Brain Drain and Capacity Building in Africa*, Sibry J.M. Tapsoba, Sabiou Kassoum, Pascal V. Houenou et al., eds, United Nations Economic Commission for Africa, pp. 92–109. Available online: idl-bnc.idrc.ca/dspace/bitstream/10625/28020/1/118149.pdf (October 2012).

Buchan, James (2008). "How Can the Migration of Health Service Professionals Be Managed So As to Reduce Any Negative Effects on Supply?," World Health Organization, Copenhagen. Available online: www.euro.who.int/__data/assets/pdf_file/0006/75453/E93414.pdf (October 2012).

Bueno de Mesquita, Judith and Matt Gordon (2005). "The International Migration of Health Workers: A Human Rights Analysis." Medact, London. Available online: www.medact.org/content/Skills%20drain/Bueno%20de%20Mesquita%20and%20Gordon.pdf (October 2012).

Cerna, Lucie (2007). "The Politics of Coalitions for High-Skilled Immigration Policies in Europe and North America." Paper presented at the Midwest Political Science Association Conference, 12 April, Chicago. Available online: www.allacademic.com/meta/p199328_index.html (October 2012).

Chicha, Marie-Thérèse and Éric Charest (2008). "L'intégration des immigrés sur le marché du travail à Montréal: Politiques et enjeux." *Choix IRPP* 14(2). Available online: www.irpp.org/fr/choices/archive/vol14no2.pdf (October 2012).

Chikanda, Abel (2004). "Skilled Health Professionals' Migration and Its Impact on Health Delivery in Zimbabwe." Policy and Society Working Paper No. 4, Centre on Migration, University of Oxford. Available online: hdl.handle.net/10646/48 (October 2012).

Chou, Meng-Hsuan (2006). "EU and the Migration-Development Nexus: What Prospects for EU-Wide Policies?" Working Paper No. 37, Centre on Migration, Policy, and Society, University of Oxford. Available online: www.compas. ox.ac.uk/fileadmin/files/Publications/working_papers/WP_2006/WP0637-Chou.pdf (October 2012).

Clemens, Michael A. and Gunilla Pettersson (2007). "A New Database of Health Professional Emigration from Africa." Working Paper No. 95, August, Center for Global Development. Available online: www.cgdev.org/files/9267_file_CGDWP95_Feb_2007.pdf (October 2012).

Commission of the European Communities (2003). "Communication from the Commission to the Council, the European Parliament, the European Economic and Social Committee, and the Committee of the Regions on Immigration, Integration, and Employment." COM (2003) 336 final, June 3, Brussels. eur-lex.europa.eu/LexUriServ/LexUriServ.do?uri=COM:2003:0336:FIN:EN:PDF (October 2012).

Commission on Social Determinants of Health (2008). *Closing the Gap in a Generation: Health Equity through Action on the Social Determinants of Health. Final Report of the Commission on Social Determinants of Health.* Geneva: World Health Organization. Available online: www.who.int/social_determinants/thecommission/finalreport/en/index.html (October 2012).

Dayton-Johnson, Jeff, Louka T. Katseli, Gregory Maniatis et al., eds (2007). *Gaining from Migration: Towards a New Mobility System.* Paris: Organisation for Economic Co-operation and Development. Available online: www. migrationpolicy.org/pubs/Gaining_from_Migration.pdf (October 2012).

Diallo, Khassoum (2004). "Data on the Migration of Health-Care Workers: Sources, Uses, and Challenges." *Bulletin of the World Health Organization* 82(8): 601–7. Available online: www.who.int/bulletin/volumes/82/8/601.pdf (October 2012).

Docquier, Frederic and Abdeslam Marfouk (2004). "Measuring the International Mobility of Skilled Workers (1990–2000): Release 1.0." World Bank, Washington, DC. doi: 10.1596/1813-9450-3381. Available online: elibrary. worldbank.org/content/workingpaper/10.1596/1813-9450-3381 (October 2012).

Dovlo, Delanyo (2003). "The Brain Drain and Retention of Health Professionals in Africa." Case study prepared for a conference on "Improving Tertiary Education in Sub-Saharan Africa: Things That Work!," 23–25 September, Accra. Available online: www.medact.org/content/health/documents/brain_drain/Dovlo%20-%20brain%20drain%20and%20retention.pdf (October 2012).

Dumont, Jean-Christophe, Pascal Zurn, Jody Church et al. (2008). "International Mobility of Health Professionals and Health Workforce Management in Canada: Myths and Realties." Working Paper No. 40, Organisation for Economic Co-operation and Development, Paris. Available online: www.oecd. org/canada/41590427.pdf (October 2012).

Easterly, William and Yaw Nyarko (2008). "Is the Brain Drain Good for Africa?" Global Working Paper 18, Brookings Institution. Available online: www. brookings.edu/research/papers/2008/03/brain-drain-easterly (October 2012).

Fritzen, Scott A. (2007). "Strategic Management of the Health Workforce in Developing Countries: What Have We Learned?" *Human Resources for Health* 5(4). doi: 10.1186/1478-4491-5-4. Available online: www.human-resources-health.com/content/5/1/4 (October 2012).

Gardner, Bob (2008). "Health Equity Discussion Paper." Toronto Central Local Health Integration Network. Available online: www.torontocentrallhin.on.ca/uploadedFiles/Home_Page/Report_and_Publications/Health%20Equity%20Discussion%20Paper%20v1.0.pdf (October 2012).

Gerlinger, Thomas and Rolf Schmucker (2007). "Transnational Migration of Health Professionals in the European Union." *Cadernos de Saúde Pública* 23(2): S184–S92. Available online: www.scielosp.org/pdf/csp/v23s2/07.pdf (October 2012).

Girardin, Brigitte (2006). "And If Immigration Benefitted Everyone?" *Les Echos*, April 12. Available online: www.ambafrance-ca.org/spip.php?article1151 (October 2012).

Grant, Mary L. (1999). "Evidence of New Immigrant Assimilation in Canada." *Canadian Journal of Economics* 32(4): 930–55. Available online: economics.ca/cgi/xms?jab=v32n4/04.pdf (October 2012).

International Conference on Primary Health Care (1978). "Declaration of Alma-Ata." Alma-Ata, September 12. Available online: www.who.int/publications/almaata_declaration_en.pdf

International Organization for Migration (2005a). *The Berne Initiative: International Agenda for Migration Management*. Geneva: International Organization for Migration. Available online: publications.iom.int/bookstore/free/IAMM.pdf (October 2012).

International Organization for Migration (2005b). "Policy Approaches to Migration and Development." MC/INF/281, November 9, International Organization for Migration, Geneva. Available online: www.iom.int/jahia/webdav/site/myjahiasite/shared/shared/mainsite/policy_and_research/policy_documents/MCINF281.pdf (October 2012).

Johnson, Maureen (2007). "The Challenge of Achieving Health Equity in Africa." International Development Research Centre, Ottawa. Available online: www.idrc.ca/EN/Resources/Publications/Pages/ArticleDetails.aspx?PublicationID=702 (October 2012).

Kabene, Stefane M., Carole Orchard, John M. Howard et al. (2006). "The Importance of Human Resources Management in Health Care: A Global Context." *Human Resources for Health* 4(20). doi: 10.1186/1478-4491-4-20. Available online: www.human-resources-health.com/content/4/1/20 (October 2012).

Laganà, Giulia (2007). "Co-development: 'Win-Win' Solution for All or Burden-Shifting Opportunity for the Developed World?," Solidar, Brussels. Available online: cms.horus.be/files/99931/MediaArchive/migration/Solidar_co_development_paper.pdf (October 2012).

Lochhead, Clarence (2003). "The Transition Penalty: Unemployment among Recent Immigrants to Canada." Canadian Labour and Business Centre. Available online: www.clbc.ca/files/Reports/Fitting_In/Transition_Penalty_e-CLBC.pdf (October 2012).

Mensah, Kwadwo, Maureen Mackintosh, and Leroi Henry (2005). "The 'Skills Drain' of Health Professionals from the Developing World: A Framework for Policy Formulation." Medact, London. Available online: www.medact.org/content//Skills%20drain/Mensah%20et%20al.%202005.pdf (October 2012).

Mullan, Fitzhugh (2005). "The Metrics of the Physician Brain Drain." *New England Journal of Medicine* 353: 1810–18. Available online: www.nejm.org/doi/full/10.1056/NEJMsa050004 (October 2012).

Munga, Michael A. and Deogratius R. Mbilinyi (2008). "Non-financial Incentives and the Retention of Health Workers in Tanzania." Equinet Discussion Paper No. 61. Available online: www.equinetafrica.org/bibl/docs/DIS61HRmunga.pdf (October 2012).

Nair, Sami (1997). "Rapport de bilan et d'orientation sur la politique de codéveloppement liée aux flux migratoires." Paris. Available online: www.ladocumentationfrancaise.fr/rapports-publics/984000139/index.shtml (October 2012).

Newland, Kathleen (2003). "Migration as a Factor in Development and Poverty Reduction." Migration Policy Institute. Available online: www.migrationinformation.org/feature/display.cfm?ID=136 (October 2012).

Newland, Kathleen (2004). "Migration as a Factor in Development and Poverty Reduction: The Impact of Rich Countries' Immigration Policies on the Prospects of the Poor." In *Impact of Rich Countries' Policies on Poor Countries: Towards a Level Playing Field in Development Cooperation*, Robert Picciotto and Rachel Weaving, eds. New Brunswick, NJ: Transaction Publisher, pp. 187–214.

Ogilvie, Linda, Judy E. Mill, Barbara Astle et al. (2007). "The Exodus of Health Professionals from Sub-Saharan Africa: Balancing Human Rights and Societal Needs in the Twenty-First Century." *Nursing Inquiry* 14(2): 114–24.

Organisation for Economic Co-operation and Development (2003). "Policy Coherence: Vital for Global Development." *OECD Observer*. Available online: www.oecd.org/pcd/20202515.pdf (October 2012).

Østergaard-Nielsen, Eva (2005). "Co-development Policies and the Role of Migrants' Transnational Networks." Abstract for intervention at Roundtable on "Migrations and Development: Transnational Networks, Remittances, Civil Society, and Human Capital Potential," 19–21 September.

Padarath, Ashnie, Charlotte Chamberlain, David McCoy et al. (2003). "Health Personnel in Southern Africa: Confronting Maldistribution and Brain Drain." Equinet Discussion Paper No. 3. Available online: www.equinetafrica.org/bibl/docs/DIS3hres.pdf (October 2012).

People's Health Movement, Medact, and Global Equity Gauge Alliance (2005). *Global Health Watch 2005–2006: An Alternative World Health Report.* New York: Zed Books.

Picciotto, Robert (2004). "Institutional Approaches to Policy Coherence for Development." Room Document 2, May 18–19, Organisation for Economic Co-operation and Development, Paris. Available online: www.oecd.org/pcd/31659358.pdf (October 2012).

Quartey, Peter, Evelyn Kwakye, and Gifty Merdiemah (2008). "The Impact of Rich Countries' Policies on Poverty in LDCs: The Case of Migrant Nurses from Ghana." *Research Monitor* 5: 19–21. Available online: cloud2.gdnet.org/CMS/getFile.php?id=rm_issue5 (October 2012).

Robinson, Rudi (2007). "A Framework for Benchmarking Progress on Policy Coherence in the Migration and Development Domain in OECD Countries." Unpublished.

Robinson, Rudi (2009). "Engaging African Diaspora Communities as Partners in Health System Strengthening in Their Countries of Origin." Workshop proposal, North-South Institute, Ottawa.

Teelucksingh, Cheryl and Grace-Edward Galabuzi (2005, November). "Impact of Race and Immigrants Status on Employment Opportunities and Outcomes in the Canadian Labour Market." *Policy Matters* 22. Available online: www.ceris.metropolis.net/wp-content/uploads/pdf/research_publication/policy_matters/pm22.pdf (October 2012).

Teferra, Damtew (2000). "Revisiting the Doctrine of Human Capital Mobility in the Information Age." Regional Conference on Brain Drain and Capital Building in Africa, 22–24 February, Addis Ababa. Available online: www.iom.int/africandiaspora/pdf/TEFERRA.pdf (October 2012).

Tettey, Wisdom J. (2003). "Africa's Options: Return, Retention, or Diaspora." May 1, Science and Development Network. Available online: www.scidev.net/en/policy-briefs/africa-s-options-return-retention-or-diaspora-.html (October 2012).

von Zweck, Claudia (2006). "Enabling the Workforce Integration of International Graduates: Issues and Recommendations for Occupational Therapy in Canada." CAOT Publications ACE, Ottawa. Available online: www.caot.ca/pdfs/wip/WIP%20Report.pdf (October 2012).

World Bank (2012). "World Development Indicators 2012." Washington, DC. Available online: data.worldbank.org/sites/default/files/wdi-2012-ebook.pdf (October 2012).

World Health Organization (2002). "Human Resources for Health: Developing Policy Options for Change." Draft discussion paper, November, Geneva. Available online: www.who.int/hrh/documents/en/Developing_policy_options.pdf (October 2012).

World Health Organization (2004). "Recruitment of Health Workers from the Developing World." EB114/5. Report by the Secretariat, April 19, Geneva.

Available online: extranet.who.int/iris/restricted/bitstream/10665/20165/1/
B114_5-en.pdf (October 2012).
Zurn, Pascal, Mario R. Dal Poz, Barbara Stilwell et al. (2002). "Imbalances in the
Health Workforce." March. Available online: www.who.int/hrh/documents/en/
imbalances_briefing.pdf (October 2012).

Chapter 5

International Migration, the Health of Migrants, and Global Health Governance

Anita A. Davies

Today, international migration is a phenomenon of globalization and contributes to increasing trade and investment. This accelerating global economic integration influences both legal and unauthorized migration patterns and migration policies. Migration is not new: it has been a feature of human life since ancient times. Migration is a process that consists of a point of origin, transit, and destination; it can have a return phase, and the process can be repeated.[1] Migration flows in the twenty-first century are much more complex, and the magnitude, density velocity and ease of travel have greatly increased (Nyberg-Sorensen et al. 2002).

As a global phenomenon, migration poses major challenges for health and global governance. First, a more mobile global population has an increased potential to spread infectious diseases. Second, there is growing concern that the health needs of migrants are not adequately addressed. These issues need to be addressed by governments of both sending and receiving countries. Multisectoral, regional, and subregional approaches are required to address migration, health, and governance.

This chapter addresses the issue of international migration and its links with health and global governance in a twenty-first century context, with a focus on sub-Saharan Africa. First, it provides an overview of international migration patterns and define migration and different categories of migrants. Second, it addresses migration health and its relationship to the migration process, migrants' legal status, and access to healthcare services. Third, the chapter refers to critical infectious diseases that are important to public health in order to illustrate the need for states to provide migrants and mobile populations' access to health and social services irrespective of their legal status as a way of inclusion, and to promote good health governance for the host community. Fourth, the chapter highlights migrants' right to health and proposes an innovative approach to engage with the diaspora for development, the promotion of good public health governance, and

---

1 The *Glossary on Migration,* published by the International Organization for Migration (IOM), defines migration as a process of moving, either across an international border, or within a state (IOM 2004a). It is a population movement, encompassing any kind of movement of people, whatever its length, composition, and causes; it includes migration of refugees, displaced persons, uprooted people, and economic migrants.

the strengthening of public health systems in Africa. The chapter concludes by stressing the need for evidenced-based migration and health governance policies in Africa.

Migration Overview

International migrants come from all over the world and travel to all parts of the world.[2] Each year, between five and 10 million people cross an international border to take up residence in a different country. In 2010, of the 6.9 billion people in the world, some 214 million individuals, or approximately 3.1 percent, was an international migrant (United Nations 2012b). Only 40 percent of global migration takes place into industrialized countries, the other 60 percent taking place between developing countries (International Organization for Migration [IOM] 2005c). The largest numbers of international migrants are in Asia, Europe, and North America (with equal numbers), followed by Africa, Latin America, and Oceania, with progressively fewer numbers. More than half of all international migrants live in developing countries, and migration often occurs within the same continent.

Significant population mobility takes place within countries, commonly from rural to urban areas, and from poorer rural areas to more prosperous ones. This is often the first step in a long sequence of migration patterns.

Several different forms of population mobility take place. Some migrants are forced from their communities, fleeing political instability, conflict, environmental degradation, and natural disasters. The United Nations High Commissioner for Refugees (2012) listed 42.5 million refugees, asylum seekers, internally displaced persons, and "others of concern" in 2011. Others crossed border for happier reasons: the World Tourism Organization (2012) estimated that there were 467 million international tourist arrivals in the first half of 2012, with the year's total anticipated to reach one billion.

The causes and effects of international migration are complex issues for both source and destination countries, with global implications. The impact of migration cannot be characterized as solely positive or negative. Factors that create benefits for one country can cause a loss for other countries. The migration of health workers is recognized as a loss to the source country and a benefit to the destination country. However, migrant health workers in the diaspora can contribute toward strengthening the health systems and developing capacity in their countries of origin. In many cases the skills of migrant health workers are

---

2 At the international level, no universally accepted definition of migrant exists. The term is usually understood to cover all cases where the decision to migrate is taken freely by the individual concerned for reasons of "personal convenience" and without intervention of an external compelling factor. It therefore applies to persons and family members moving to another country or region to better their material or social conditions and improve the prospect for themselves or their family (IOM 2004a).

often not utilized by the health workforce of the destination country, thus creating a loss of health skills in both countries.

Migrants can be classified into two broad groups: voluntary migrants and forced migrants. Voluntary migrants include people who move for employment, study, family reunification, or other personal factors. Forced migrants leave their places of origin to escape persecution, conflict, repression, natural and human-made disasters, ecological degradation, or other situations that endanger their lives, freedom, or livelihood. Migrants can also be classified by their legal status in a country as regular or irregular migrants.[3] Regular migrants are those persons who migrate through the legal migration channels. Migrants can often move from a regular status to an irregular status depending on various circumstances. The legal status of a migrant often influences their access to health and social services in many countries.

Internal migration is often the first move in the migration process. Worldwide, rural to urban migration has been noted for economic migrants as the first migration phase. The more adventurous migrants then move across international borders with regular or irregular status. The largest volume of migrants from Africa leave Europe for North America.

Migration in Africa

Different categories of migrants can be found in sub-Saharan Africa. These migrants are pushed by the current social, political, economic, ecological, and ethnic situations in many of the countries in the region. The vast majority of Africans migrating in recent years have been due to forced movements of refugees and internally displaced persons.[4] This forced movement of people has occurred in Burundi, the Democratic Republic of Congo, Ethiopia, Liberia, Sierra Leone, Somalia, Sudan, Uganda, and, most recently, Zimbabwe. Migration in Africa has also been due to economic reasons involving temporary labour. Major host countries of labour migrants are Côte d'Ivoire in West Africa, Gabon in Central Africa, and Botswana and the Republic of South Africa in Southern Africa. The

---

3 Irregular migrants are persons who, owing to illegal entry or the expiry of a visa, lack legal status in a transit or host country. The term applies to migrants who infringe a country's admission rules and any other person not authorized to remain in the host country (also called clandestine, illegal, undocumented migrants or migrants in an irregular situation) (IOM 2004a).

4 A refugee can be defined as a person who meets the criteria of the UNHCR Statute and qualifies for the protection of the United Nations provided by the High Commissioner, regardless of whether that person is in a country that is a party to the Convention relating to the Status of Refugees, 1951 or the 1967 Protocol relating to the Status of Refugees, or whether that person has been recognized by the host country as a refugee under either of these instruments.

major countries of origin are Mali, Burkina Faso, and Lesotho. Ghana, Nigeria, and Senegal are considered both receiving and sending countries.

Nomadic tribes are found in many countries in sub-Saharan Africa. These people have traditionally moved and continue to do so, often in response to climatic changes in the environment. This mobile population has no regular access to health and social services in their countries of origin, transit, or destination.

In recent years there have been gender changes in migration worldwide. Migration used to be seen as dominated by men, but women now make up 50 percent of all migrants.[5] In Africa more women are migrating independently. Often children are left behind to be cared for by their fathers or older relatives. This has created a change in the dynamic of child rearing.

Many countries in Africa have now become countries of origin, transit, and destination. For example, migrants from sub-Saharan Africa might have to go through Tunisia or Libya to get to Italy or Malta (BBC News 2007). Consequently African governments must address the needs of different categories of migrants and the different effects of migration when developing their health, development, migration, and other national strategies.

Migration Health

The health of migrants has always raised the fear of importing unknown diseases in host communities. Very little has been documented about the fact that the regular migration process often requires rigorous health assessments on individuals who tend to be young and healthy. Irregular migrants who often do not have access to health care can pose a public health hazard.

Migration health addresses the physical, mental, and social needs of migrants, and the public health needs of hosting communities through policies and practices corresponding to the emerging challenges facing mobile populations today (IOM 2004b).

Migrants who are healthy when they leave their countries of origin can be exposed to hazardous health conditions in the process of migration. Those hazards differ in the pre-migration, transit, post-arrival, and return phases. Regarding the pre-migration phase, although disease prevalence in the country of origin has consequences for the vulnerability of the migrant, migrants do not necessarily bring disease to the country of destination, as is often implied.

In the transit phase, hazardous exposure tends to occur to irregular migrants, such as trafficked or smuggled persons. Irregular migrants usually travel using unusual and dangerous methods of transportation. Once they have arrived in the host country, having survived the journey, the migrants often live in unsanitary,

---

5 Migration-related policies and regulations have not taken the needs of female migrants into consideration and are not gender sensitive. Female migrants often face a double vulnerability of being a woman and a migrant.

overcrowded conditions and work in unsafe environments; they do not have access to health and social services. Irregular migrants are excluded from preventive clinical services for legal, cultural, social, economic, and political reasons (Gushulak and MacPherson 2006). Illegal migrants do not have health insurance, lack information in cases when health services are free, and are afraid of being discovered and deported by the authorities.

The health of migrants has several other determinants than the epidemiology of disease in their host countries. Migrants are often marginalized and can be an invisible group with limited access to health and social services. Health status can change after migrants have spent some time in their host environment, where they are exposed to new pathogens and to lifestyle and social determinants that promote ill health. It is in the interest of public health that migrants have access to basic healthcare services. Tuberculosis, HIV/AIDS, and other communicable diseases as well as reproductive health are of utmost concern in migrant populations. Migrants are also susceptible to chronic and noncommunicable diseases, and often take on the prevalence rates of the disease in their host community.

In recognition of the importance of the health of migrants today, the members of the World Health Organization (WHO) discussed this issue at the 2008 World Health Assembly (World Health Assembly 2008).[6] This resolution encouraged members to:

- promote equitable access to health promotion and care for migrants;
- identify the gaps in service delivery in order to improve the health of all populations, including migrants;
- gather, document, and share information and best practices for meeting migrants' health needs in countries of origin or return, transit, and destination;
- raise cultural and gender sensitivity to migrants' health issues among health service providers and professionals; and
- train health professionals to deal with the health issues associated with population movements.

Infectious Disease and Population Mobility in Africa

Conditions of the migration process can increase the vulnerability and health risks associated with the transition and acquisition of many infectious diseases. Migrant receiving industrial countries have thus developed strategies to safeguard the health of their populations and reduce the burden on their healthcare systems. This has not been the case when there is migration and population mobility within and

---

6 The health of migrants is now on the WHO agenda. This was brought to the World Health Assembly during Portugal's presidency of the European Union. Portugal is one of Europe's migrant-receiving countries.

across country borders in Africa. However, travellers to South Africa require proof of vaccination, for example, before they are allowed to enter the country from a zone known to have yellow fever.

Nonetheless, African countries have weak public health systems that are poorly financed, and do not have adequate staff or materials of public health governance in place. States have the duty to enable people to live healthy lives. National governments in partnership with a wide range of stakeholders including civil society must practise good stewardship to ensure careful management of their health system to address the populations' health needs. National strategies should focus on the reduction of health inequalities for both nationals and non-nationals to maintain a healthy country (Travis et al. 2002).

WHO works with both migrant-sending and -receiving countries to promote health for all. Its 2005 revision of the International Health Regulations (IHR), the 2007 World Health report that focuses on improving global health security, and the 2008 World Health report that revisits primary health care all provide guidance and insights to good global public health governance (WHO 2005, 2007b, 2008b).[7]

There has always been an interest in the relationship between population mobility and global public health (Gushulak et al. 2007). This interest has grown since the 1990s with concern for in emerging and re-emerging diseases, such as malaria, tuberculosis, and HIV/AIDS. In recent years more attention has been drawn to population mobility, avian influenza, and severe acute respiratory syndrome (SARS). Surveillance and reporting of all reportable diseases is the global public health responsibility of all countries. Cross-border collaboration is of utmost importance, and surveillance should be conducted among migrant and mobile populations. The need for migrants to be able to access health services cannot be overemphasized. It would be unethical to monitor a disease in a population and not offer treatment.

---

7   The revised IHR contribute to the resilience of society and health systems to respond to many crises within the context of the international health. They came into force in 2007 and provide guidance for countries to work together to identify health risks and act to contain and control them. The regulations are needed because no single country, regardless of capability or wealth, can protect itself from outbreaks and other hazards without the cooperation of others. The "World Health Report 2007—A Safer Future: Global Public Health Security in the 21st Century" marks a turning point in the history of public health, and signals what could be one of the biggest advances in health security in half a century (WHO 2007b). It shows how the world is at increasing risk of disease outbreaks, epidemics, industrial accidents, natural disasters, and other health emergencies that can rapidly become threats to global public health security. The "2008 World Health Report—Primary Health Care (Now More Than Ever)" brings primary health care back to the forefront of the political arena (WHO 2008b). Globalization and migration put the social cohesion of many countries under stress, and health systems are not meeting healthcare needs.

Malaria, Tuberculosis, HIV/AIDS, and Population Mobility

Every year, malaria kills one million people—mostly children. Globalization and population mobility increase the number of cases of malaria in some parts of the world. Global climate change has increased mosquito reproduction rates, and mosquitoes are now found in new locations worldwide. Non-immune people are at risk when they move to areas where malaria is prevalent. Rural-to-urban migration has been known to contribute to the malaria epidemics in some parts of Africa. International migration can facilitate the import of malaria to developed countries. Population movement is also increasingly implicated in the spread of drug resistance in malaria. The relationship between malaria transmission and population mobility is complex. To succeed, strategies to eradicate or control malaria should consider the link between migration and the spread of disease (Hall and Martens 2000).

Tuberculosis, a re-emerging disease, is a major global concern: one third of the world population are infected. It is the second leading infectious disease causing mortality, after HIV (WHO 2011a). The disease killed 4,000 people a day and approximately 1.45 million in 2010. A significant proportion of migrants travel from countries with a high incidence to countries with low incidence. As migrants make up 30 percent of the world's population, it is imperative that they can access treatment for tuberculosis and that prevention facilities are available worldwide. Treatment should be completed in order to discourage drug resistance.[8] The burden of multidrug-resistant tuberculosis (MDR-TB) in 2010 was 650,000 cases, or 5.4 percent, of the 12 million prevalent cases (WHO 2011a). Less than 5 percent of patients are tested for MDB-TB because of the constrained capacity of tuberculosis laboratories.

In South Africa, of 1,539 tuberculosis patients in KwaZulu Natal tested for drug resistance, 221 patients were MDR-TB, and 53 had extensively drug-resistant tuberculosis (XDR-TB) (Gandhi et al. 2006). WHO first announced XDR-TB in 2006. Both forms of drug-resistant tuberculosis seriously threaten global control.

HIV and tuberculosis co-infection are producing explosive epidemics. Increasing co-infection means that people living with HIV/AIDS are dying from tuberculosis. It is thus of global public health interest to strengthen the capacity of laboratory facilities in Africa.

With regard to HIV/AIDS, significant evidence links HIV and population mobility in Africa. In East Africa, the incidence is higher near roads and among people who have either migrated or have sexual partners who are migrants (Biddlecom and Brockerhoff 1999). In Southern and West Africa, migrant workers

---

8 There are several barriers to migrants' access continuous tuberculosis treatment (WHO 2012b). For the good of all, migrants should have free access to tuberculosis services. Migrants often move from high endemic areas to low endemic areas or vice versa. Migrant health determinants and risk factors often predispose them to the disease.

and their sexual partners have higher levels of infection than the general population. For example, itinerant traders and long-distance truck drivers have shown to be at increased risk to contract HIV infection. Border towns have high rates of HIV prevalence, being places where transient populations such as truckers encounter a more stable local population, and which are often not reached by national HIV and AIDS intervention programs (Anarfi 1993).

The highest incidence of HIV is not in Africa's poorest countries, however, but in Southern African countries such as South Africa and Botswana, which have sufficient transport infrastructure, relatively high levels of economic development, and considerable internal and cross-border migration. Strategies to address the current AIDS pandemic in Africa should therefore be multiregional, cross-border, and multi-sectoral. The management of the HIV/AIDS pandemic is an excellent example of a global public health issue.

SARS and the avian influenza are examples of newly emerging diseases of the twenty-first century. Both diseases are associated with population mobility and occurrence in more than one continent. In 2003, the outbreak of SARS in Asia and its arrival in Canada clearly demonstrated how international population mobility, human behaviour, and an inadequate understanding of the disease facilitated its spread. In the wake of avian influenza, there are many lessons to be learned from the SARS experience.

The prevention and control of avian influenza and human influenza pandemic preparedness should be a priority for global health governance. Many African governments with competing health burdens may not see an influenza pandemic as an imminent threat, but this is to their detriment. Avian influenza in the poultry population has been reported in several African countries and human cases have been reported in Egypt, Nigeria, and Djibouti. Given the increased mobility of people within Africa and the migratory route between Africa and Asia and Africa and the Middle East and Europe, it is worth strengthening the capacity at the community level for surveillance, home-based care, and the prevention and control of influenza-like illnesses. A human influenza pandemic in Africa, where health and social services are weak, could bring disastrous results. Co-morbidity with HIV/AIDS, tuberculosis, and malaria will also take its toll on an unprepared population. Countries all around the world have been urged by Margaret Chan, director general of WHO, not to let down their guard and to prepare for a human influenza pandemic. African states should come together to strengthen their humanitarian and crisis preparedness plans that can be used for any disaster caused by a disease.

Migration and the Right to Health

This chapter has highlighted migrants' lack of access to healthcare and preventive services due to reasons such as legal status, education, inadequate finances, and stigma. Global health governance should have a positive impact on migration health, through advocacy for migrants' rights to being health members of their host communities. Access to health care must be seen as a public good. Healthy migrants make a healthy world. In most cases, migrants, irrespective of their legal status, contribute to the economy of their host communities and should have access to health services.

Migrants, first and foremost, are human beings who have the right to health. Governments have an obligation to uphold this right in the interest of good public health governance. The right to health is a fundamental human right that applies to every human being regardless of migration status.

The right to health includes underlying preconditions necessary for health: food and nutrition, housing, access to safe and potable water and adequate sanitation, safe and healthy working conditions, and a healthy environment.

Several legal instruments exist at the regional, national, and international levels that can be used to advocate migrants' right to health. The international code of human rights consists of legally binding international components. The International Covenant on Economic, Social, and Cultural Rights and the Convention on the Rights of the Child can be used to advocate for migrants right to health. The IOM (2007) reviewed the instruments that apply to European states and recommended that states ensure that migrants' right to health are formally recognized in national laws, and obstacles to this are eliminated. Similar recommendations can be made to African states, as many have signed on to human rights international and national instruments. Virtually all African countries have signed up to the 1981 African Charter on Human and Peoples' Rights (the Banjul Charter) and the 1990 African Charter on the Rights and Welfare of the Child. They are obliged to respect migrants' right to health and refrain from denying or limiting equal access to preventive, curative, and palliative health services regardless of legal migration status.

African governments should therefore recognize health as a basic human right for its citizens and the migrants that it hosts. National health development and migration policies should be developed and implemented in the spirit of solidarity and equity to ensure health, development, and social stability. Health providers, policy makers, health management planners, and other professionals need to be trained to address healthcare issues associated with population mobility. Information is also needs to be provided to migrants. Governments of both sending and receiving countries must take a multi-sector approach to partner with different migrant and mobile communities to protect and promote the health of those people. Developed countries must strengthen developing countries' capacity for good public heath governance through innovative initiatives. An integrated and globally focused approach is required to address migration health issues into national foreign policy initiatives (Gushulak et al. 2007).

An Innovative Approach

Remittances for Development in Africa

It is difficult to address health governance in Africa when the overburdened health systems are crumbling due to the lack of human and financial resources and adequate facilities. New solutions are needed to address this issue. In the bid for development and capacity building in Africa, members of the African diaspora have contributed through financial remittances, the transfer of skills and knowledge, and the development of businesses.[9] Financial remittances by migrants to their countries of origin account for more income than foreign aid in some countries. Table 5.1 shows remittance as percentages of gross domestic product (GDP) in some parts of Africa.

Table 5.1   Remittances inflows from the African diaspora, 2010

Country	Total (US$ million)	Share of Gross Domestic Product (%)
Côte d'Ivoire	185	0.8
Ethiopia	345	0.9
Kenya	1,777	5.4
Lesotho	746	28.6
Mauritius	226	2.3
Nigeria	10,045	4.5
Senegal	1,350	11.0
South Africa	1,119	0.2
Sudan	1,420	3.1
Uganda	915	4.3

Source: Annual Remittances Data: Inflows, World Bank (2010).

The diaspora can influence development through other forms of remittances, such as social, political, governance, technological, medical, and other needed skills. In many cases remittances have been transferred in an unstructured manner.

---

9   The AU defines the African diaspora as "peoples of African descent and heritage living outside the continent, irrespective of their citizenship and who remain committed to contribute to the development of the continent and the building of the African Union" (AU 2005b). In 2007 the African diaspora was estimated to consist of about 112.6 million people in South America (primarily Brazil, Colombia, Venezuela), 39.2 million people in North America (United States and Canada), 13.5 million people in the Caribbean, and about 3.5 million people in Europe (World Bank 2007).

Diaspora contributions do not necessarily fit into the national strategic development and health plans. It has thus been difficult to determine the specific impact of remittances on strengthening health systems and development in the country of origin. It is therefore necessary to channel all diaspora initiatives through a multi-sectoral government structure that ensures that activities contribute to national strategic plans. The IOM has developed a framework to engage with the diaspora and countries of origin and destination to contribute to development in Africa. Other organizations such as the World Bank, which held the second annual Global Diaspora Forum in 2012 supported by its African Diaspora Program, are exploring innovative programs with the diaspora.

Migration for Development in Africa

The IOM's Migration for Development in Africa (MIDA) initiative facilitates the return of members of the African diaspora from Europe and North America to their countries of origin in order to contribute to development. It has launched projects in several African countries. Some of these projects have involved the return of health workers and supported hospital twinning and other diaspora activities. The main objective is to promote strategic dialogue and cooperation between stakeholders, at the national level as well as at the regional level through the New Partnership for Africa's Development (NEPAD), the AU, nongovernmental organizations (NGOs), multilateral organizations, and UN agencies to discuss the implementation of government policies addressing migration, health, and development issues in Africa. The Ghana MIDA Project, for example, has facilitated the transfer of diaspora skills and knowledge to Ghana through periodic, temporary, or circular return.[10]

The MIDA initiative demonstrates the capability of countries of origin, countries of destination, members of diasporas, and international organizations to work together to achieve a common goal of strengthening human resource capacity in developing countries through the transfer of knowledge and skills found in migrant and diaspora populations (IOM 2004a). The MIDA initiative is driven by needs. Projects are based on results of needs assessments conducted in collaboration with the government in the countries of origin (see Table 5.2).

---

10 More information on the MIDA Initiative can be found on the IOM website at www.iom.int/MIDA.

Table 5.2   International Organization for Migration's migration for development in africa initiative

> The MIDA initiative has been used for the development of different sectors. It works with national governments of both the countries of origin and the countries of destination. The following steps are essential for the success of a MIDA project:
>
> - identify skills and resources available in the diaspora;
> - identify resource needs of participating countries;
> - matching the identified skill/resource needs of target countries with appropriate skills/resources of nationals in the diaspora in order to engage the diaspora in the development process of the countries of origin;
> - explore the most beneficial ways to channel and invest migrant remittances for development of countries of origin and to advocate for the creation of conducive environment for such investments; and
> - build synergies between governments at the national as well as the local level (regions and municipalities), civil society, and academic and research institutions.

Conclusion: The Need for Evidenced-Based Policy, Stewardship, and Public Health Governance in Africa

From the issues highlighted in this chapter, it is clear that global health governance has a cross-cutting nature that affects the people's mobility, which is often driven by economics and trade. Health governance is also driven by human security and linked with global crime, which includes the human smuggling and trafficking. Given climate change, there are elements of disease control and disaster preparedness and response that should be considered. These issues all have a profound effect on the epidemiology of global infectious diseases and noncommunicable conditions in migrants, mobile populations, and host communities. Further research is needed on migration, health, and governance in Africa to provide information for evidence-based policy at the government, regional, and sub-regional levels to advocate for the public health rights of migrants and mobile populations, to facilitate integration, and to avoid stigma.

African governments, in the bid to implement a stewardship public health model, should reduce inequalities in access to health services and recognize the needs of migrants and include their needs in national health strategic plans. The governments should exercise their mandate and responsibility for public health legislation, regulation, and the enforcement of policies related to migration health. These policies should be based on evidence drawn from information gathered on migration and the social, economic, and environmental determinants of health. There should be a provision made for both international and internal migrants. The health sector should be governed properly at all levels to attain the health system goals. For a stewardship public health model to be success, health policies must be clear, constructive, and strategically driven by the state (Saltman and Ferroussier-Davis 2000).

African countries need to show good stewardship and better coordination within each country, within each region, and with the rest of the world to contribute to global health governance, as health threats and risks are increasingly associated with international population mobility. Such stewardship and coordination will drive the development of national and international border disease control and migration policies. These policies reflect the volume and diversity of populations moving within countries and between regions with disparities in disease risk, prevalence, and availability of health services. Global health governance policies should address migrants' access to health care for the common good.

Evidence-based policies in migration, health, and development in Africa can influence global public health governance. Governments of both sending and receiving countries should also engage with members of the African diaspora for sustainable development. Health governance and capacity-building strategies can be developed to strengthening health systems in Africa.

References

African Union (2005). "Report of the Meeting of Experts from Member States on the Definition of the African Diaspora." April 11–12, Addis Ababa. Available online: www.africa-union.org/organs/ecossoc/Report-Expert-Diaspora%20 Defn%2013april2005-Clean%20copy1.doc (October 2012).

Anarfi, John K. (1993). "Sexuality, Migration, and AIDS in Ghana: A Socio-Behavioural Study." *Health Transition Review* 3: 45–67.

BBC News (2007). "Key Facts: Africa to Europe Migration." July 2. Available online: news.bbc.co.uk/2/hi/europe/6228236.stm (October 2012).

Biddlecom, Ann E. and Martin Brockerhoff (1999). "Migration, Sexual Behavior, and the Risk of HIV in Kenya." *International Migration Review* 33(4): 833–56.

Gandhi, Neel R., Anthony Moll, A. Willem Sturm et al. (2006). "Extensive Drug Resistant Tuberculosis as a Cause of Death in Patients Co-infected with Tuberculosis and HIV in a Rural Area of South Africa." *Lancet* 368(9547): 1575–80. Available online: ftp.cdc.gov/pub/nchstp/tb/ who_cc_latvia/present/Articles/Gandhi_XDR%20TB%20HIV%20in%20 KZN_Lancet.pdf

Gushulak, Brian D., Liane Macdonald, and Douglas W. MacPherson (2007). "Health and Foreign Policy: Influences of Migration and Population Mobility." *Bulletin of the World Health Organization* 85(3): 200–206. Available online: www.who.int/bulletin/volumes/85/3/06-036962.pdf (October 2012).

Gushulak, Brian D. and Douglas W. MacPherson (2006). *Migration Medicine and Health: Principles and Practice*. Hamilton: BC Decker.

Hall, Lisbeth and Pim Martens (2000). "Malaria on the Move: Human Population Movement and Malaria Transmission." *Emerging Infectious Diseases* 6(2): 103–9. Available online: wwwnc.cdc.gov/eid/content/6/2/contents.htm (October 2012).

International Organization for Migration (2004a). "Glossary on Migration." Geneva. Available online: publications.iom.int/bookstore/free/IML_1_EN.pdf (October 2012).

International Organization for Migration (2004b). "Migrant Health for the Benefit of All." MC/INF/275, November 8, Geneva. Available online: www.iom.int/jahia/webdav/shared/shared/mainsite/about_iom/en/council/88/MC_INF_275.pdf (October 2012).

International Organization for Migration (2005). "World Migration Report 2005: Costs and Benefits of International Migration." Geneva. Available online: publications.iom.int/bookstore/free/wmr_2005.pdf (October 2012).

International Organization for Migration (2007). "Migration and the Right to Health: A Review of European Community Law and Council of Europe Instruments." Geneva. Available online: publications.iom.int/bookstore/free/IML_12_EN.pdf (October 2012).

Nyberg-Sorensen, Ninna, Nicholas Van Hear, and Poul Engberg-Pedersen (2002). "The Migration-Development Nexus Evidence and Policy Options." July, International Organization for Migration, Geneva. Available online: iom.ch/jahia/webdav/site/myjahiasite/shared/shared/mainsite/published_docs/serial_publications/mrs_8.pdf (October 2012).

Saltman, Richard B. and Odile Ferroussier-Davis (2000). "The Concept of Stewardship in Health Policy." *Bulletin of the World Health Organization* 78(6): 732–9. Available online: www.who.int/bulletin/archives/78%286%29732.pdf (October 2012).

Travis, Phyllida, Dominique Egger, Philip Davies et al. (2002). "Towards Better Stewardship: Concepts and Critical Issues." WHO/EIP/DP/02.48, World Health Organization, Geneva. Available online: www.who.int/healthinfo/paper48.pdf (October 2012).

United Nations, Department of Economic and Social Affairs, Population Division. (2012). "Trends in International Migrant Stock: The 2008 Revision." United Nations database, POP/DB/MIG/Stock/Rev.2008, October 6. Available online: esa.un.org/migration/p2k0data.asp (October 2012).

United Nations High Commissioner for Refugees (2012). "UNHCR Global Trends 2011: A Year of Crises." Geneva. Available online: www.unhcr.org/4fd6f87f9.pdf (October 2012).

World Bank (2007). "World Bank Officials Engage African Diaspora in Development Efforts." Washington, DC, December 3. Available online: go.worldbank.org/TNAUDP28A0 (October 2012).

World Bank (2010). "Migration and Remittances Data." Washington, DC. Available online: go.worldbank.org/092X1CHHD0 (October 2012).

World Health Assembly (2008). "Health of Migrants." WHA61-17, May 24, World Health Organization, Geneva. Available online: apps.who.int/gb/ebwha/pdf_files/A61/A61_R17-en.pdf (October 2012).

World Health Organization (2005). "Revision of the International Health Regulations." Geneva, May 23. Available online: www.who.int/entity/csr/ihr/IHRWHA58_3-en.pdf (October 2012).

World Health Organization (2007). "The World Health Report 2007—A Safer Future: Global Public Health Security in the 21st Century." Geneva. Available online: www.who.int/whr/2007/en (October 2012).

World Health Organization (2008). "The World Health Report 2008—Primary Health Care (Now More Than Ever)." Geneva. Available online: www.who.int/whr/2008/en (October 2012).

World Health Organization (2011). "Global Tuberculosis Control: WHO Report 2011." Geneva. Available online: www.who.int/tb/publications/global_report/2011/gtbr11_full.pdf (October 2012).

World Health Organization (2012). "Tuberculosis Care and Control in Refugee and Displaced Populations." Geneva. Available online: www.who.int/tb/challenges/refugees/en/ (October 2012).

World Tourism Organization (2012, September). "22 Million More International Arrivals in the First Half of 2012." *UNWTO World Tourism Barometer* 10(September). Available online: dtxtq4w60xqpw.cloudfront.net/sites/all/files/pdf/unwto_barom12_05_sept_excerpt.pdf (October 2012).

PART IV
National and Regional Policy Responses and Innovation

Chapter 6

Integrating Science and Community Development: The Practice of Traditional Medicine in Fighting HIV and AIDS

Jane Adar

At the High-Level Meeting on AIDS at the 2006 United Nations General Assembly, the member states agreed to work toward the universal access to comprehensive prevention programs, treatment, care, and support by 2010. Yet millions of people are still without basic health care, particularly in Africa.

UNAIDS's (2005) "Three Scenarios" project asks if, by 2025, millions of Africans are still becoming infected with HIV, what would be the main reasons? Would it be because there was no choice, or a lack of understanding of the consequences of the decisions and actions being taken now? Or would it be because the lessons of more than two decades of the epidemic were not learned or were not applied effectively? The answer to these questions is that in 2025, there may be millions more Africans affected by HIV/AIDS because there is insufficient political will to change behaviour and to halt the forces driving the epidemic in Africa.

What we do today will change the future. The world will have to deal with HIV/AIDS for some time to come, and the extent of its impact will depend on the response and investment made now. Applying and sustaining the knowledge of almost three decades will make a fundamental difference to Africa's future. As the epidemic continues to devastate the continent, it becomes increasingly clear that different strategies are required to confront the wide range of complex social, cultural, and environmental impacts. Furthermore, the economic contexts in which HIV/AIDS continues to spread must be researched, tested, evaluated, modified, and adopted.

Globalization has not made addressing the epidemic any easier. Driven by sustained neoliberal economic policies, it has had negative impacts on Africa due to structural adjustment and debt in poor countries. These factors have forced countries to cut funding and to privatize public health systems. Consequently, resources for basic health care must compete with the meagre available resources for other priorities, such as infrastructure and education. Privatization of public healthcare systems in Africa has also meant that people who cannot afford the cost have had to do without. The mobility of people migrating from South to North or South to South as a result of globalization has increased the brain drain of qualified health professionals from developing countries to developed countries, which has resulted in the further weakening of already weak health systems.

Despite the many challenges facing the African continent, significant progress has been made in the fight against the HIV/AIDS epidemic (World Health Organization et al. 2011). Nonetheless, even with increases in treatment coverage, 53 percent of people needing antiretroviral treatment (ART) in 2010 went without. According to the 2011 progress report published by the World Health Organization (WHO), UNAIDS, and UNICEF, efforts to increase access to treatment were hampered by weaknesses in health systems, uncertain financing for HIV treatment, and insufficient integration of HIV/AIDS with other aspects of healthcare delivery. Many developing countries are struggling to find innovative and cost-effective strategies that are relevant to their local HIV/AIDS epidemic situation. For example, in mostly resource-constrained settings, the integration of traditional medicine into health systems should be investigated, specifically in Africa. Although access to treatment has increased in recent years, and the number of new infections has stabilized since 2007, far too many people are getting sick and dying. This underscores the urgent need to strengthen HIV/AIDS prevention and treatment efforts.

This chapter discusses the role of traditional medicine in increasing access to universal HIV/AIDS prevention programs, treatment, care, and support through its integration into mainstream health systems. The chapter maps out Resolution AF/RC50/R3 on Promoting the Role of Traditional Medicine in Health Systems: A Strategy for the African Region, which lists four priority interventions of the implementation strategy, and the 2001 Abuja Declaration on HIV/AIDS, Tuberculosis, and Other Infectious Diseases of the Organization of African Unity—now transformed into the African Union (AU). It will focus on the 46 countries of the WHO Regional Office for Africa.[1]

The chapter outlines some of the reasons why traditional medicine must be integrated into health systems in the African region, and describes the integration that has already taken place. It then outlines implementation strategies, the status of further integration, and some of the responses and innovations that countries have used so far. Next, research, developments, and challenges facing traditional medicine are discussed with reference to existing initiatives and studies. Finally, it concludes with a discussion of some of the specific challenges facing countries in the integration of the health system and suggestions on a way forward for effective

---

1   The 46 countries in the WHO African Region are Algeria, Angola, Benin, Botswana, Burkina Faso, Burundi, Cameroon, Cape Verde, Central African Republic, Chad, Comoros, Congo, Côte d'Ivoire, Democratic Republic of Congo, Equatorial Guinea, Ethiopia, Eritrea, Gabon, Gambia, Ghana, Guinea, Guinea-Bissau, Kenya, Lesotho, Liberia, Madagascar, Malawi, Mali, Mauritania, Mauritius, Mozambique, Namibia, Niger, Nigeria, Rwanda, São Tomé and Principe, Senegal, Seychelles, Sierra Leone, South Africa, Swaziland, Togo, Tanzania, Uganda, Zambia, and Zimbabwe.

integration. The chapter argues, from an African perspective, that traditional medicine practice can no longer be left behind by science.

Justification for Integrating Traditional Medicine into the Health System

WHO defines traditional medicine as "the total combination of knowledge and practices, whether explicable or not, used in diagnosing, preventing or eliminating physical, mental or social diseases and which may rely exclusively on past experience and observation handed down from generation to generation, verbally or in writing" (WHO Regional Office for Africa [WHO/AFRO] 2000). In Africa it is estimated that up to 80 percent of the population uses traditional medicine for their primary healthcare needs (Homsy et al. 2004; UNAIDS 2000; WHO/AFRO 2010).

The percentage of people who use traditional medicine varies from country to country. For example, traditional medicine use in Uganda and Tanzania is at 60 percent; Benin, Cameroon, and Rwanda are at 70 percent; Côte d'Ivoire, Kenya, Mauritania, Zimbabwe, Zambia, Mozambique, Senegal, and South Africa are at 80 percent; and Ethiopia is at 90 percent (Chatora 2003; Pope et al. 2009; WHO/AFRO 2010). It is also estimated that three out of four people with HIV/AIDS rely on some form of traditional medicine for treating the symptoms of HIV and AIDS. In many parts of Africa, traditional health practitioners far outnumber conventional health practitioners. In 2003, the ratio of conventional western-trained general practitioners was 1:20,000 whereas the availability of traditional medical practitioners was 1:200 or 1:400 (Chatora 2003).

The practice remains widespread; people seek traditional health care along with, or even before, they approach conventional or western medical services. This is the reality of pluralism in medical practices in Africa, irrespective of whether it is acknowledged at the formal level. The advent of colonialism and subsequent introduction of conventional or western medicine exposed traditional medical practitioners to ridicule and stiff competition—their practices were considered heathen, unscientific, backward, and crude. In many countries traditional medical practice was made illegal by the colonial rulers, despite the fact that it had existed long before conventional medicine, and attempts by colonial governments and early religious missionaries to suppress were unsuccessful. The practice was and still is deeply rooted and widespread.

In Africa, most people with HIV/AIDS depend on and trust traditional medical practitioners and herbal treatments. In many rural areas, the only access to health care is through traditional medicine practitioners, who share the same cultural values and belief systems as their patients. People are deterred from going to major centres to seek conventional treatment because of the prohibitive cost and the long distances. The majority of those who seek services from traditional medicine practitioners believe in the effectiveness of those treatments. In addition to being accessible and affordable, traditional medicine is also part of a wider belief system, and considered integral to the everyday life and well-being of a community. Conventional health care has never been, and probably never will be, adequately and equitably provided anywhere in Africa. This is due to the reality of capitalism, financial limitations related to rapid population growth, political instability, and poor economic performance.

Those with people with access usually consult both traditional and conventional systems, although it is for different reasons and during different stages of the disease. Certain aspects of HIV/AIDS are believed to be better treated by one or the other system. In spite of increased interest in the traditional medicine, true cooperation between the two systems is rare (Bodeker et al. 2000; Homsy et al. 2004; Kayombo et al. 2007; Nyumbu et al. 2000; Peltzer et al. 2008; Puckree et al. 2002; UNAIDS 2000, 2002). Traditional health practitioners may refer to conventional health systems, but the reverse is rarely the case (Peltzer et al. 2006). The world needs to accept that many Africans will continue consulting traditional medicine practitioners either because of the inaccessibility of conventional medicine or personal choice. Traditional medicine has its faults just as conventional medicine is not perfect. However, while the benefits revealed by conventional medicine have been extensively utilized, the same cannot be said for traditional medicine. The negative view of traditional medicine that has remained for over 100 years has resulted in a lack of integration into health systems. Indeed, in an increasingly diverse world, why is something as valuable as traditional medicine not part of modern science, or integrated into global health governance?

In this context, integrating science and community development refers to incorporating research, biomedical science, and traditional medicine to fight infectious diseases. The WHO/AFRO definition refers to increased healthcare coverage through collaboration, communication, harmonization, and partnership building between conventional and traditional systems of medicine while ensuring intellectual property rights and protection of indigenous knowledge (see Sambo 2003; WHO/AFRO 2000). Traditional medicine and practices is supported only when there is available evidence on safety, efficacy, and quality, and when such evidence is generated when it is lacking.

Traditionally, the systems of integration of traditional medicine have taken four different forms (Sambo 2003). These are a monopolistic or exclusive system, a tolerant system, an inclusive system, and an integrative system.

In a monopolistic or exclusive system, only conventional medical doctors have the right to practise medicine. No country in Africa falls into this category.

In a tolerant system or a system of coexistence, traditional health practitioners—while not formally recognized—are permitted to practise in an official capacity. Most African countries have not formally recognized traditional medicine through the formulation of national policies or legal and regulatory frameworks for regulating the practice, practitioners, and products (that is, medicines). Nevertheless, traditional medicine is practised.

In an inclusive system, both conventional and traditional medicines are separate components of the national health system. National authorities officially recognize traditional medicine, but some aspects are not yet incorporated into the national system. In some cases, the national authorities are developing the appropriate framework for traditional medicine with regards to policy, regulation, practice, health insurance coverage, research, and education. Benin, Burkina Faso, Cameroon, Equatorial Guinea, Guinea, Côte d'Ivoire, the Democratic Republic of Congo (DRC), Niger, Nigeria, Madagascar, Mali, Mozambique, Swaziland, Tanzania, and Zimbabwe have inclusive systems (Sambo 2003).

An integrative system fully recognizes traditional medicine and incorporates it into all areas of healthcare delivery including national medicines policy, registration of traditional medicine products, regulation of traditional medicine practice, establishment of traditional medicine hospitals, inclusion of traditional medicine in national insurance schemes as reimbursable items, establishment of relevant research institutions on traditional medicine, and training of traditional medicine practitioners at all levels of education including universities. Integration also assumes the visibility of traditional medicine in national health programs and its reflection in national planning and budgeting schemes. Only four countries in the world—the People's Republic of China, the Democratic Republic of Korea, the Republic of Korea, and Vietnam—have integrated traditional medicine into their national healthcare systems.

The freedom of choice for individuals to select their treatment modality and the individual's right according to Universal Declaration of Human Rights guarantees the right to be provided with all the necessary information to enable choices. It is therefore crucial that conventional and traditional medicine practitioners are both equipped with the adequate knowledge and skills necessary to assist people in making a reasonably informed choice of either traditional medicine or conventional medicine, or a combination, depending on the prognosis. Should the choice be to use traditional medicine, then a person has that right, with a reciprocal duty from the government in its obligation to make the treatment safe and effective and to maintain quality standards.

Researchers in several countries have conducted clinical pilot studies on traditional medicine. Outcomes of some of the studies on using traditional medicine to treat HIV/AIDS in Zimbabwe, South Africa, Kenya, Uganda, Zambia, and Burkina Faso have provided very promising results (UNAIDS 2002; Kasilo 2003). In some studies traditional medicine proved to be effective, while others showed presence of toxicity when used in certain doses or if used for a prolonged period. Toxicity can also be present in many conventional medicines, but the issue has been addressed with good research that uses acceptable scientific protocols. Rigorous clinical trials have allowed conventional medicine to improve on the safety, efficacy, and quality. Accordingly, problems raised against traditional medicine can be addressed in the same manner in order to eliminate practices that are not safe or effective, and do not meet quality standards, especially since well over 50 percent of Africans use traditional medicine. In addition to research and studies, the inclusion of traditional health practitioners in a number of policymaking committees and programs, such as national AIDS councils or committees, would alleviate some of the challenges crippling integration.

Implementing Traditional Medicine in Healthcare Systems

Different strategies for formulating policies, laws, and legislation have been developed since Declaration of Alma-Ata in 1978. The AU launched the "Decade of Traditional Medicine" in 2001. Its plan of action had 11 strategic priority areas: building awareness of traditional medicine; enacting legislation; making institutional arrangements; informing, educating, and communicating; mobilizing resources; engaging in research and training; cultivating and conserving medicinal plants; protecting traditional knowledge; producing standardized African traditional medicine locally; developing partnerships; and establishing evaluation, monitoring, and reporting mechanisms (AU 2005a).

In 2002, WHO (2002b) published a strategy for 2002 to 2005 that set out the priority intervention areas of policy formulation, capacity building, research promotion, and the development of the local production of traditional medicines and the protection of intellectual property rights (IPRs).

These two strategies are very similar. The five WHO interventions cover areas similar to those raised by the AU Plan of Action. The AU's plan prioritizes the issue of sensitization of society on traditional medicine, partnerships, evaluation, and monitoring and reporting mechanisms, which were not clearly highlighted in the WHO strategy. If countries in the African region are to succeed in integrating traditional medicines into the health systems, therefore, the first steps are to formulate effective policies, build capacity, promote research, develop the local production of traditional medicines, and protect IPRs. Threats brought by the scourge of infectious diseases such malaria, tuberculosis, HIV, and AIDS provide an opportunity to integrate the two systems, which must be made a priority by African leaders. The issue of integrating traditional medicine with conventional medicine faces many challenges that are discussed below.

Different components of the integration strategy have been implemented since the adoption of the resolution on promoting the role of traditional medicine in health systems and the 2001 Abuja declaration. Research, studies, and programs have been carried out or are currently being conducted across the region.

Various responses and innovations are used to establish and integrate traditional medicine into the health system. In light of the above implementation strategies, some of these are discussed here.

Formulating Policy on Traditional Medicine

Policy provides a country with a plan for managing with certain affairs. Increasingly, countries have clearly defined the role that traditional medicine plays in national healthcare delivery systems. In 1984 WHO/AFRO (1984) passed resolution

AFR/RC34/R8, which urged member states to prepare specific legislation to govern the practice of traditional medicine as part of national health legislation and ensure adequate budget allocation that makes effective development of traditional medicine.

Benin, Côte d'Ivoire, DRC, Equatorial Guinea, Ethiopia, Ghana, Guinea, Mozambique, Togo, and Tanzania have a national policy on traditional medicine in place. However, Botswana, Burkina Faso, Burundi, Cameroon, Central Africa Republic, Chad, Congo, Gambia, Kenya, Madagascar, Mali, Mauritania, Niger, Nigeria, Rwanda, São Tomé and Principe, Seychelles, Sierra Leone, South Africa, and Uganda are in the process of developing traditional medicine policies.

Comoros and Guinea Bissau have neither any policy on traditional medicine nor plans to develop one. Gabon and Zambia use existing national drug policies.

More than 39 countries in the region had finalized the development of the national policy on traditional medicine by the end of 2010. Among the key priorities of the AU's action plan are the facilitation, recognition, acceptance, development and institutionalization of traditional medicine by all members into the region's public health systems. Progress has been made by a number of countries in policy formulation but much still needs to be done, as some developed policies have not been translated into implementation.

Because the use of locally available or imported traditional medicine is widespread and growing, a national policy that governs the practice is crucial. The absence of such a policy is a public health challenge in terms of regulating the safety, efficacy, quality, access, and rational use.

Regulating Traditional Medicine

The establishment of rules governing traditional medicine provides a framework for developing the practice while ensuring safety measures are respected. For those countries that are committed to integrating traditional medicine into their health systems, the first steps include creating laws and regulations. From an African perspective, pride in the generational knowledge of traditional health care should be protected by law to prevent the abuse of traditional medicine practitioners. In many countries, such as Kenya, policy documents such as the Sessional Paper on National Pharmaceutical Policy give little or no attention to traditional medicine practitioners—who are the custodians of traditional medicine (Republic of Kenya 2010).

Conventional medical practitioners and critics of traditional medicine have also argued that there is no way to monitor the work of traditional medicine practitioners. Some countries have established traditional healers associations, through which traditional medical practitioners can be monitored. These associations also provide an infrastructure for building capacity. Traditional medical practitioners in Zambia, Kenya, and South Africa have indicated that it has been difficult to harmonize the legal and regulatory frameworks because of draconian laws such as Kenya's 1925 Witchcraft Act that have not been repealed.

In Benin, Burkina Faso, Cameroon, Côte d'Ivoire, Equatorial Guinea, Ethiopia, Kenya, Ghana, Guinea, Madagascar, Malawi, Mali, Mozambique, Nigeria, Senegal, South Africa, Tanzania, Togo, Uganda, Zambia, and Zimbabwe, some laws and regulations have been enacted to govern traditional medicines. Angola, Central African Republic, Chad, DRC, Equatorial Guinea, Gambia, Rwanda, São Tomé and Principe, and Seychelles are developing laws and regulations (AU 2007).

National Offices for Traditional Medicine

Since the practice of traditional medicine is well recognized by both the AU and WHO, it is important to establish a national office, department, or directorate. The presence of such an office offers the opportunity to have the personnel and infrastructure required to implement any initiative. The office would formulate, implement, and monitor policies, laws, and regulations pertaining to traditional medicine. In 2010, 39 of 46 countries had established national office of traditional medicine in the Ministry of Health.

Expert Committees for Traditional Medicine

An expert committee is convened by the national government for the purpose of making, reviewing, providing technical advice, and making recommendations on policy issues pertaining to traditional medicine. Angola, Benin, Burundi, Central Africa Republic, Côte d'Ivoire, DRC, Ethiopia, Ghana, Guinea, Mozambique, Nigeria, Sierra Leone, and South Africa have such a committee. Several countries use existing relevant expert committees rather than establish a separate one, which is sensible provided that traditional medicine is not overlooked. A few countries are in the process of establishing expert committees.

National Research Institutes and Training Institutions for Traditional Medicine

Burundi, Cameroon, Chad, DRC, Gabon, Ghana, Guinea, Nigeria, and Tanzania have established national research institutes to deal specifically with traditional medicine. Such institutions may exist in a number of countries but have not been identified. Kenya, South Africa, Rwanda, Mozambique, Mali, Madagascar, Ethiopia, Equatorial Guinea, and DRC use existing research institutions to conduct traditional medicine research.

Developments, Research, and Challenges

Although traditional healers and conventional health providers do not collaborate frequently, there is enthusiasm on the part of traditional health practitioners, who remain willing to learn from their conventionally trained counterparts. Such collaboration is essential, given the current trends of the HIV epidemic and the dynamics between the traditional medicine and the health systems (Kayombo et al. 2007; Mills et al. 2006; Nyumbu et al. 2000; Puckree et al. 2002). Collaboration and capacity-building projects provide conventional medical practitioners with opportunities to equip traditional medicine practitioners with the knowledge and skills currently lacking among traditional medicine practitioners. Only through such initiatives can negative practices such as the use of unsterilized instruments and wife inheritance be addressed.[2]

There is very little information on whether research findings on knowledge, attitudes, and practice have been used to develop any intervention that addressed capacity building. In cases where training was reported, it was found to be short term as the training of traditional medicine practitioners ended once the funding was exhausted. No information was found to show progress made on developing a code of ethics to guarantee the safety and quality of traditional medical services or on incorporating aspects of traditional medicine into the curriculum of health professionals or in continuing education and skills development programs. Few reports have reported collaboration initiatives.

There have been several studies on the safety, effectiveness, and quality of traditional medicine (Kayombo et al. 2007; Mills et al. 2005; Nyumbu et al. 2000; Owira and Ojewole 2008; Pope et al. 2009; Tshibangu et al. 2004; UNAIDS 2002). Some have found that certain traditional medicines were effective against herpes zoster, chronic diarrhea associated with HIV and AIDS, and weight loss, and have also shown increased white blood cells important to the immune system and improvements in HIV-related illnesses and fungal infections. There is mounting evidence of the importance of involving traditional medicinal practitioners in managing the HIV and AIDS epidemic both to share their potential benefits and to reduce the possible negative impact of some traditional health interventions on the spread of the disease and the unsafe treatment of infected individuals.

Despite the promise of such studies, there remain concerns about their short duration, limited sample sizes, and lack of control groups. Studies in Eastern, Western, and Southern Africa are attempting to address safety, efficacy, and quality. Even though there are concerns, these efforts must be recognized and encouraged. In order to improve the standard of safety, effectiveness, and quality, traditional medicines must undergo extensive research.

Some countries in the African region are producing pilot projects to use various plant-based preparations to treat various ailments (Kasilo 2003; Odongo 2002; Pope et al. 2009). The Institute of Tropical Medicines and Infectious Diseases at the Jomo Kenyatta University of Agriculture and Technology in collaboration with the Kenya Medical Research Institute, is involved in identifying the plants used

---

2   Wife inheritance is a cultural practice of taking over the wife of a deceased brother or relative even when either partner is infected by HIV. Traditional medicine practitioners are strong advocates of wife inheritance. Illnesses, death, and other misfortune and treatment have been linked the practice of wife inheritance, which has contributed to the spread of HIV.

in traditional medicine, determining the toxicity levels for various medicines, and calculating appropriate dosages. The Southern African Network for Biosciences, South Africa's Council for Scientific and Industrial Research, and traditional healers are also collaborating to test different plants used in Angola, Botswana, Lesotho, Malawi, Mauritius, Mozambique, Namibia, Seychelles, South Africa, Swaziland, Zambia, and Zimbabwe.

While there are many initiatives to find effective traditional medicine treatment for infectious diseases such as HIV and AIDS, the discovery of a potential product will only happen with investment in rigorous research, capacity building, and the development of local production. Much remains to be done.

Specific Responses and Challenges

Traditional medicine is here to stay. Populations with strong beliefs in traditional medicine will continue to use it, as they have for centuries. As part of community development, effective strategies that include all role players must be developed to incorporate science into the practice of traditional medicine. A few countries in Africa have integrated traditional medical practitioners into their healthcare systems, promoted investment in the research of traditional medicines and the development of traditional remedies, and have protected related IPRs.

The vital role of traditional medicine in global healthcare governance has long been recognized. The 1978 Alma-Ata Declaration acknowledged the role of traditional medicine and its practice in achieving health for all. The AU's (2007) Africa Health Strategy provides a framework for action to promote the use of traditional medicine in reducing mortality and morbidity. Other partner agencies, such as USAID, European Union, Africa Development Bank, as well as UN and AU agencies, have also acknowledged the role of African traditional medicine in providing health care throughout the continent.

Critics of integration have disapproved of bringing traditional medicine and practitioners into mainstream health systems as a hoax that should not be left unchallenged or as a sign of lack of leadership. Such arguments recall a time when traditional medicine practice was outlawed by the colonial masters that viewed such practices as backward and uncivilized, forgetting that the practice of traditional medicine is deeply rooted in African culture and, most importantly, holds value for the progression of medicine.

Structured, institutionalized collaboration of traditional medicine practitioners and conventional medical practitioners that shows respect for each discipline, with adequate funding from the governments—both bilaterally and multilaterally—must be developed. For such collaboration to work effectively, an independent body that reports either to the office of top level of government would give this body the prominence and power to scale up the integration of traditional medicine in more African health systems.

Proper scientific scrutiny must still be part of the integration. Conventional medicine undergoes extensive studies, testing the risks and benefits, making it almost impossible to contest its effectiveness. Traditional medicine should also undergo the same process using acceptable, well-designed protocols. Formats to assist registration of traditional medicine must be developed, as has been done with registering medicines in the pharmaceutical industry. The slow rate of integration indicates that some challenges remain, for example in the areas of safety, efficacy, and quality as well as intellectual property and indigenous knowledge as discussed below.

Safety, Efficacy, and Quality Standards

There is little scientific literature on the safety and efficacy of traditional medicine. A growing number of reports have documented sometimes fatal adverse effects of misuse of traditional therapies as well as therapies that lack sufficient safety information or are misrepresented by quack traditional healers, or that involve substances such as bleach, flowers, and human parts.

Studies have shown that when the right to choose whether to believe in traditional medicine or conventional medicine is compromised, people will secretly use what they believe without disclosing its use to either the healthcare provider or the traditional medicine practitioner. Such a decision may prove detrimental to the practice of medicine and indeed fatal to the individual, as some traditional medicines may interact negatively with conventional medicine when taken together (Pope et al. 2009). Given that the field of traditional medicine has not yet generated enough research interest, especially with respect to safety, efficacy, and standards, there is insufficient evidence for authoritative deliberations.

Without the scientific tests required to prove safety and efficacy, it becomes difficult for governments to support traditional medicine initiatives. Secrecy also makes it challenging for conventional medical practitioners to treat people who use both types of medicine. The lack of trust among traditional medicine practitioners, researchers, and biomedical scientists makes it difficult for traditional medicinal practitioners to disclose the composition of what is in the medicine used for fear that their IPRs will be violated.

Intellectual Property and Indigenous Knowledge

In the African tradition, traditional knowledge is passed from generation to generation to a specific individual within the family. One medicinal plant may be used to treat various ailments by different practitioners. Therefore, there are often many people involved in the discovery of a drug, particularly since the long chain of discovery may start with traditional healers and lead from community members to several different types of scientists, including phytochemists and clinicians. The result is an incredibly complex process for deciding how intellectual property is shared down the chain.

That process is hampered in Africa because of persistent underfunding for research, leading to a fundamental lack of the equipment necessary to conduct research. Without the right equipment or expertise to carry out different elements of research, many scientists are often forced to give their discoveries to institutions that possess the right tools and equipment. The most hopeful compounds are usually handed over to pharmaceutical companies to develop drugs that can be manufactured on a large scale. Uncertainties over intellectual property often mean that many potential drugs never get off the ground.

Another challenge is inadequate protection or preservation of traditional medicinal plants and knowledge. Protection is essential to ensure access to traditional health care and respect for those who hold the knowledge. IPR issues require national and international attention. Moreover, overharvesting medicinal plants and using poor harvesting methods threaten ecosystems throughout the region.

With regard to traditional medicine, intellectual property is relatively a new subject in the region. As a result only a few countries such as Eritrea, South Africa, Uganda, and Zimbabwe have developed or reviewed their legislation to include the safeguards provided for in the World Trade Organization's Trade-Related Aspects of Intellectual Property Rights Agreement as of 2010. In addition, Cameroon and Ghana have developed a national framework for IPRs on traditional medicine, while South Africa has developed a traditional knowledge bill. Nigeria has developed national legislation as well as a bill on IPRs. International rules have been built upon national laws with the aim of harmonizing existing regulations or internationalizing certain legislative models (Kebede 2010). The traditional medicines market is currently unregulated in nearly all African countries, which leaves consumers vulnerable to ineffective and potentially dangerous treatments. Countries that claim to regulate traditional medicine often tailor those regulations to support conventional medicine. Unregulated or inappropriate use of traditional medicine can also have side effects that may result in death. Yet most African governments have done very little to regulate traditional medicine. Without regulation, any person who claims to possess knowledge of traditional medicine can sell or distribute traditional medicine or claim to be a traditional medicine practitioner. Because traditional medicine is so widely used, the need for regulation must be addressed not just as a matter of safety but as a matter of progress for medicine itself.

With the uncertain status of traditional medicine and the lack of coordination among institutions, the endangerment of medicinal plant species and spread of bad harvesting practices remain extensive.

Conclusion

Africa is more affected by diseases such as tuberculosis, malaria, and HIV/AIDS than any other continent in the world. There is an urgent need for its countries to be at the forefront of discovering viable, safe, effective, and good-quality traditional medicine. Africa has an abundance of natural resources; it can no longer argue that it lacks specialized knowledge or skills. Attitudes toward traditional medicine must be addressed, not only as conventional medicine practitioners perceive it, but, most importantly, as Africans perceive it. Many Africans grew up with access only to traditional medicines to treat many diseases. Many childhoods have been marked with bitter-tasting remedies or initial stings from an ointment that seemed to be punishment. Nonetheless, it is important to take pride in the many effective traditional medicines that are the result of generations of knowledge. Many people will continue to use effective traditional medicine.

In the early days of conventional medicine, accepted practices included draining a person's blood, drilling holes into skulls to relieve headaches, sweating away the fever, and many other practices that now, after research and testing, explain many deaths and are now considered not only barbaric but also unscientific. The same esteem that allows for development and discovery in conventional medicine should be afforded to traditional medicine. Is Africa's legacy the notion that traditional medicine is backward until it is packaged in a western-type pill? Or will Africans develop their own beliefs and practices?

Apart from a day commemorating African traditional medicine each year and signing resolutions and declarations, African leaders must follow the examples of China, India, and Japan, which have developed evidence-based, accessible, and affordable traditional medicine. Countries that are stuck in the developmental stages of drafting policies and regulations must prioritize the issues of traditional medicine and speed up the process. Such policies and regulations must also be supported with adequate budgets.

Existing national and international studies must be consolidated and new research is needed to fill the evidence gaps. There needs to be collaboration among researchers, biomedical scientists, and traditional medicine practitioners in order to identify medicinal properties, to test the safety, efficacy, and limitations of traditional medicine and to address false claims of cure, weed out charlatans, build the knowledge capacity of traditional medicine practitioners with correct information on HIV and AIDS, provide patients with quality health care, and address the issue of IPRs and indigenous knowledge.

The subject of intellectual property and indigenous knowledge remains under debate in a number of countries. Traditional medicines may also be found in different families or communities and in many different countries. The chain of discovery is long and made more complicated if such a discovery is handed over to pharmaceutical companies and overseas companies. Nevertheless, Africans must unite with a central goal and even compete with each other to develop the wonders of traditional medicine. Africa should actively integrate science and traditional medicine as a priority. The future of medicine lies in integration.

References

African Union (2005). "Plan of Action on the AU Decade of Traditional Medicine (2001–2010): Implementation of the Decision of the Lusaka Summit of Heads of State and Government." October 10–12, Gabarone. Available online: www.africa-union.org/Social%20Affairs/African%20Ministers%20of%20Health%20 2005/PLAN%20OF%20ACTION-TRADITIONAL%20MEDICINE.pdf (October 2012).

African Union (2007). "Africa Health Strategy: 2007–2015." April 9–13, Johannesburg. Available online: www.africa-union.org/root/UA/ Conferences/2007/avril/SA/9-13%20avr/doc/en/Health_Strategy_Min_Draft. pdf (October 2012).

Bodeker, Gerard, Donna Kabatesi, Rachel King et al. (2000). "A Regional Task Force on Traditional Medicine and AIDS." *Lancet* 355(9211): 1284.

Chatora, Rufaro (2003). "An Overview of the Traditional Medicine Situation in the African Region." *African Health Monitor* 4(1): 4–7. Available online: www.afro.who.int/index.php?option=com_docman&task=doc_ download&gid=501&ItemId=2111 (October 2012).

Homsy, Jaco, Rachel King, Joseph Tenywa et al. (2004). "Defining Minimum Standards of Practice for Incorporating African Traditional Medicine into HIV/AIDS Prevention, Care, and Support: A Regional Initiative in Eastern and Southern Africa." *Journal of Alternative and Complementary Medicine* 10(5): 905–10.

Kasilo, Ossy M.J. (2003). "Enhancing Traditional Medicine Research and Development in the African Region." *African Health Monitor* 4(1): 15–18. Available online: www.afro.who.int/index.php?option=com_ docman&task=doc_download&gid=501&ItemId=2111 (October 2012).

Kayombo, Edmund J., Febronia C. Uiso, Zakaria H. Mbwambo et al. (2007). "Experience of Initiating Collaboration of Traditional Healers in Managing HIV and AIDS in Tanzania." *Journal of Ethnobiology and Ethnomedicine* 3(6). doi: 10.1186/1746-4269-3-6. Available online: www.ethnobiomed.com/ content/3/1/6 (October 2012).

Kebede, Derege, ed. (2010). *African Health Monitor*. Special Issue 14: African Traditional Medicine Day, August 31. Available online: ahm.afro.who.int/ special-issue14/ahm-special-issue-14.pdf

Mills, Edward, Curtis Cooper, Dugald Seely et al. (2005). "African Herbal Medicines in the Treatment of HIV: *Hypoxis* and *Sutherlandia*. An Overview of Evidence and Pharmacology." *Nutrition Journal* 4(19). doi: 10.1186/1475-2891-4-19. Available online: www.nutritionj.com/content/4/1/19 (October 2012).

Mills, Edward, Sonal Singh, Kumanan Wilson et al. (2006). "The Challenges of Involving Traditional Healers in HIV/AIDS Care." *International Journal of STD & AIDS* 17(6): 360–63. doi: 10.1258/095646206777323382.

Nyumbu, Mutinta, E. Bwalya, and N. Orabaton (2000). "Referral Practices among Zambian Traditional Health Practitioners to Health Delivery Points: Has the HIV/AIDS Pandemic Changed the Practice." 13th International AIDS Conference, 9–14 July, Durban. Available online: ww1.aegis.org/conferences/iac/2000/WePeD4730.html (October 2012).

Odongo, Eunice A. (2002). "Women Fighting AIDS in Kenya, Traditional Medicine and HIV/AIDS." 14th International AIDS Conference, 7–12 July, Durban. Available online: www.iasociety.org/Abstracts/A9559.aspx (October 2012).

Owira, Peter M.O. and John A.O. Ojewole (2008). "'African Potato' (*Hypoxis hemerocallidea* corm): A Plant-Medicine for Modern and 21st Century Diseases of Mankind? A Review." *Phytotherapy Research* 23(2): 147–52. doi: 10.1002/ptr.2595.

Peltzer, Karl, Nolwandle Mngqundaniso, and Gebrewold Petros (2006). "HIV/AIDS/STI/TB Knowledge, Beliefs, and Practices of Traditional Healers in KwaZulu-Natal, South Africa." *AIDS Care* 18(6): 608–13.

Peltzer, Karl, Natalie F. Preez, Shandir Ramlagan et al. (2008). "Use of Traditional Complementary and Alternative Medicine for HIV Patients in KwaZulu-Natal, South Africa." *BMC Public Health* 8(255). doi: 10.1186/1471-2458-8-255. Available online: www.biomedcentral.com/1471-2458/8/255 (October 2012).

Pope, Cynthia, Renée T. White, and Robert Malow, eds (2009). *HIV/AIDS: Global Frontiers in Prevention/Intervention.* New York: Routledge.

Puckree, Threethambal, Melody Mkhize, Zama Mgobhozi et al. (2002). "African Traditional Healers: What Health Care Professionals Need to Know." *International Journal of Rehabilitation Research* 25(4): 247–51.

Republic of Kenya. Ministry of Medical Services and Ministry of Public Health and Sanitation (2010). "Sessional Paper on National Pharmaceutical Policy." June. Available online: apps.who.int/medicinedocs/documents/s18697en/s18697en.pdf (October 2012).

Sambo, Luis G. (2003). "Integration of Traditional Medicine into National Health Systems in the African Region: The Journey So Far." *African Health Monitor* 4(1): 8–11. Available online: www.afro.who.int/index.php?option=com_docman&task=doc_download&gid=501&ItemId=2111 (October 2012).

Tshibangu, K.C., Z.B. Worku, M.A. de Jongh et al. (2004). "Assessment of Effectiveness of Traditional Herbal Medicine in Managing HIV/AIDS Patients in South Africa." *East African Medical Journal* 81(10): 499–504.

UNAIDS (2000). "Collaboration with Traditional Healers in HIV/AIDS Prevention and Care in Sub-Saharan Africa: A Literature Review." Geneva. Available online: data.unaids.org/Publications/IRC-pub01/jc299-tradheal_en.pdf (October 2012).

UNAIDS (2002). "Ancient Remedies, New Disease: Involving Traditional Healers in Access to AIDS Care and Prevention in East Africa." UNAIDS Case Study, June, Geneva. Available online: data.unaids.org/Publications/IRC-pub02/jc761-ancientremedies_en.pdf (October 2012).

UNAIDS (2005). "AIDS in Africa: Three Scenarios to 2025." Geneva. Available online: data.unaids.org/Publications/IRC-pub07/jc1058-aidsinafrica_en.pdf (October 2012).

World Health Organization (2002). "WHO Traditional Medicine Strategy: 2002–2005." Geneva. Available online: apps.who.int/medicinedocs/pdf/s2297e/s2297e.pdf (October 2012).

World Health Organization, UNAIDS, and UNICEF (2011). "Global HIV/AIDS Response: Epidemic Update and Health Sector Progress Towards Universal Access." Progress Report 2011, Geneva. Available online: whqlibdoc.who.int/publications/2011/9789241502986_eng.pdf (October 2012).

World Health Organization Regional Office for Africa (1984). "Final Report of the Regional Committee." 34th Session of the WHO Regional Committee for Africa, September 12–19, October, Brazzaville. Available online: www.afro.who.int/en/downloads/doc_download/5226-thirty-fourth-session-of-the-who-regional-committee-for-africa-final-report.html (October 2012).

World Health Organization Regional Office for Africa (2000). "Promoting the Role of Traditional Medicine in Health Systems: A Strategy for the African Region." AFR/RC50/9, March 9, Brazzaville. Available online: www.afro.who.int/index.php?option=com_docman&task=doc_download&gid=872&Itemid=2111 (October 2012).

World Health Organization Regional Office for Africa (2010). "Guidelines for Registration of Traditional Medicines in the WHO African Region." Brazzaville. Available online: www.afro.who.int/index.php?option=com_docman&task=doc_download&gid=6152 (October 2012).

Chapter 7

Health Professionals and Sustainable Economic Development in the Horn of Africa

Mengsteab Tesfayohannes

The Horn of Africa is one of the most troubled parts of the world. For a long time, the region has been ravaged with recurrent drought and famine, brutal civil conflicts (Somalia and Sudan), interstate armed conflicts (Ethiopia and Eritrea), internal displacement, and widespread, abject poverty, and disease. This situation is due to internal and external destabilizing factors related to ethnicity, tribalism, resource sharing, poverty, strategic international interests, porous borders, and hegemonic desires. The Horn is also one of the most geopolitically important regions of the world. It is located along the busiest shipping routes between the Red Sea basin and the Indian Ocean. The region produced the second highest number of refugees (after the Central and Great Lakes regions) in sub-Saharan Africa (United Nations High Commissioner for Refugees [UNHCR] 2009). It is a sad scenario to see crises of extensive magnitude in countries that share many common sociocultural and linguistic heritages.

For the purposes of this chapter, the Horn of Africa refers to four countries: Djibouti, Eritrea, Ethiopia, and Somalia. Many of the facts and figures are estimates as it is difficult to obtain accurate data from the region. Accordingly, the region has over 100 million people (World Bank 2012c). With regard to socioeconomic indicators, about 24 percent of the total population in sub-Saharan Africa lives below the poverty line of less than $1.25 a day (United Nations 2012a). Although the gross domestic product (GDP) per capita on a purchasing power parity basis varies slightly from country to country, the average for the region was estimated to be around $1,250 in 2010 (Central Intelligence Agency 2012). This is low even in comparison with sub-Saharan Africa's average of more than $2,200 (World Bank 2012d). In terms of demography, women account for more than 50 percent of the population. (World Bank 2012d). Gender disparity in education and economic opportunities is prevalent in the region at all levels, be at the country, community, or personal levels. More women than men are victims of abject poverty.

As a vivid sign of a classical underdeveloped regional economy, more than 80 percent of the labour force in the Horn of Africa is engaged in subsistence agricultural and nomadic activities (Central Intelligence Agency 2012). The rest is involved in other economic sectors, including the informal economy. Currently, the region's countries are attempting to reverse their bleak socioeconomic status by undertaking some fundamental reforms that allow them to make a noticeable headway in attaining at least some of the United Nations Millennium Development Goals (MDGs) by 2015. As a result of support from the international community at least two of the MDGs have already been met: the targets of reducing by half the proportion of people living on less than $1.25 per day and the proportion of people without access to improved sources of water (UN 2012a). Some progress is still being made on the goals of achieving university education and overall human development, promoting gender-aware development processes that empower women, improving health and reducing child mortality, ensuring environmental sustainability, and promoting innovation and appropriate technology.

Like other vital socioeconomic sectors such as agriculture, industry, and education, the healthcare system in the Horn of Africa is in a precarious situation. Service-providing capacity is extremely low and outreach across the region is extremely limited (UNICEF 2012). Health significantly affects the productivity and well-being of the bulk of the population of any country. Therefore, an all-out effort is needed to advance the capacity to provide better health services to society at large. Unfortunately, the healthcare sectors in the Horn have suffered from years of neglect and lack of attention, due to inadequate resources allocation, poor governance, and sociopolitical instability. The current dilapidated conditions of the region's healthcare systems deprive the majority of the population of even rudimentary health services. There is an extreme critical shortage of qualified healthcare professionals and basic medical supplies and facilities throughout the region. Many highly qualified health workers such as doctors, health officers, medical technologists, and registered nurses have left in large numbers for several affluent countries, in search of a better life by gaining financial and non-financial incentives.

During the last 40 years, the countries in the Horn of Africa produced huge numbers of refugees and highly skilled emigrants particularly in the strategically vital sectors such as health. From 1990 to 2005, more than 40 percent of those locally trained medical doctors, and nurses left the region to work outside of their countries. More than 80 percent of them settled in North America and Europe (Clemens and Pettersson 2007). The availability of a strong and modern healthcare system is one important attribute of the developmental dynamics in democratic state building. Unfortunately, massive brain drain has left the Horn countries with underdeveloped and debilitated healthcare systems, which has been detrimental to their developmental endeavours. Healthy human ingenuity is the most important input in the sustainable economic development dynamics and wealth creation process. Policies, strategies, and action plans that are specific, measurable, attainable, realistic, timely, effective, and resourceful are needed to tackle and reverse the massive brain drain of qualified healthcare professionals from the Horn of Africa.

Such plans demand a radical reform of the current archaic and inefficient healthcare governance and management systems, which would discourage the continuing brain drain of qualified healthcare professionals and its consequential effects and would contribute to promoting brain gain. This chapter therefore deals with the major causes of brain drain and its prevalence in the Horn of Africa. It considers the negative impacts of brain drain on the region's overall sustainable development efforts and the reasons behind the failure to reduce the mass exodus. It discusses the observed weaknesses and strengths of current policies, strategies, and action programs and provides reasons and recommendations for Horn countries making healthcare systems a high priority in their core development agendas and for attracting the diaspora to come home.

Rather than provide an empirical survey, this chapter focuses on the conceptual discourse supported by research-based anecdotal facts, observational realities, and figures. In this way, it seeks to reveal the weaknesses of the existing policies, strategies, and action programs (if any) for retraining healthcare professionals in the region. This preliminary conceptual study can thus help policy makers and other stakeholders improve the functionality of the region's healthcare systems. This chapter will follow an exploratory and conceptual methodology using dialectical inquiry and a holistic approach in its analysis and strategic considerations. Brain drain problems stem from the failure to take decisive strategic actions at the right time, of the right type, at the desired level, and at various stages of developmental continuum. The recommendations contained in this chapter are conceptual and subjective, and open for further discussion, evaluation, and analysis.

The Contribution of Health to Sustainable Economic Development

There is a strong link between health and economic growth. Health affects the national economic dynamics of any country directly and indirectly. The productivity of the workforce depends on its physical and mental developmental welfare. Health is not only the absence of illness; being healthy is a source of well-being. The individual's capacity for physical and mental development throughout life is the best asset for the continuity of economic prosperity at all levels of societal structural hierarchy. In this rational sense, promoting proper health protection is a valuable national investment with its intrinsic and extrinsic instrumental values (Beine et al. 2001; Mexican Commission on Macroeconomics and Health 2004). For example, healthy workers are more productive and less absent from work due to health-related issues. Students with good nutrition can concentrate better and learn and retain knowledge better. Accordingly, they tend to contribute more to socioeconomic endeavours later as better skilled and more productive workers.

Good healthcare provision has played a cardinal role in the developmental of industrialized countries. The 1993 Nobel laureate Robert W. Fogel (2002), who studied the impact of health on economic growth, confirmed that between one third and one half of the achieved economic growth in England in the last 200 years has been due to improved nutrition and health protection provided to the bulk of the population. Other noteworthy studies have confirmed the positive impact of large-scale health services provision on socioeconomic growth (Commission on Macroeconomics and Health 2001). For example, an increase in life expectancy from 50 years to 70 years (an increase of 40 percent) would tangentially raise the growth rate by 1.4 percentage points annually (Barro 1996). A 10 percent decrease in malaria is associated with an increased annual growth of 0.3 percent (Gallup and Sachs 1998). The existing level of global malnutrition causes a decrease in the annual GDP per capita worldwide of between 0.23 percent and 4.7 percent (Arcand 2001). All these findings indicate a powerful link between health and socioeconomic growth. For very poor countries such as those in sub-Saharan Africa, the impact of health care on sustainable economic development is more prevalent as an important part of the national socioeconomic pyramid (Beine et al. 2001).

The inadequate provision of health services is a major contributor to the continuing poverty cycle, as illustrated in Figure 7.1. Better health services would enhance the resourcefulness of the economically active population. As C.K. Prahalad (2010) has said, "if we stop thinking of the poor as victims or as a burden and start recognizing them as resilient and creative entrepreneurs and value-conscious consumers, a whole new world of opportunity can open up."

However, the region's national economies are dominated by macroeconomic management focused on wasteful rent-seeking interactions and the excessive dualism of the extreme economic dominance of a few alongside the majority poor. The result is an effective bottleneck in socioeconomic growth. In classical dualistic cities such as Nairobi, Lagos, Johannesburg, and Addis Ababa, it is not surprising to see extraordinary modern communication facilities, exotic cars, expensive private schools, hospitals, and other luxury facilities sometimes not even easily found in developed countries. These expensive trappings are surrounded by the abject poverty of the majority of city dwellers. Dualism provides the opportunity for the few who are economically dominant to waste scarce national wealth in order to meet their own narrow needs at the expense of basic development spending earmarked for improving the lives of the poor. In many low-income countries, what limited healthcare provision facilities exist are usually concentrated in major urban areas. For example, in Nairobi, there is one physician for 300 people, while in the nearby rural area the ratio is one medical doctor for more than 20,000 people (Republic of Kenya, Ministry of Public Health and Sanitation 2006). Health care should be a right, not a privilege. This kind of excessive dualism should not be permitted to deprive the majority of the population from getting relatively better health care. The poor represent not only a disgraceful human condition but also a huge potential force for a sustainable development if they can be helped in their self-help endeavours (Kotler and Lee 2009).

Indeed, unless the Horn countries expand their basic health services to include the majority at the bottom, they cannot achieve the necessary socioeconomic growth. The overall performance and outreach of the healthcare system of any country have a direct impact on the sustainable economic development and welfare of that society.

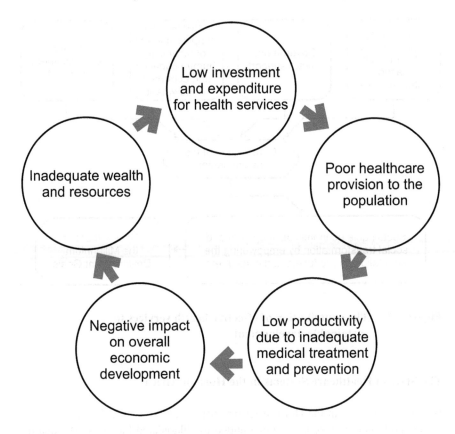

Figure 7.1   The health-related poverty trap

In the democratic state-building process, it is a Herculean task to create an effective and well-governed national healthcare system. Figure 7.2 shows the intricacy of the healthcare capacity-building process, which requires the contribution of all stakeholders including government departments and ministries, international partners, nongovernmental organizations (NGOs), professional associations, community organizations, and many others. Capacity building in health care is a strategic investment with potentially higher returns. The returns are the well-being of citizens, which is vital in any development dynamics. The countries in the Horn of Africa need to invest resources to advance their national healthcare systems to smooth the road map to sustainable socioeconomic development.

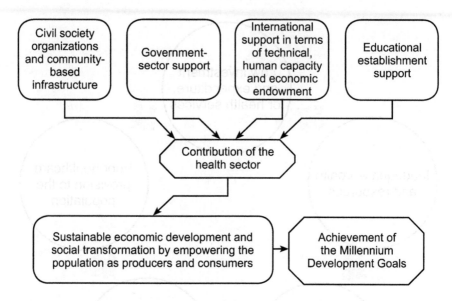

**Figure 7.2   The contribution of effective health services to
sustainable development**

The State of Healthcare Systems in the Horn of Africa

Healthcare systems in the Horn of Africa suffer from a chronic shortage of both
human and material resources compounded by dilapidated facilities. The quality
of healthcare services can be assessed in terms of both preventive and treatment
services provided to the population at large. According to the World Health
Organization (2012a) the following are the building blocks of a health system:

- a well-performing and responsive healthcare workforce;
- a well-functioning healthcare system that ensures equitable access to
  essential medical products, vaccines, and technologies of assured quality,
  safety, and efficacy;
- appropriate and affordable financing system that supports adequate
  healthcare services and helps protect the needy from financial catastrophe
  or impoverishment associated with paying for healthcare services;
- a functioning health information system that ensures the production,
  analysis, dissemination, and use of reliable and timely information on
  health determinants, health system performance, and health status; and
- an effective and able healthcare governance system that involves workable
  strategic policies and action programs that promote a framework for
  effective oversight, coalition building, sound regulation, and accountability.

These five building blocks contribute to the quality of the healthcare system, which has been defined as "the degree to which health services for individuals and populations increase the likelihood of desired health outcomes and are consistent with current professional knowledge" (Institute of Medicine 2001). The quality of health care itself is expressed in an integrated framework that incorporates structure, process, and outcome elements. As John Peabody and his colleagues (2006) write:

- *Structure* refers to stable, material characteristics (infrastructure, tools, technology) and the resources of the organizations that provide care and the financing of care (levels of funding, staffing, payment schemes, incentives).

- *Process* is the interaction between caregivers and patients during which structural inputs from the health care system are transformed into health outcomes.

- *Outcomes* can be measured in terms of health status, deaths, or disability-adjusted life years—a measure that encompasses the morbidity and mortality of patients or groups of patients. Outcomes also include patient satisfaction or patient responsiveness to the healthcare system.

As shown in Table 7.1, the overall status of the healthcare systems in the four countries in the Horn of Africa is very poor. In sum, their extremely meagre spending per capita is unsustainable and very low by any given standard. The adult mortality rate is also excessively high, which indicates the rudimentary nature of healthcare provision in terms of outreach and quality.

The effectiveness of healthcare provision depends on the adequate supply of qualified healthcare professionals at all levels and specializations. The region continues to suffer from a chronic shortage of healthcare professionals including doctors, pharmacists, healthcare officers, laboratory technicians, and registered nurses. The region's healthcare sector is severely understaffed and poorly organized and has woefully inadequate resources compared to the universally accepted benchmark for basic healthcare provision. Table 7.2 illustrates that the sparse availability of healthcare professionals and their inability to serve even 20 percent of the population.

The Horn of Africa is among the worst place in the world to find a doctor and other healthcare professionals (WHO 2006). WHO recommends a minimum ratio for developing countries of 1:10,000. However, in Ethiopia, for example, the ratio is one doctor for 47,000 people. This critical shortage is aggravated by the rural-urban disparities. In major urban areas such as Addis Ababa, Asmara, Djibouti, and Mogadishu, the concentration of the healthcare professionals is very high compared to the rural areas: in Ethiopia, more than half the doctors working are in Addis Ababa and other bigger cities. Moreover, more than 60 percent of them work in private hospitals and clinics, because public hospitals and clinics pay extremely

Table 7.1 Basic health indicators in the Horn of Africa

Country	Population, 2011 (millions)	GNI per capita, 2011	Life expectancy male/female at birth (years), 2011	Child mortality under age five (years per 1,000), 2011	Adult mortality rate (male/female per 1,000), 2010	Total health expenditure per capita, 2010	Total health expenditure as percentage of GDP, 2010
Djibouti	0.9	1,270[a]	56.5/59.4	89.5	321.2/278.7	$91.7	7.2
Eritrea	5.4	430	59.1/63.8	67.8	344.8/261.3	$11.9	2.7
Ethiopia	84.7	400	57.7/60.9	77.0	304.3/258.9	$15.7	4.9
Somalia	9.6	N/A	49.6/52.8	180.0	367.6/311/6	N/A	N/A

Note: No recent data on Somalia are available. GNI = gross national product; GDP = gross domestic product.
[a] Most recent data are from 2009.
Source: World Bank (2012d, 2012b).

Table 7.2   Human resources for health in the Horn of Africa

	Djibouti (2012)	Eritrea (2011)	Ethiopia (2012)	Somalia (2012)	WHO African Region (2012)
Physicians	185	215	1,806	300	118,621
Density per 10,000 population	2.3	0.5	0.2	0.4	2.2
Nurses and Midwifery personnel	666	2,505	19,158	965	467,487
Density per 10,000 population	8.0	5.8	2.4	1.1	9.0
Dentistry personnel[a]	99	16	N/A	N/A	16,732
Density per 10,000 population[a]	1.2	0.05	N/A	N/A	0.4
Pharmaceutical personnel	266	107	1,201	50	34,223
Density per 10,000 population	3.2	0.2	0.2	0.1	0.7

Notes: N/A = not available; WHO = World Health Organization.
[a] Data are for 2005–10.
Sources: World Health Organization (2011b, 2012c).

low salaries, require long working hours without adequate compensation for overtime, and have discouraging working environments fraught with bureaucratic red tape and inefficiency. There are also many other demotivating reasons, such as understaffing (Berhan 2008). The situation is similar in Eritrea, Somalia, and Djibouti. Attention dedicated to health care is obviously weak, despite the vicious cycle of poverty. However, within the limits of available capacity, these four countries should make it a priority to provide the basic healthcare services to the bulk of their populations. It should be a mandatory precondition for the acceleration of socioeconomic development.

Over the past 40 years, Ethiopia and Somalia have attempted to establish healthcare training institutional capacities such as medical and nursing schools and other training establishments. Ethiopia successfully trained more than 4,000 doctors, including specialists, and 19,000 qualified nurses between 1968 and 2006 (Berhan 2008). However, less than half of them currently work in the country. Furthermore, only 638 of those working in Ethiopia are engaged in public hospitals and clinics. The situation in Somalia is even worse due to political crises and civil war. There are only 300 doctors in the whole country (WHO 2012c). This is a vivid evidence of the severity of the situation. Until 2003, Eritrea did not have its own medical school (AMES 2010). The majority of doctors in Eritrea received their training in Ethiopia, as Eritrea was part of it until 1991. Eritrea has now established the Orotta School of Medicine. However, the government and the public must nurture the medical school and other training facilities to function properly and produce qualified doctors. The Medical School of Djibouti and the Higher Institute of Health Sciences were founded only in 2007 (WHO 2010a). Meanwhile, there are more Ethiopian medical specialists working in Chicago area alone than working in the country. Even many of the newly trained doctors migrate without even serving locally for a brief period.

It is difficult to track down the resource outlay for training doctors and other healthcare professionals, but these countries spend a lion's share of their meagre training resources on capacity building in their healthcare sector. Nonetheless, they fail to implement effective retention strategies for their professionals to stay at home and serve the local population. Indeed, the people of the Horn have sacrificed what little they have to train young healthcare professionals just to see them leave to pursue both financial and non-financial incentives. However, there are known push and pull factors for this unwanted scenario.

The Whys and Hows of Brain Drain

The brain drain issue has become a major concern in both developed and less developed countries. The flow is not only from developing to developed countries, but also from developed to developed and from developing to developing countries. Because it is case specific, there is no commonly accepted universal definition. For example, B. Lindsay Lowell and Allan Findlay (2001) defined brain drain as the emigration of tertiary-educated persons at such levels and for such lengthy durations that their losses are not offset by the benefits they bestow. The potential benefits are remittances, technology transfer, and the promotion of investment or trade from the recipient country. Brain drain exists in all areas but is more severe in the health sector as the developed countries themselves have substantial shortages of qualified healthcare professionals.

Brain drain also occurs within a country. Intra-country or internal brain drain can happen into two forms: from rural to urban and from public to the private establishments. There are ample possibilities for highly qualified healthcare professionals such as doctors to leave their practices and engage in other non-medical activities, particularly in politics, business, and the bureaucracy. A common scenario is external brain drain, when healthcare professionals migrate to other countries because of financial and non-financial incentives and better professional opportunities. External brain drain can also happen into two ways. The first and more popular one is African healthcare professionals migrating to the more affluent countries such as the United Kingdom, France, Canada, and the United States. The second but less popular is the so-called inter-developing countries brain drain, with healthcare professionals migrating from one African country to another with better endowments. Many highly qualified Ethiopian doctors now work in Botswana because it offers more monetary and non-monetary incentives and better working conditions.

Brain drain is detrimental to the originating country, although a debate continues over how to measure the negative impact of migration versus the tangible benefits to the countries of origin. Generally, it is easier to assess internal brain drain: while service provision is national it may not be as desired. For example, internal brain drain includes flows from rural to urban areas in pursuit of better opportunities and from public to private healthcare facilities in pursuit of better pay and professional development. However, for the purposes of this chapter, the discussion will focus on the external brain drain.

Several factors are involved in inter-country brain drain (Meeus 2003). Earlier studies have already identified numerous push and pull factors for brain drain, which are generally common in several development countries (Adredo 2000; Brown 2000; Dovlo 2004; Edokat 2000; Goma 1990; Lowell and Findlay 2001; McAuliffe and Maclachlan 2005; Meeus 2003; Mutume 2003; Scott et al. 2004; Teferra 2000; Teferra 2005; UN Economic and Social Council 2000). Therefore, for clarity in the context of the Horn of Africa, these factors are discussed here in a hierarchal framework at the national, sectoral, and institutional levels.

Push and Pull Factors at a National Level

National Governance and Political Stability

The countries in the Horn suffer tremendously from bad governance, hegemonic rules, excessive administrative bureaucracy, corruption, nepotism, misrule, and lack of basic democratic rights. The perennial nature of all these disadvantages has contributed to the huge brain drain of qualified human resources in the region. This problem persists despite continuous attempts by these countries to develop retention strategies such as offering compensation raises (salary increments), improving bureaucratic inefficiencies, and providing more facilities for professional development. Nonetheless, the pull factors in the receiving countries have so far managed to win, thanks to factors such as a conducive and politically stable atmosphere, responsible and relatively accountable governance, assurance of basic human and democratic rights for residents and citizens, good healthcare governance, highly developed medical schools, high-level use of technology, a well-integrated network, and effective coordination among healthcare training and caregiving establishments.

The Sociocultural Environment

Many countries spend a significant portion of GDP to protect the health and well-being of their citizens. Both developed and developing countries make health care a high priority in their national development agendas as the corner stone of multi-fold societal progress. This is particularly true in the industrialized countries, where healthcare systems are well structured and socially inclusive. Healthcare professionals at all levels enjoy incremental monetary benefit, social respect, and professional recognition. Such a motivating and professionally supportive, benevolent atmosphere is, of course, more attractive to health workers. However, in underdeveloped and conflict-ridden and post-conflict fragile states, as in the

Horn of Africa, there is paltry recognition and respect for healthcare professionals, who are also considered marginally important by the bureaucracy. Although many efforts are underway, even in the Horn, to improve their situation and status, qualified healthcare professionals leave for countries that provide financial and non-financial incentives such as suitable working environment, opportunities for professional recognition and development, higher monetary compensation, shorter and less challenging working hours, adequate benefits, sufficient resources, and better working conditions. The Horn countries have not yet created a conducive environment to the extent of their ability in many aspects, as discussed below. They so far have not done well in using the professional capacity and talent of their healthcare workforce due to weak governance and institutional capacity. Doctors and nurses, particularly those working in rural areas, are forced to work under duress. Their working conditions diminish their professional calibre and ambition. These are some of the numerous push factors that cause healthcare workers to migrate to other countries at an alarming rate.

National Regulatory Problems

The Horn countries have failed to streamline their healthcare regulatory framework. Many governance regulations are excessively bureaucratic, under-coordinated, and not well synchronized. There are deficiencies in the top-down and bottom-up communication and administrative systems, resulting in discouragement and mayhem in the medical profession. In reality, there is a dualistic environment that allows for a few to benefit unreasonably at the expense of many. The national healthcare regulatory frameworks are designed and implemented so that so-called concerned government organs wield excessive bureaucratic power over the healthcare regulatory systems in terms of service provision, resource allocation, and administrative performance and coordination. Industrialized countries such as Germany, Canada, the United States, and Japan have established well-functioning healthcare systems with professional societies and supporting associations suitably organized to play a pivotal role in the professional development of medical sciences. Emerging countries such as Korea, Singapore, Brazil, and China have also managed to do so. In the Horn, these types of healthcare professional accreditation and governing associations and boards are at an embryonic stage. Governments give little respect and recognition to their important role and their independent status and indeed often interfere. Healthcare professionals are also prone to manipulation to collaborate in unethical activities and zero-sum games played by the political power holders through corruption and bad governance. These arduous push factors at home coupled with the favourable working conditions and affluence abroad have created the current massive brain drain scenario in the Horn of Africa.

Push and Pull Factors at the Sectoral Level

Health Sector Institutional Governance

Healthcare governance in the Horn, particularly at the sectoral level, is very poor. Governmental involvement dominates in the governance, provision, and financing activities in almost all sectors, be it public, semi-public, or private. The level of involvement is intensive and coercive to the extent of dictating hospitals and other institutional capacities, resource allocation, and service provision to the public. Ministries of health have the sole authority to develop policies and strategies, to administer and govern, and to guide and control the activities of both public and private healthcare providers and trainers. These command-and-control mechanisms include both urban and rural areas.

However, the region's governments have failed to make adequate efforts to empower their healthcare ministries. The ministries themselves should also do their best to meet their obligations. They are expected to be administratively efficient, technically qualified, and strategically effective to attract preferential treatment by the central governments. They should not expect preferential treatment unless they seriously try to marginalize their weakness and enhance their strength.

Moreover, health ministries are forced to function under heavy political influence and budgetary constraints as the governments in the region give priority to other agendas such as military concerns. These capacity limitations have left healthcare professionals under-remunerated and desperate for coping strategies. As a result, highly qualified doctors become dissatisfied with their pay, workload, and the resources available to them. As in many other countries, the region's healthcare-governing bureaucrats have failed to address job and professional dissatisfaction of healthcare professionals, creating an inconvenient situation for retention of healthcare professionals. Brain-receiving countries have successfully attracted healthcare professionals to their workforce by providing better opportunities, helped by their well-developed healthcare governance structures.

Institutional Capacity, Income, and Job Satisfaction

Qualified healthcare professionals in the Horn of Africa have long suffered from disproportionally low remuneration, poor working conditions, low job satisfaction, and inadequate professional development. The extremely limited opportunities for upgrading skills and the critical shortage of other supportive facilities such as modern medical equipment and cutting-edge healthcare technology have become major stumbling blocks for retention endeavours. For example, many hospitals, medical schools, and other healthcare facilities in the region still operate with rudimentary and insufficient X-ray equipment, operating room facilities, and surgical tools. These limitations prevent them from enhancing their performance and providing better service. The inability to implement performance-based healthcare management systems has also been detrimental. These impediments contribute to the failure of exercising judicious promotional and encouragement approaches at sectoral levels.

Push and Pull Factors at Institutional and Departmental Levels

Poor Organization of Healthcare Providers

Service providers such as hospitals, clinics, health centres, and laboratories are the prime actors in a national healthcare system. Their outreach, performance, and resourcefulness are the indicators of the functionality of the system in any given environment. Healthcare providers in the Horn operate within a cumbersome top-down administrative hierarchy of the supreme national healthcare governance bodies such as the national ministries of health. This bureaucratic working environment has become so complex and excessive that many medical doctors and other qualified healthcare workers lose interest and concentrate instead on finding ways to leave the region and work elsewhere.

Inadequate Coordination and Collaboration

It is very expensive to train medical doctors and other highly qualified healthcare professionals. For example, in 2002 the estimated cost of training a generalist medical doctor was between $50,000 and $60,000 and takes a minimum of six years (Shinn 2002). Although the training is expensive yet inadequate, the Horn countries have managed to train healthcare professionals at both generalist and specialist levels. However, there is still lack of effective complementarity between training establishments and service providers such as hospitals and health centres. This deficiency negatively affects the professional development of medical doctors in particular, providing an excuse to leave their countries of origin. Medical schools are expected to establish collaborative links with the appropriate ministries, the business community and international partners. However, they are not yet successful in expanding their specialization programs to upgrade skills in line with the local short- and long-term needs. Some of the reasons might be the lack of coordination and the chronic deficiency of governance coupled with lack of resources.

Challenges in Promoting National and International Networks, Collaboration and Partnership

The Horn countries have a poor reputation for promoting national and international networks and cooperative partnership initiatives in many academic and developmental activities. This has become one of the main non-financial demotivating factors for healthcare professionals. For example, many doctors have taken their own initiatives to establishing networks with medical schools, research centres, and other healthcare development centres around the world. The partnership between Addis Ababa University Faculty of Medicine and German, British, and American universities and between Eritrea's Orotta School of Medicine relationship and Santa Clara University in Cuba and George Washington University in the United States have been fruitful examples (AMES 2010; George Washington University 2009). Such initiatives have laid the groundwork to extend easily to the institutions of brain-receiving countries.

Thanks to the global dissemination of technology in general and information technology in particular, even poor countries can afford to make modern technological tools and multimedia locally available at affordable cost. Governments need to take bold action to make such facilities accessible by allocating more resources, which could be generated through savings, diversion of resources from other sectors, public and private partnerships, and foreign investment and support. Governments should encourage private sector involvement as well as public-private partnership in healthcare provision, governance, and administration. Hence, healthcare providers and training institutions should endeavour to make modern technology and communication systems widely available to mitigate the arduous consequences of brain drain.

RELIANOMICS in the Health System for Brain Retention and Gain

This section contains strategies to improve the effectiveness and outreach of health care in the Horn of Africa. These strategies and arguments are theoretical in their content and limited in their scope. In order to encourage new ideas that promote more innovation and continuous improvement, this section relies on a methodological approach and conceptual analysis called "RELIANOMICS." It advocates building internal capacity to serve as the foundation for achieving success. Strengthening internal capacity and attracting external capacity create a win-win outcome. In other words, external support should complement internal capacity building within a holistic framework.

RELIANOMICS is framed to answer three fundamental questions: What is the true desired end point—what is worthy of ambitions and efforts? What is the full value to be created—not just economic value but social value as well? What is the total equation—the full framework—by which efforts and tradeoffs must be measured, and how can the solution be made sustainable? The concept adheres to the holistic approach with top-down, bottom-up, and side-support links and interdependence. RELIANOMICS focuses on making the balance right to achieve better results, because, as Carly Fiorina (2001) says, if the balance between what is local and what is global, between what is economic benefit and what is societal benefit, between what is held sacred and what is invented a new is not balance right, it is not possible to gain access to the world's thinking, talent, ideas, and know-how.

RELIANOMICS goes beyond expressing how to make activities and their results more effective, efficient, affordable, and far reaching. Figure 7.3 illustrates the coordination of healthcare provision and financing within the RELIANOMICS conceptual framework. To reframe the content and form of any system, there must be an inquiry into the details of the whole system and the mandates of important stakeholders and task executors. The stakeholders are the healthcare providers and financiers (or actors) in the top-down healthcare system. The cardinal questions are: How are the most important functions of the healthcare system organized, coordinated, governed, and managed? What effective policies, strategies, and action plans should be developed to enhance the quality, effectiveness, efficiency, outreach, and affordability of health care for all citizens?

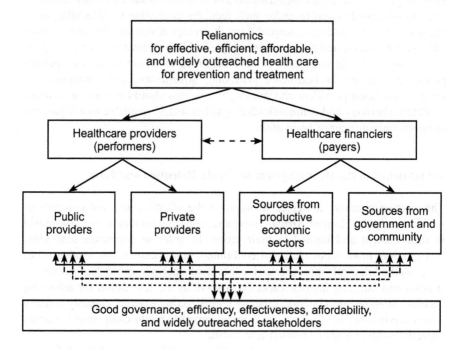

Figure 7.3   RELIANOMICS **framework**

These questions trigger a need to evaluate the past practices in order to identify weaknesses and formulate a better and more practical strategic framework that can upgrade the governance and management of the healthcare system within the limits of available resources. This in turn paves the way to develop the ability to retain healthcare professionals. Figure 7.4 depicts proposed methodological steps to serve as a road map for improving healthcare provision, outreach, and governance. Improvements can be implemented with the joint collaboration of government, the private sector, and international partners. As mentioned earlier, a significant improvement in the building blocks necessary for a functioning health system is essential if to improve the brain drain situation in the Horn of Africa.

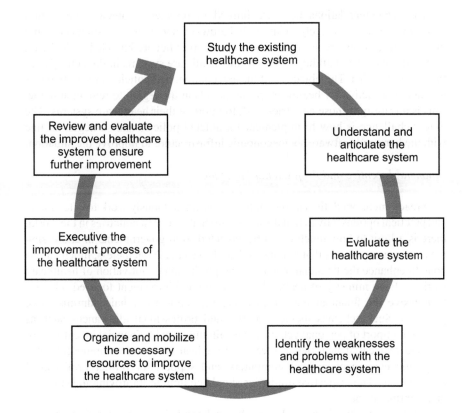

Figure 7.4   Healthcare improvement steps

Appropriate Retention Strategies

This section focuses on appropriate brain retention strategies in line with the RELIANOMICS conceptual framework. The proposed strategies deal with:

- the formulation and recommendation of proactive and reactive smarter policies, strategies, and focused action plans and schemes;
- the promotion and building of local socioeconomic infrastructural and institutional capability and support (bottom up, side support);
- the promotion of collaborative socioeconomic infrastructural and institutional support and partnership (bottom up, side support); and

- implementation approaches expressed in terms of action–events–outcomes–evaluations and control–continuous improvement.

The recommendations here are limited to policies, strategies, and action plans that deal exclusively with both hardware and software socioeconomic infrastructure. They are not remedies by themselves but are intended to deal with improving the basic building blocks of the healthcare systems in the countries of the Horn of Africa. The objective of these recommended policies and strategies is to make it attractive for healthcare professionals in the region to remain at home. This is a priority if those countries wish to improve their healthcare systems. The bigger challenge is how to implement formulated policies and strategies in line with the hard and software socioeconomic infrastructure to improve the situation.

Financial Incentive and Professional Motivation

As already mentioned, the Horn countries should assiduously work to offer sound and practical options. Given that these are among the poorest countries in the world, there is a limit to how much could be expected from governments in addressing the resource constraints that plague the health systems. Nonetheless, much can be done to enhance the financial incentive and professional motivation of healthcare workers. Each ministry of health should design and implement focused schemes to improve the financial incentives rather that cling to archaic administrative practices. Such schemes include salaries and professional allowances such as duty-free import of personal vehicles, land allotments with financial incentives for building residential facilities, professional medical tools and equipment, books, electronic equipment such as computers, and support for further professional development. The respective ministries should commit to improving the situation on a continuous basis.

While capacity issues should be acknowledged, cooperation among government organs, the private sector, and other international partners is mandatory in generating the necessary resources. The current salary scales cannot reasonably allow medical doctors to have a decent life and concentrate on what they can contribute to the needy population. Younger and recently graduated doctors especially need support to settle properly into their places of assignment. The Horn governments and relevant ministries should establish a permanent task force with members representing stakeholders from all sectors to work out the regulatory details and financial and non-financial incentives for retaining qualified healthcare workers and enticing those who have already left to return home. Such incentives include professional privileges and improved working conditions. To fulfil these requirements necessitates undertaking a concerted effort, dedication, and contribution from all concerned parties.

Fiscal Improvement

Statistics have revealed that the budgetary allocation for healthcare systems in the Horn of Africa is inadequate even at the current levels for sub-Saharan Africa. This fiscal limitation further diminishes the ability of the healthcare system to meet its mandated obligation of protecting the health of the population. Health is one of the five foundations of socioeconomic development dynamics. The other four foundations are electricity, water, education, and transportation and communication. Governments in the Horn and their international supporting partners and aid donors should consider the importance of health care in terms of basic survival and well-being. They should give preferential treatment for national health care in their budgetary resources.

Inter-country conflicts, destructive interference, perennial civil wars, and political instability have forced the region's countries to waste the bulk of their meagre resources on national defence. Those countries should instead be encouraged to divert those resources to the most vital socioeconomic development sectors such as health care, education, agriculture, and industrial development. Countries in the Horn regularly receive massive external support earmarked for developmental assistance, which should be directed to developing healthcare-related projects and schemes. In sum, healthcare governing bodies and providers in each country should efficiently manage the resources earmarked for their national health care through projects and schemes that strengthen the incentives for healthcare professionals. These efforts would curb brain drain and even promote brain gain. Sample efforts include workload and overtime incentives, professional development incentives, global opportunity and network development incentives and allowances, sabbatical leaves, housing allowances, equipment upgrade allowances, and research and scholarship allowances.

A Conducive Environment for Scientific and Technological Development

Science and technology play a pivotal role in the knowledge creation and application process. The introduction of new ideas and technological resources bolsters competitiveness, quality, and efficiency. It also improves productivity, work performance, and work methods. The application of new methods and implementation of new and better technologies directly contributes to retention endeavours. Moreover, the use of technology enhances the quality of training and production of better qualified healthcare professionals at all levels. The current technological revolution and increased availability of electronic technologies at affordable cost have greatly contributed to advancing the quality of healthcare services in industrialized countries. With the help of such technologies, many developing countries have also dramatically improved their healthcare systems (WHO 2008a). The countries of the Horn should therefore introduce more appropriate, updated, and affordable technology in healthcare provision and appropriate training, focusing on public health outreach, acute and chronic health problems, health extension services, and so on. These countries have been slow to introduce affordable and significant technologies such as mobile medical services providers for remote areas or mobile small-scale health services that are durable and affordable for rural healthcare outreach. They should ensure that such supportive technology as well as appropriate and effective working methods are introduced and used in their healthcare systems. Those responsible for governing the healthcare systems should support these modernization efforts. The countries should also formulate comprehensive schemes to improve and implement healthcare technology such as phase-by-phase upgrades of general and specialized medical facilities, establishing referral hospitals equipped with up-to-date medical equipment and facilities, creating lead healthcare research centres that maintain links with peers in the developed countries. Improving healthcare systems is a continuous process that demands constant efforts. The Horn countries should continue to upgrade their healthcare systems by all affordable means.

Training and Capacity Building

In the Horn of Africa, countries are responsible for modernizing and expanding their healthcare training and capacity-building establishments. This helps them produce adequate numbers of new healthcare professionals, including medical doctors. Medical schools are expensive to run, but the countries can modernize them phase by phase as has been done in Egypt, Korea, Singapore, South Africa, and several other emerging countries (Deloitte PLC 2009). Medical schools should be a place for knowledge creation, application, and dissemination. They are thus expected to improve their scholastic quality and organizational leadership structure in order to provide better learning facilities. They should also create an environment conducive to applying it for social good. Modern training technologies such as telemedicine have made it possible for medical school academics and practising medical doctors to consult with peers in the diaspora. These types of partnerships are flourishing in many African countries. Through these communication systems, participants can collaborate with their foreign experts if the need arises. Moreover, curricula should be reformed so it prepares future medical graduates to provide more qualified service and also improves the working environment (Boelen and Hack 1995).

Medical education helps create a system that retains its graduates to serve needy communities. Furthermore, medical schools can enhance their reputations as well as quality and cost-effectiveness. They foster the promotion of brain sharing through technical cooperation and partnership exchange programmes in areas such as research and development and teaching-learning activities. At the local level, through links with the needs and aspirations of the local community, medical schools contribute to the retention and brain gain endeavours by attracting qualified candidates, especially in underserved rural localities. This strategy can help produce qualified professionals willing to serve the community of their origin. A good example is Ethiopia's Jimma University, which adopted an innovative and student-centred curriculum for its medical school that reflects the local realities. This approach enhances the school's influence over the trainees to establish emotional links, affiliation, and sympathy with their community, and this feeling of belongingness motivates the trainees to stick together with the community. This kind of curriculum has the potential to produce highly qualified but grassroots-based medical doctors. It has already enjoyed wide-ranging praise and recognition for producing professionals with locally relevant skills and community-based services (Dovlo 2004). After all, qualified healthcare workers should be able to provide relevant services by responding to the specific needs of the local population.

In fact, the penetration of the so-called rich-country attitudes, values, and standards has contributed to the overall intellectual migration of qualified professionals in terms of orientation and life style. This reality has made the consequence of brain drain much deeper than merely the loss of qualified professionals. It has already had a forceful impact on the style and approach of education systems in sub-Saharan Africa (Todaro and Smith 2006). Healthcare training institutions must streamline their programs in line with accepted professional quality standards.

Medical science, like other disciplines, has seen massive progress over the last 60 years. Many medical schools, research centres, and hospitals are now equipped with the state-of-the-art facilities even in many developing economies. Therefore, it is possible for medical schools in the Horn of Africa to improve their quality and capacity by introducing modern technology-aided training methods integrated with relevant practical internships. This is, of course, a step-by-step process that should correspond with available resources. Partnership and collaboration between medical schools is possible in both developed and developing countries. Healthcare training institutions, particularly medical schools, should benefit from this opportunity by linking themselves with their counterparts in other developed and developing countries for mutual benefits.

Follow-up, Information Sharing, and Networking

Networking is a powerful tool. It helps to update information and benefits from newly developed technology. It is highly desirable for improving internal functions and working conditions. In countries with well-functioning healthcare systems, healthcare providers, healthcare financiers, and training establishments are well integrated in an interconnected network and sophisticated framework that extends from the broad picture to the grassroots level in both urban and rural settings. In the Horn of Africa, healthcare providers should establish strong local networks as well as international networks. There are clear mutual advantages to local-local and local-international linkages and partnerships, which can advance the national healthcare systems. Healthcare professionals in particular should establish a strong links with medical schools and research centres. Professors and researchers should share new ideas, new technologies, and discoveries.

The establishment of effective and well-organized professional medical associations and societies is also helpful for nurturing professional development by disseminating information about new developments in all structures of the healthcare system. They are also instrumental in providing professional guidance and ethical standards. The challenges of establishing the desired integrated system necessitate collaboration among all stakeholders in both the public and private sectors. Information sharing and networking should follow top-down and bottom-up approaches to connect all echelons in the hierarchy, which is an important precondition for responsiveness of the healthcare system. Doctors and medical schools need to know about new drugs, newly discovered diseases, new treatment methods, better diagnostic methods, and other vital innovations in medical sciences. Horn governments and their aid donors should try their best to create a suitable environment, which in turn will help motivate qualified healthcare professionals to remain at home and continue to contribute to the betterment of public health.

Improving Health Sector Governance

The Horn countries should endeavour to streamline their healthcare governance systems. Good governance is a prerequisite for establishing a well-integrated and responsive healthcare system. This in turn promotes sustainable socioeconomic growth and the retention of healthcare professionals. Improvement in healthcare governance includes the following tasks: formulating appropriate regulations and work procedures, establishing organization-based governance, overseeing the administration of healthcare training establishments, formulating and implementing appropriate training programs, executing training activities to produce qualified healthcare professionals at different levels, appointing the right people to the right positions, designing programs for skill upgrading and professional development programs, implementing modern and affordable technologies that facilitate performance effectiveness and efficiency, implementing well-coordinated and integrated management in all components of a national healthcare system, and establishing a managerial chain of command that promotes backward and forward managerial and operational links. In sum, the countries of the Horn must improve their healthcare governance by accomplishing these challenging tasks in order to lay the foundations necessary for a well-governed and modern healthcare system. Zambia, Ghana, Kenya, and Botswana have done well in enhancing the governance and effectiveness of their healthcare systems.

Internal and External Socioeconomic Infrastructure

The support of socioeconomic sectoral infrastructure is essential for a well-governed and sustainable healthcare system. The healthcare system of any country must be vertically and horizontally integrated with the other sectors including education, agriculture, industry, transport and communication, finance, and construction. Therefore, collaborative links must be made with other economic sectors in a national economy. In the same way, external or international links are also necessary. Healthcare issues are complex and demand international cooperation, support, and partnership, including sharing of information and innovation. For example, diseases such as malaria, HIV/AIDS, and cancer have international impacts. All countries need to collaborate to eliminate or manage them because of their global reach. Various global initiatives exist. For example, the UN, WHO, the William J. Clinton Foundation, and the Bill and Melinda Gates Foundation play pivotal roles in reducing the negative impacts of HIV/AIDS on the less developed countries predominantly in sub-Saharan Africa. Moreover, broad local community participation at the grassroots level is necessary in order to improve the quality and outreach of health care. The countries of the Horn of Africa should coordinate the supportive links of the socioeconomic infrastructure with the national healthcare systems. Such collaborative work can produce effective schemes and feasible strategies for tackling the problem.

Figure 7.5 shows the conceptual framework containing critical determinants of a viable national healthcare system at the macro and micro levels. Governments and other stakeholders in the Horn should formulate feasible action programs in line with these determinants to advance their healthcare provision and governance. Various forms are appropriate for their objectives. This is part of the comprehensive activities needed to create conducive environment for retention of qualified healthcare professionals in the region. These clustered determinants are complex, hierarchal and mutually inclusive, and are critical to success. The Horn governments and their international collaborative partners should address prudently in developing a sustainable and wider outreached healthcare system at the national, sectoral, and institutional (or departmental) levels. Stakeholders need to formulate and implement policies, strategies, and action plans dealing with each of them in priority sequence. It is much easier to develop appealing policies and strategies on paper, but the challenge is to design and apply mechanisms for successful implementation. If implementation mechanisms and modalities cannot be established, no positive results are possible regardless of how good the policies and strategies are. The countries need to apply the commonly accepted cycle of implementation process of actions, events, outcomes, evaluation, and control for continuous improvement.

Many countries in sub-Saharan Africa have exerted much effort into designing lasting and meaningful development policies to advance their socioeconomic development. However, none of the grand policies and strategies has come to fruition except for some strategies that materialized temporarily but vanished due to failure to use skilful implementation techniques, mechanisms, and procedural modalities (Araia 2001). Policy formulation complements policy implementation, and this reality must be understood in the broader scope of a macroeconomic management framework. Policy makers in the Horn of Africa should recognize the importance of considering the objective realities and cultural values of the local environment in the development and implementation of policies and strategies.

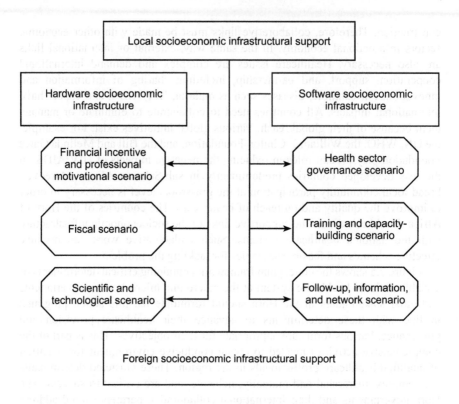

Figure 7.5   RELIANOMICS **for retention and brain gain in the health sector**

A country must use its own traditions, culture, values, institutions, and history to create and achieve its own process of developmental democratic state building (Sunkel 1972). Lessons can be learned from the experiences of others, but trying to transplant what has succeeded elsewhere to a different environment and socioeconomic situation may not work. The lessons need to be adapted.

   Appropriate and locally initiated policies, strategies, and action plans in health care can pave the way to successful policy implementation. In the developmental process, it is fundamentally necessary to formulate and implement effective, complementary policies and strategies, as reflected in Figure 7.6. The Horn countries have experienced policy implementation problems due to inadequately coordinated or harmonized implementation strategies (Nwankwo and Richards 2004; Wolgin 1997). Previous studies have acknowledged that the formulation of policies and strategy should be complemented by implementation modalities and appropriate institutional arrangements (Nugent and Yhee 2002). But articulated and logically synchronized policies, strategies, schemes, action plans, and regulatory acts are required to achieve success in implementation. Success requires dedicated good governance, superior technocratic ability,

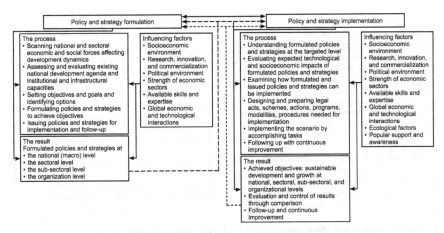

Figure 7.6   The complementarity of policies and strategies in developmental continuum

and able leadership. Figure 7.7 articulates how the process of policy and strategy formulation and implementation should complement one another in an integrated system.

Conclusion

In 2009, Eritrean television broadcast the inauguration of a recently constructed road. At the ceremony, an elder in a Eritrean village said, "The degree of independence and sovereignty of a given country is measured by its ability to make five of the most basic infrastructural facilities ready to the local population: roads for easy communication, schools for basic education, healthcare services, clean water, and electrification." The countries in the Horn of Africa ought to provide at least the basic healthcare services to their citizens. This is possible only by strengthening their healthcare sectors to provide at least basic services in both rural and urban areas. The expansion of healthcare capacity depends on numerous factors including training more qualified healthcare professionals and improving the governance and institutional functions and management systems.

Successful capacity building in the health sector and retention of healthcare professionals in poor countries like those in the Horn is a huge challenge that requires a massive investment as well as broad and smart efforts. Poor countries are more vulnerable to the powerful economic and political forces outside their control, which can have a decisive and dominating influence on their economic and social well-being (Todaro and Smith 2006). Those countries require joint efforts and the active support of international partners and vital stakeholders at all levels. Healthcare workers themselves should play a principal role in the process. The

National level • Sociocultural environment • Good governance and political stability • Political, economic, and cultural foundations (organizations), sustainable socioeconomic development • Constitutional-based democratic guarantee and social welfare	Stakeholders at all levels • Central government through its institutional capacity • Regional governments through their institutional capacity • Community institutional structures • Public and private partnerships • Self-help organizations • Local and foreign nongovernmental organizations • Business sector and representative agencies • External bilateral technical assistance agencies • Academic and research institutes • Private consultants and business incubators and promoters • Banks and other financial institutions • Diaspora communities

Sectoral level (e.g., health and education)
• Effective, appropriate, and benevolent policies
• Effective and efficient administration policies and regulations
• Qualified, suitable, and implementable institutional and regulatory framework
• Regional sectoral development policies and strategies
• Good governance of health and education services
• Effective, long-term human resources development
• Scientific and technological division and dissemination strategies
• Establishment of lean, clean, efficient administrative bureaucracy
• Design of financial incentive and professional motivation
• Indigenization of training and skill upgrading programs
• Promotion of international networks, partnerships, collaboration, and exchange programs

Institutional and department levels (micro level)
• Legal framework regulating and promoting health and educational services
• Focused policies and strategies for technical and managerial aspects of service provision
• Upgraded institutional capacity to provide:
  - training
  - research and advisory services
  - information services
  - technical services
  - financing services
  - network and linkage services
• The level of effectiveness of the sectorally based incentive programs enhancing the activities of the units, which can include

Figure 7.7   Determinants of health sector development as a contribution to retention of healthcare professionals

tasks of important players such as concerned government sectors, donors, non-governmental organizations and the business community must be co-ordinated (Henderson and Tulloch 2008). There must also be coordination in formulating and implementing policies and strategies and implementation dynamics relating to the healthcare systems. After all, the Horn countries are obliged ensure that qualified packages of financial and non-financial incentives are in place to respond realistically to the needs of healthcare professionals. If the countries are unable to properly plan, lead, manage, monitor, evaluate, and control the activities of their healthcare systems, their efforts will fail. They need to design an effective healthcare governance and management system at all hierarchical levels. The Horn countries must strengthen the managerial abilities of their healthcare institutional structures.

There is no a universal readymade strategy or model to curb brain drain and strengthen the healthcare sector in every country. The region's countries should continue to develop strategies and tactics for dealing directly with the healthcare sovereignty agenda. Because the challenge to retain healthcare professionals is more formidable for these poor countries, they have increased responsibility not to lose those professionals in whom they have already invested heavily. Their tax payers deserve to receive the services of those trained with their hard-earned money. There are, of course, limits to capacity, but the countries should make every effort to train more medical workers and successfully retain them at home.

The issue of brain drain continues to attract international attention, because the most important asset for any socioeconomic development effort is a country's people. If countries fail to provide the necessary protection for the well-being of their citizens, the result is nothing short of disaster and stagnancy in socioeconomic development. The countries in the Horn of Africa have ample opportunity to resolve their external conflicts, civil wars, and internal instability with civility and dialogue instead of wasting hundreds of millions of dollars on armaments and war. They should divert their meagre resources to other vital development endeavours including producing and retaining qualified healthcare professionals.

References

Adredo, Dejene (2000). "Human Capital Flight from Africa: An Assessment of Brain Drain from Ethiopia." In *Brain Drain and Capacity Building in Africa*, Sibry J.M. Tapsoba, Sabiou Kassoum, Pascal V. Houenou et al., eds. United Nations Economic Commission for Africa, pp. 122–47. Available online: idl-bnc.idrc.ca/dspace/bitstream/10625/28020/1/118149.pdf (October 2012).

AMES (2010). "Partnership for Eritrea: Graduate Medical Education Program." April 18. Available online: www.samss.org/samss.upload/wysiwyg/Presentations%20from%20AMES/Eritrea%20-%20George%20Washington%20Postgrad.pdf (October 2012).

Araia, Ghelawdewos (2001). "Development Policy Shift for Africa." *African Link Magazine*. Available online: www.africanidea.org/african_development.html (October 2012).

Arcand, Jean-Louis (2001). "Undernourishment and Economic Growth: The Efficiency Cost of Hunger." FAO Economic and Social Development Paper No. 147. Available online: www.fao.org/docrep/003/X9280E/X9280E00. HTM (October 2012).

Barro, Robert J. (1996). "Health and Economic Growth." Prepared for the Pan American Health Organization, November. Available online: www.paho.org/english/hdp/hdd/barro.pdf (October 2012).

Beine, Michel, Frederic Docquier, and Hillel Rapaport (2001). "Brain Drain and Economic Growth: Theory and Evidence." *Journal of Development Economics* 64: 275–89.

Berhan, Yifru (2008). "Medical Doctors Profile in Ethiopia: Protection, Attrition, and Retention. In Memory of 100 Years Ethiopian Modern Medicine and the New Ethiopian Millennium." *Ethiopian Medical Journal* 46(1): 1–77.

Boelen, Charles and Jeffery E. Hack (1995). "Defining and Measuring Social Accountability of Medical Schools." World Health Organization, Geneva. Available online: whqlibdoc.who.int/hq/1995/WHO_HRH_95.7.pdf (October 2012).

Brown, Mercy (2000). "Using Intellectual Diaspora to Reverse the Brain Drain: Some Useful Examples." In *Brain Drain and Capacity Building in Africa*, Sibry J.M. Tapsoba, Sabiou Kassoum, Pascal V. Houenou et al., eds. United Nations Economic Commission for Africa, pp. 92–109. Available online: idl-bnc.idrc.ca/dspace/bitstream/10625/28020/1/118149.pdf (October 2012).

Central Intelligence Agency (2012). "The World Factbook." Washington, DC. Available online: www.cia.gov/library/publications/the-world-factbook (October 2012).

Clemens, Michael A. and Gunilla Pettersson (2007). "A New Database of Health Professional Emigration from Africa." Working Paper No. 95, August, Center for Global Development. Available online: www.cgdev.org/files/9267_file_CGDWP95_Feb_2007.pdf (October 2012).

Commission on Macroeconomics and Health (2001). "Macroeconomics and Health: Investing in Health for Economic Development." World Health Organization, Geneva. Available online: www.cid.harvard.edu/archive/cmh/cmhreport.pdf (October 2012).

Deloitte PLC (2009). "A Report on Healthcare Quality." Deloitte Development LLC.

Dovlo, Delanyo (2004). "The Brain Drain in Africa: An Emerging Challenge to Health Professionals' Education." *Journal of Higher Education in Africa* 2(3): 1–18. Available online: www.codesria.org/IMG/pdf/02-dovlo.pdf (October 2012).

Edokat, Tofah (2000). "Effects of Brain Drain on Higher Education in Cameroon." In *Brain Drain and Capacity Building in Africa*, Sibry J.M. Tapsoba, Sabiou Kassoum, Pascal V. Houenou et al., eds. United Nations Economic Commission for Africa, pp. 174–85. Available online: idl-bnc.idrc.ca/dspace/bitstream/10625/28020/1/118149.pdf (October 2012).

Fiorina, Carly (2001). "Policymaking in an Internet Age." Speech delivered at the "Progress and Freedom Foundation Summit," August 19, Aspen. Available online: www.hp.com/hpinfo/execteam/speeches/fiorina/aspen_01.html (October 2012).

Fogel, Robert W. (2002). "Nutrition, Physiological Capital, and Economic Growth." Lecture prepared for presentation at the Senior Policy Seminar on Health, Human Capital, and Economic Growth: Theory, Evidence, and Policies of the Pan American Health Organization and the Inter American Development Bank, October 3. Available online: www.paho.org/english/HDP/HDD/fogel.pdf (October 2012).

Gallup, John Luke and Jeffrey Sachs (1998). "The Economic Burden of Malaria." October, Center for International Development at Harvard. Available online: www.earth.columbia.edu/sitefiles/file/about/director/pubs/mal_wb.pdf (October 2012).

George Washington University (2009). "GW Helps African Nation Double Its Pediatricians." Washington, DC, December 15. Available online: gwtoday.gwu.edu/gw-helps-african-nation-double-its-pediatricians (October 2012).

Goma, Lameck (1990). "The African Brain Drain: Investment in and Utilization of Human Capital." In *Capacity Building and Human Resource Development*, Alexander A. Kwapong and Barry Lesser, eds. Halifax: Lester Pearson Institute for International Development.

Henderson, Lyn N. and Jim Tulloch (2008). "Incentives for Retaining and Motivating Health Workers in Pacific and Asian Countries." *Human Resources for Health* 6(18). doi: 10.1186/1478-4491-6-18. Available online: www.human-resources-health.com/content/pdf/1478-4491-6-18.pdf (October 2012).

Institute of Medicine (2001). *Crossing the Quality Chasm: A New Health System for the 21st Century*. Washington, DC: National Academy Press.

Kotler, Philip and Nancy R. Lee (2009). *Up and Out of Poverty: The Social Marketing Solution*. Upper Saddle River, NJ: Pearson Education.

Lowell, B. Lindsay and Allan Findlay (2001). "Migration of Highly Skilled Persons from Developing Countries: Impact and Policy Responses." Synthesis Report. International Migration Papers No. 44., International Labour Organization, Geneva. Available online: www.ilo.org/public/english/protection/migrant/download/imp/imp44.pdf (October 2012).

McAuliffe, Eilish and Malcolm Maclachlan (2005). "'Turning the Ebbing Tide': Knowledge Flows and Health in Low-income Countries." *Higher Education Policy* 18(3): 231–52.

Meeus, Wilma (2003). "'Pull' Factors in International Migration of Health Professionals: An Analysis of Developed Countries' Policies Influencing Migration of Health Professionals." Unpublished master's thesis, University of the Western Cape, Cape Town. Available online: etd.uwc.ac.za/usrfiles/modules/etd/docs/etd_gen8Srv25Nme4_8927_1216732945.pdf (October 2012).

Mexican Commission on Macroeconomics and Health (2004). "Investing in Health for Economic Development." Instituto de Políticas Públicas y Estudios del Desarrollo, Mexico City.

Mutume, Gumisai (2003). "Reversing Africa's 'Brain Drain': New Initiatives Tap Skills of African Expatriates." *African Recovery* 17(2).

Nugent, Jeffrey B. and Seung-jae Yhee (2002). "Small and Medium Enterprises in Korea: Achievements, Constraints and Policy Issues." *Small Business Economics* 18(1–3): 85–119.

Nwankwo, Sonny and Darlington Richards (2004). "Institutional Paradigm and the Management of Transitions: A Sub-Sahara African Perspective." *International Journal of Social Economics* 31(1/2): 111–30.

Peabody, John W., Mario M. Taguiwalo, David A. Robalino et al. (2006). "Improving the Quality of Care in Development Countries." In *Disease Control Priorities in Developing Countries*, Dean T. Jamison, Joel G. Breman, Anthony R. Measham et al., eds. Washington, DC: World Bank. Available online: www.ncbi.nlm.nih.gov/books/NBK11790/#A10280 (October 2012).

Prahalad, C.K. (2010). *The Fortune at the Bottom of the Pyramid: Eradicating Poverty Through Profits*. Upper Saddle River, NJ: Pearson Education.

Republic of Kenya. Ministry of Public Health and Sanitation (2006). "Annual Health Report." Nairobi.

Scott, Mark L., Anna Whelan, John Dewdney et al. (2004). "'Brain Drain' or Ethical Recruitment." *Medical Journal of Australia* 180(4): 174–76. Available online: www.mja.com.au/journal/2004/180/4/brain-drain-or-ethical-recruitment (October 2012).

Shinn, David H. (2002). "Reversing the Brain Drain in Ethiopia." Paper presented to the Ethiopian North American Health Professionals Association, November 23, Alexandria, VA. Available online: chora.virtualave.net/brain-drain8.htm (October 2012).

Sunkel, Osvaldo (1972). "Latin American Under Development in the Year 2000." In *Economics and World Order from the 1970s to the 1990s*, Jagdish N. Bhagwati, ed. New York: Macmillan, pp. 199–231.

Teferra, Damtew (2000). "Revisiting the Doctrine of Human Capital Mobility in the Information Age." Regional Conference on Brain Drain and Capital Building in Africa, 22–24 February, Addis Ababa. Available online: www.iom.int/africandiaspora/pdf/TEFERRA.pdf (October 2012).

Teferra, Damtew (2005). "Brain Circulation: Unparalleled Opportunities, Underlying Challenges, and Outmoded Presumptions." *Journal of Studies in International Education* 9(3): 229–50.

Todaro, Michael P. and Stephen C. Smith (2006). *Economic Development.* 9th ed. Boston: Pearson Addison Wesley.

UNICEF (2012). "Response to the Horn of Africa Emergency: A Continuing Crisis Threatens Hard-Won Gains." April, Addis Ababa. Available online: www.unicef.org/esaro/HOA_2012_Report.pdf (October 2012).

United Nations (2012). "The Millennium Development Goals Report 2012." New York. Available online: www.undp.org/content/dam/undp/library/MDG/english/The_MDG_Report_2012.pdf (October 2012).

United Nations Economic and Social Council (2000). "Report of the Regional Conference on Brain Drain and Capacity Building in Africa." February 24. Available online: www.iom.int/africandiaspora/pdf/Braindrain. pdf (October 2012).

United Nations High Commissioner for Refugees (2009). "2008 Global Trends: Refugees, Asylum-Seekers, Returnees, Internally Displaced and Stateless Persons." June 16, Geneva. Available online: www.unhcr.org/4a375c426.html (October 2012).

Wolgin, Jerome M. (1997). "The Evolution of Economic Policymaking in Africa." *American Economic Review* 87(2): 54–7.

World Bank (2012b). "Health Nutrition and Population Statistics." Database, Washington, DC. Available online: databank.worldbank.org/Data/Views/VariableSelection/SelectVariables.aspx?source=Health%20Nutrition%20and%20Population%20Statistics (October 2012).

World Bank (2012c). "World Development Indicators 2012." Washington, DC. Available online: data.worldbank.org/sites/default/files/wdi-2012-ebook.pdf (October 2012).

World Bank (2012d). "World Development Indicators and Global Development Finance." Database, Washington, DC. Available online: databank.worldbank.org/Data/Views/VariableSelection/SelectVariables.aspx?source=World%20Development%20Indicators%20and%20Global%20Development%20Finance (October 2012).

World Health Organization (2006). "The World Health Report 2006: Working Together for Health." World Health Organization, Geneva. Available online: www.who.int/whr/2006/en/ (October 2012).

World Health Organization (2008). "Maximizing Positive Strategies between Health Systems and Global Health Initiatives." Geneva. Available online: www.who.int/entity/healthsystems/New-approach-leaflet-ENv2-p4p.pdf (October 2012).

World Health Organization (2010). "Country Cooperation Strategy at a Glance: Djibouti." Geneva. Available online: www.who.int/countryfocus/cooperation_strategy/ccsbrief_dji_en.pdf (October 2012).

World Health Organization (2011). "World Health Statistics 2011." Geneva. Available online: www.who.int/gho/publications/world_health_statistics/EN_WHS2011_Full.pdf (October 2012).

World Health Organization (2012a). "Health Systems Topics." Geneva. Available online: www.who.int/healthsystems/topics/en/ (October 2012).
World Health Organization (2012b). "World Health Statistics 2012." Geneva. Available online: www.who.int/healthinfo/EN_WHS2012_Full.pdf (October 2012).

Chapter 8

Strengthening Health Capacity in Sub-Saharan Africa: A Millennium Development Challenge

Nelson K. Sewankambo[1]

The centrality of health as a key determinant of economic growth, labour force productivity, and poverty reduction is increasingly recognized and growing in prominence in development discussions by the global community. At the same time, health outcomes in sub-Saharan Africa are in many instances regressing, while in other instances they are not progressing fast enough to achieve economic growth or development (Sanders et al. 2009).

It is therefore of great importance to Africa that the eight Millennium Development Goals (MDGs) relate to health outcomes either directly (MDG 4 and 5, to reduce child mortality and improve maternal health respectively, and 6, to combat HIV/AIDS, malaria, and other diseases) or indirectly (the remaining five). An example of the latter is MDG 1 on the eradication of poverty and hunger. Achieving this goal can be affected by the ill health of individuals or families, which may push them into poverty because of catastrophic healthcare costs since most people in sub-Saharan Africa pay out of pocket for health services. The reverse is also true: the loss of earnings resulting from poor health can throw families into poverty and hunger.

Many have argued that the development failures of the 1990s led to the MDGs. Indeed, the MDGs represent a diplomatic truth (i.e. a reality) since they were a negotiated compromise at the 2000 United Nations Millennium Summit, even though they may not be exactly what the G77 developing countries wanted (Tandon 2008). Moreover, they do not address the root causes of underdevelopment in many countries, particularly in Africa.

Irrespective of whether the MDGs represent a diplomatic truth or social reality they are a welcome agenda for action. Whereas efforts to achieve them in sub-Saharan Africa are unlikely to succeed, they have nonetheless highlighted the developmental challenges that Africa continues to face in this millennium (Bryce et al. 2006). There have been advances in the health sector of low- and

---

1   The views expressed in this chapter do not represent those of Makerere University College of Health Sciences, the United States National Institutes of Health, or the US Department of Health and Human Services.

middle-income countries, but this progress has been slower than expected, and health inequities are widening (Kruk and Freedman 2008; United Nations 2011). Weaknesses in the health system—particularly the inadequacies of the health workforce—are recognized as formidable impediments, underlying the above failures, to achieving the MDGs (Corkery 2000). Health systems need both vertical and horizontal programs that work in harmony to deliver effective, equitable, and affordable health services (Reich et al. 2008). To this end, the diagonal approach that has been gaining attention may attend better to both disease-specific and system priorities (Ooms et al. 2008).

Health Workforce Constraints in African Countries

It is necessary to appreciate the gravity of the problem at hand in order to make appropriate interventions to strengthen health capacity in Africa. The population of sub-Saharan Africa totals more than 874.8 million, with an estimated ratio of less than 0.2 physicians per 10,000 (World Bank 2012a). The region needs approximately 700,000 physicians to meet the MDGs. Accurate information is difficult to come by because of absence of country by country reliable data. In 2004 the two-year global Joint Learning Initiative (2004) reported that an estimated additional one million health workers will be needed over the next decade to deliver basic health interventions in sub-Saharan Africa. The Joint Learning Initiative concluded that the future of global health and development in the twenty-first century lies in the management of the crisis in human resources for health.

Globally, there is awareness of a lack of capacity and failure of African countries to strengthen their health systems and develop a strong, well-trained public health workforce that can provide quality and equitable service. Similarly, there is inadequate capacity of many African universities to contribute to academic rigours of training more and more health professionals as well as generating new knowledge for health (Omer 2005). A country's capacity for having adequate health workers is a determinant of equitable national development that provides for not only those who can afford or have connections in the system but also the poor, weak, and vulnerable. Africa's shortage of health workers has been neglected for decades by state governments, donor agencies, and global health initiatives. The shortfall is due to a number of factors identified by the Joint Learning Initiative, including lack of long-term investments in health and higher education sector, unsuccessful reforms, poor stewardship, and governance (Joint Learning Initiative 2004; Liese et al. 2003). Understaffing has resulted in stress and increased workloads among health professionals, who are in any case also poorly paid, poorly equipped, and have limited career opportunities. In addition, the HIV/AIDS epidemic has caused wastage due to deaths and ill health, in addition to stigma and fear of infection, burnout, absenteeism, increased workloads, and stress—which all affect productivity. Persistent outmigration of health personnel from Africa to the rich North has made the situation worse and is clearly a response to inaction or inadequate action to address the workforce challenges in sub-Saharan Africa. In recognition of the enormous challenge posed by such migration, the World Health Organization (WHO) proclaimed 2005–15 the decade of human resources for health.

In addition to the Joint Learning Initiative's efforts to highlight the urgent need for human health resources, the United Kingdom's Commission for Africa (2005) called upon the world's richest countries to provide \$7 billion to develop Africa's health infrastructure. The 2006 *World Health Report: Working Together for Health*, published by WHO (2006), advanced the urgency to yet a higher level. It identified 57 countries as having critical shortages of health workers, 36 of which were in sub-Saharan Africa. In yet another development in 2006 the Global Health Workforce Alliance was established and guided by the belief that "every person in every village everywhere has access to a skilled, motivated and supported health worker" (Omaswa 2009). At its first global forum on human resources for health held in 2008, the alliance issued the Kampala Declaration and agenda for Global Action with 12 immediate and urgent actions that needed to be taken (Global Health Workforce Alliance 2008). Four months later the world leaders taking part in the G8 Toyako Summit supported the declaration, making more specific financial and technical commitments for health workforce than they did for any of the other building blocks of the WHO health system framework, namely health services, health information, medical products, vaccines and technologies, health financing, and leadership and governance (Jimba 2009). In order not to lose momentum, there remains a need for innovative and radical ideas that are focused and more appropriate to local situations as viable solutions that individual countries themselves can implement while assisted by the international community. Otherwise Africa will slowly reach a time where without the ingenuity that Thomas Homer-Dixon (2001) points to, it will not be able to close the widening gap between the health worker challenges it faces and its ability to address them.

A Systems Approach: The Starting Point to Addressing African Health System Issues

In 1991 Milton Roemer (1991) defined a health system as "the combination of resources, organization, financing and management that culminates in the delivery of health services to the population." In 2007 WHO (2007a) expanded the definition to a system that "consists of all organizations, people and actions whose *primary intent* is to promote, restore or maintain health." Its goals are to improve "health and health equity, in ways that are responsive, financially fair, and make the best, or most efficient, use of available resources."

An attempt to unpack a health system indicates that it is an open system (subject to influence from outside factors such as politics, education, poverty, infrastructural context) that has many component parts. Those parts include but are not limited to ministries of health, health services and organizations of all sorts, patients, pharmaceutical and non-pharmaceutical health-related companies, health service providers, patients, families, and academic health institutions. Enhancing the capacity of health systems is fundamental to strengthening service delivery in order to improve health outcomes in Africa. This requires strengthening of the different parts of the system, which has been described as a complex adaptive system that is constantly in flux (Plsek 2001).

Due to space limitations, however, this chapter focuses on one aspect: the health workforce. Addressing the challenges of enhancing the health workforce should be viewed through a systems-thinking lens. Health workers and the organizations they may be a part of are prone to change from within, without external imposition, and are therefore adaptive and self-organizing. Their behaviour, which is influenced by context, is generally non-linear and thus may not be predictable. Over time globalization has gradually but steadily added complexity to the phenomenon of health system change.

Stewardship: A Challenge for African States

In many African countries, stewardship—defined as the overall system oversight—is generally weak. It remains a fragile function due to lack of state capacity driven by political, resource, administrative, and information constraints. Sub-Saharan African governments should set the context and policy framework for the overall health system including supporting the health worker component, generating appropriate data and systematic information for policy making, and setting and enforcing rules and incentives that define the environment and guide the behaviour of health system players (with incentives and disincentives). Otherwise, it will remain difficult to strengthen African health capacity appropriately and sufficiently to assure that equity and quality of services exist on the continent. It is imperative for African governments to undertake major reforms to ramp up their oversight role for both public and the private sector, which generally provides 50 percent of health services in the countries. The debate on the roles of public and private sectors in health system financing and service delivery in developing countries has re-emerged because of the interest in how to best achieve health for all (Lagomarsino, de Ferranti, et al. 2009; Lagomarsino, Nachuk, et al. 2009; Nishtar 2007).

Whatever the outcome of this debate, good stewardship will remain an important pre-requisite for enhancing the human resource capacity of well-functioning health systems in Africa. There is hardly any monitoring, regulation, or control by governments of formal and informal workers who participate in delivery of public and private health services in Africa, which consist of a mix of public and private practitioners, hospitals, health clinics, and community health worker initiatives run by nongovernmental organizations (NGOs), local drug shops, traditional healers (Lagomarsino, de Ferranti, et al. 2009). Practitioners of alternative medicine including traditional medicine exist widely in Africa and are more accessible, particularly in rural populations where they provide care probably to most of the population. While these types of health providers should be encouraged and supported to provide the best care they can, they pose very challenging practical issues that governments must address as part of the stewardship agenda. Those issues range from standard setting to regulation and control in order to protect the population from exploitation and any harmful practices (Fink 2002; WHO Regional Office for Africa 2000).

Stewardship for enhancing health workforce capacity should be guided continuously by data and information derived from questions such as which institutions and actors are involved in training and employment and how multi-sectoral collaboration and participation can be improved so that indeed every person, in every village, everywhere has access to a skilled, motivated, and supported health worker. Other questions include: What are the financial, management, and resource needs (for example, skills, quantity) for a particular country or the region in which it is located? What are the important trends in resource needs or availability? What health priorities are relevant for the immediate, mid-term, and long-term future that affect human resource needs? What other information is needed, and from where, to ensure effective decision making on matters related to recruitment and promotion and to the maintenance of discipline and quality performance? What are the infrastructural and financial needs required to ensure optimal health workforce capacity and quality performance on the job? What kinds of providers exist, what types of services do they provide, and to whom and with what results?

Without such information, it is difficult—if not impossible—to achieve effective monitoring, regulation, and enforcement. There are, however, also ethical challenges that need to be critically examined and whose solutions inform the stewardship processes (Cash 2005).

The challenge of health workforce inadequacy in sub-Saharan Africa goes beyond numbers of health workers to include other problems such as failure to utilize the existing trained personnel to the best advantage due to a number of constraints. Those constraints include the inability to absorb health workers or significant delays in deploy despite existing shortages in the health system, insufficient supervision and incentives, or poor motivation resulting in underperformance, double employment, unsatisfactory work environments, low salaries that may sometimes be delayed for months, inadequate training because of poorly resourced tertiary education institutions, poor retention that leads to internal (in-country) and external migration, inequitable rural–urban distribution, unsatisfactory skills mix or availability, and lack of access to various specialists. In general, African governments have unfortunately been unable to look after the health workers they have within their national boundaries. The incentives that (skilled) workers experience or receive significantly influence individual performance and thus have an impact on the whole health sector. Careful attention to incentives and disincentives should be a priority and include at least a work environment that is adequately resourced for both provider and patient satisfaction, attractive living conditions, and long-term benefits linked to opportunities for career advancement.

Governance

Governance and stewardship are complementary but not the same. The former is almost always context specific because it must reflect the ways in which all stakeholders interact in a particular set of societal circumstances in order to influence the outcomes of public policies. Africa, with its 53 states, presents a wide variety of contexts that differ across borders and within borders, from the Cape to Cairo and from Dakar to Mombasa. Effective leadership and management strategies are essential to effective governance for a particular country or its regions. Governmental decentralization, which has permeated African countries in the last few decades, has added to the complexity of governance challenges that must be taken into account for any health workforce reform to succeed in any country. Specific reform strategies may include formal and informal mechanisms to promote health-producing behaviour and discourage harmful behaviour.

Governance goes well beyond setting and enforcing legal norms and moral codes for workers to obey. Instead, it involves creating incentives for a wide array of actors, setting priorities for the most cost-effective interventions, coordinating increasingly fragmented activities, mobilizing international aid and technical assistance, and stimulating research (Taylor and Gostin 2008). Nothing is probably more important than a careful reflection and understanding of the country context in which enhancement of health capacity has to be undertaken. The factors that will facilitate or hinder system changes are also specific to context and depend heavily on a country's history, culture, political, and other social forces. It is therefore important that a systems approach to addressing workforce issues be applied so as to achieve greater chances of success and thus maximize benefits in the reform process.

If significant developments in human resources for health in sub-Saharan Africa are to be made there is a need to focus attention not just on national or state governance but also on global governance in relation to human resources for health. In both cases consideration should be given to understanding and defining the new roles of the state and complementary actors in developing and supporting the health workforce. This necessitates rethinking how health systems are organized for the most effective and efficient delivery of services, with a redistribution of roles based on the competitive advantage of each actor and a focus on ensuring equity in service delivery. The role of communities should not be overlooked. The capacity of African communities requires attention and efforts directed to building that capacity so that they can analyze issues better and engage policy makers.

African governments and continental organization have an opportunity to create an enabling international and national environments to harness the resources and skills of organizations such as WHO, the African Union, the New Partnership for Africa's Development (NEPAD), and the International Organization for Migration (IOM), which has recently begun funding health initiatives.

Implications of Globalization for Strengthening Health Capacity

Globalization has a profound impact on the health of the populations in Africa, as in low- and middle-income countries (LMICs) elsewhere. It is creating new challenges for Africa to develop and maintain an effective workforce within the context of international law and policy (Lee et al. 2002). For example, the processes of global change and globalization of trade are restructuring human societies, ushering in new patterns of trading in human skills and expertise, making it easier for mobility of health workers across national boundaries, and reshaping the broad determinants of health. Globalization has expanded the threats of both communicable and non-communicable diseases throughout the world including LIMCs (Beaglehole and Yach 2003; Garrett 1994). It is also likely to impose greater demands on national health systems and lead to developmental challenges, especially in LIMCs, which are likely to experience the greatest impacts. The Commission on Macroeconomics and Health (2001), chaired by Jeffrey Sachs, documented how appropriate, timely action can save up to 10 million lives a year, but this remains far from being realized.

Sovereign states or national governments are undoubtedly at the forefront of dealing with health policy in their respective countries and have the power to determine and set their priorities. They have the primary authority and responsibility for the health of their people. Many times, however, priorities for the health sector in a number of African countries may be determined and dictated by funders, including high-income countries. This is especially likely to occur if the national budgets are heavily funded from external sources. Non-state actors also increasingly affect public health nationally and internationally. Overall, the growing integration and internationalization of the determinants of health have contributed to the rapid decline in the practical capacity of sovereign states to protect the health of their populations through unilateral action. This has intensified the need for international cooperation among states (Taylor 2004).

The key participants in a system of global health governance include the public and private sectors, together with civil society. The emergence of many different players and the acceleration of globalization have heightened and considerably complicated global health governance. The need for a coherent system of international health law and governance has never been greater (Taylor and Gostin 2008). This is especially so since there is recognition that current systems of global governance are insufficient to meet the wide range of challenges and opportunities brought by globalization (Dodgson et al. 2002).

African states, like other LMICs, have to position themselves appropriately so that they are active players in global health governance and derive maximum benefit. Global cooperation is of vital importance because in this day and age no state can stand wholly alone. A sense of global responsibility is indispensable in addressing the global health challenges (High-Level Panel on Threats 2004). Global cooperation is even more important and urgent in order to address the various daunting health issues facing sub-Saharan Africa, especially as the origins of those health issues are in part rooted in national and global health governance challenges, including the changing global architecture and the shifting role of the nation-states, the rise of new actors such as private philanthropy, and the growing insecurity in global public health (Cohen 2006).

African governments should strive to have their views heard to make a difference in global governance that is in the best interests of their countries' efforts for strengthening health capacity. It should be the case even during those times when it may be necessary for states to cede a measure of their national sovereignty in favour of supranational and transnational African interests. These developments may at times lead to diminished state power to set national priorities. Recent developments have ushered in an era of heightened global health diplomacy, which, if well intentioned and utilized, could contribute to propelling African countries forward in strengthening their own health workforce capacity.

Global Health Diplomacy and International Collaboration in Strengthening Health Capacity in Africa

The Oslo Ministerial Declaration, which was issued by the foreign ministers of Thailand, Brazil, France, Indonesia, South Africa, Norway, and Senegal in 2007 (2007), called for the inclusion of global health in the scope of foreign policy. The ministers' stated desires are to encourage new ideas, seek and develop new partnerships and mechanisms, and create new paradigms of cooperation. The declaration requires new forms of global governance to address pressing health challenges and asserts a set of common values, including the belief that "every country needs a robust and responsive health system."

There is a rapidly increasing scrutiny of the processes and determinants of the global policy environment for health. Global health diplomacy offers an opportunity for meaningful and innovative collaborative action for enhancing global action and cooperation (Novotny et al. 2008). High-income countries are paying more attention to global health diplomacy with a view to maintaining and strengthening international relations while at the same time improving health. Africa, perhaps more than any other continent, has been the target of assistance and donations from a proliferating assortment of government, private sector, and large and small organizations and thus may potentially stand to benefit the most from improvements in global health diplomacy.

International collaboration and foreign assistance may be either beneficial or harmful, depending on the issue, and must strive to minimize any harmful effects. Zambia presents an important but not uncommon illustration. Its experience in complying with structural adjustments reforms imposed by the World Bank and the International Monetary Fund (IMF) as conditions to receive loans, grants, or debt relief has exacerbated its health problems, undoubtedly contributing to an exodus among its health professionals. Its attempts to curb this outflow have apparently also been hampered by ongoing conditionalities. Some existing guidelines and agreements are useful in advocating for the protection of health in low-income countries. For example, in 2000 the Committee on Economic, Social and Cultural Rights (2000) issued General Comment 14 on Article 12 regarding health as provided by states' obligations.

Learning from Successes in Other Regions of the World

Global health diplomacy and international collaboration can be a useful vehicle for learning between countries. Whereas individual African countries can design human resource development models that would work best for their respective situations, it would be prudent to examine past experiences and build upon successes from within and outside the continent. Two examples from outside Africa—namely Bangladesh and Cuba—are discussed in this section. There are, however, also worthy examples from within Africa, such as Malawi.

Bangladesh, a poor, low-income country, is home to BRAC, the world's largest indigenous development NGO, which serves poor people in Bangladesh and some sub-Saharan African countries. The organization's learning culture facilitates its learning from internally generated evidence regarding progress made. According to Lincoln Chen (2009), BRAC's successful and model health work reaches the lives of 92 million people through, for example, the development, growth, and expansion of a cadre of 74,000 female village health workers, *shasthyo shebikas,* who receive six weeks of training. These workers offer primary care services, such as oral rehydration therapy, for common ailments mostly through health education and sale of health products. In order to support the village health workers and others at lower and middle level for analysis of health challenges and planning appropriate interventions BRAC launched the James P. Grant School of Public Health with an innovative curriculum. The school is part of BRAC'S broad focus and interest of contributing to advancing higher education through BRAC's private university.

Across the globe is Cuba, a poor country with scarce resources which has for decades managed to have adequate health capacity, earning itself a place among world leaders in health workforce adequacy and has been the envy of many LMICs. The country's health outcomes match or surpass those in high-income countries, as reflected in low infant, child, and maternal mortality rates and a high healthy-life expectancy. In addition the country has had a long established program of sending Cuban doctors overseas to many African countries. This approach is being and adapted by other countries such as China (Spiegel 2006; Thompson 2005). An elective service by US health professionals, the Global Health Corps, is being discussed with the thinking that these would contribute to strengthening health capacity in under-resourced environments like sub-Saharan Africa (Institute of Medicine 2005).

Cuba's health system has several other distinguishing characteristics that are missing in most African countries. It has developed public policies that prioritize the development of human capital within a context of limited resources, making it possible to achieve an integrated and effective health service that ensures both curative and preventive services with equitable distribution of health workers across the country and ensuring universal free-of-charge health coverage (Márquez 2009; Vujicic et al. 2009). Since the 1959 revolution Cuba's public health system has acquired and sustained a diversified health workforce with adequate, staff–population ratios (for example, 6.72 physicians and 90.5 nurses or midwives per 10,000 inhabitants, compared to 17.6 physicians and 64.2 nurses or midwives in Brazil, 10.3 physicians and 1.4 nurses or midwives in Chile, 1.5 physicians and 6.2 nurses or midwives in Colombia, and 24.2 physicians and 98.2 nurses or midwives in the United States) (De Vos 2005; WHO 2012c). The services spread "along the continuum of care, particularly ambulatory services in polyclinics—the basic unit of the system—staffed with doctors, nurses, and health technicians and serving a population of 25 000–30 000, and in specialised centres and at home" (Márquez 2009). There is a primary healthcare physician and nurse in every neighbourhood, serving about 150 families. Auxiliary personnel are trained to serve in rural areas. Health technicians help meet changing needs and there is a well-established interlinked network of referral facilities (Márquez 2009).

Despite the poor economic situation in Cuba, the country has enough health workers enabling it to maintain collaboration with and provision of human resource technical assistance to those countries (De Vos et al. 2007).

Research and Research Capacity for Enhancing Africa's Health Capacity

African countries are faced with weak, fragile, and unmapped health systems. Often data are unavailable for evidence-based health policy making and action. There is an overwhelming need for an evidence base to guide policy decisions and monitoring progress. Implementation and delivery of effective interventions are frequently inadequate due to a spectrum of financial or other poorly understood issues related to infrastructure, logistics, workforce, or culture. The generation of new knowledge through research or monitoring and the evaluation of programs is therefore critical. But this also requires the presence of capable individuals who can undertake valid studies. Building human resource capacity should include enhancing research capacity.

Sub-Saharan African countries, more often than not, lack the capacity to systematically measure and understand their own general health and human resource weaknesses and constraints. This leaves policy makers in a desperate situation without scientifically sound ideas of what they can and should actually strengthen. Most African countries do not emphasize development of health research capacity as part of the overall strengthening human resources capacity or of the health system. On the contrary, Cuba has done otherwise. It has progressively developed and linked research institutions and their social and technological research innovations to public health services, and it has strengthened operational research to inform program implementation and optimize care (De Vos et al. 2005; Lage 2008; Toledo Romani et al. 2007).

To maximize learning from successes and failures, there should be deliberate efforts to conduct research or experiment with new or alternative implementation approaches. Sadly, national strategies for supporting and accelerating research activities, together with enhancing human resource research capacity, are usually omitted or overlooked in plans for development of an effective health workforce. But this should change in the near future.

Education of Health Workforce (Pre-service and In-service)

The state of the education of the health workforce is generally in a crisis across the African continent (Omer 2005). It is caused by inadequate and ever decreasing investment by African governments and also by the massive entry of the private sector in this field. Institutions that were once progressive institutions during the colonial era have suffered significant setbacks in the last 50 years, although a number are undergoing a significant revival. Institutions that train health workers should be supported better so as to develop the infrastructure and educators necessary for enriching health capacity-building efforts.

Despite the global awareness of the human resource crisis affecting Africa, there is a general lack of serious collective action by the global community. The training of health personnel takes time. Increased access to health personnel is often contingent on very long-range planning. Each country needs to determine its human resource needs for the near, mid, and long terms so that education efforts can be tailored to meet those needs.

Training auxiliary workers would be of enormous benefit to African countries, as they have already added value to the health system. This type of health workers is low cost and takes a short time to train. Auxiliary health workers are much less likely to emigrate. However, they require intense supervision. It is important that African countries and their international partners or funders do not slacken their efforts and investments into training high-level health workers such as physicians, dentists, pharmacists, nurses, health planners, and managers, who can provide the required oversight of the auxiliary workers and plan for services while also offering the high-quality services required in their respective countries.

Education provided in-country is likely to cost much less yet be more relevant to the local situation, and thus less likely to lead to external brain drain. Plans for educating and training an adequate health workforce that can provide quality services equitably must be forward-looking as well as satisfy current needs. Those in training now will provide services not today but also in years to come, which therefore necessitates an intelligent forecast of future needs in order to develop an appropriate curriculum. Since medical and other health-related knowledge and information is changing very fast, trainees must develop a culture of life-long, self-directed learning, so as to be able to acquire new knowledge as it emerges and use it to improve the quality of services they deliver.

In this millennium, Africa has to emerge as a dynamic and innovative continent using new technologies that allow educators and health specialists to overcome the old barriers such as distance and borders. Future success lies in adopting innovations in education that take advantage of effective, efficient, cost-effective new methodologies, including the use, location, and timing of information technology. A country should also have mandatory requirements for periodic, regular recertification based on a worker's evidence of continuing upgrading of knowledge and skills. To make this workable there should be in place facilities and avenues for continuing professional development that can be accessed easily by the appropriate categories of health workers.

There are anecdotal reports of deteriorating standards of professionalism among health workers throughout Africa. This trend must not be allowed to continue. Attention must be directed to ensuring the highest standards of professionalism among trainees and, equally, if not more, important, among their trainers and others who act as mentors and role models. Equally important is adequate supervision and practical experience in the course of training. The softer skills of successful practice as a health worker should not be overlooked, such as communication skills, leadership, humanism, and empathy. The breadth of skills to be learned will vary depending on the level of training. However, it is critical to train health workers in management (including human resource management) and planning because there is serious shortage of these skills across sub-Saharan Africa.

For certain procedures, the required skills have become so simplified that they can be carried out by trained mid-level providers who are not physicians. To this end task shifting has featured prominently in many recommendations on strengthening health capacity in LIMCs, in particular those of sub-Saharan Africa. And yet a decision to implement task shifting can have major implications for different aspects of the health system, such as stewardship and governance, education and training, financing, and ethical considerations. Sub-Saharan African countries need to make individual decisions based on their own circumstances whether task shifting can enhance their workforce capacity. Shifting tasks from physicians to mid-level providers requires many people in both categories. While it might not be a panacea for the human resources problems facing sub-Saharan Africa, it must be part of an overall strategy to remedy public health services (Philips et al. 2008). These efforts should therefore not cause undesirable effects on the rest of the healthcare system, including diverting human resources from other health programs or local needs, or distorting overall health services.

Indeed, there are many considerations that must go into such a policy, such as whether the quality of care and financial or other incentives can sustain health worker outputs (Berer 2009). Tasks and workloads for mid-level providers must be designed to prevent overwork and unnecessary complexity. There needs to be sufficient awareness and acceptance of mid-level staff doing the work of physicians in the community. The education system must be able to provide adequate training, supervision, and support, so these new responsibilities do not cause stress and burnout. Moreover, education and training must adjusted to allow for the implementation of this policy shift within the overall framework of pre-service and in-service education and training of health workers.

High-income countries play a role in strengthening health capacity in Africa through education and training via three approaches: stopping the unethical recruitment or Africa's trained personnel and instead taking a greater responsibility for training health workers in their home countries to at least meet their own requirements, supporting and helping to increase the training capacity of sub-Saharan African countries, and offering high-level specialized training overseas in selected fields related to sub-Saharan Africa. It is important for long-term planning and distribution of the global human resources for health workforce training to be implemented from a perspective of solidarity. Training of health workers relies on training Africa's personnel both in-country or elsewhere on the continent and in high-income countries.

Matching Future Population Needs with Health Capacity Development

African countries must each have the capacity to project their future health service needs to be able to forecast their human resource needs. The global population is projected to rise from 7 billion people in 2011 to 10.6 billion by 2050 (United Nations Population Fund 2011). Africa is home to the most rapid levels of population growth and of urbanization in the world (Cilliers 2009). For example, East Africa is the least urbanized region in the world but is also urbanizing quickly and is expected to double in less than nine years, faster than anywhere else in the world—from 50.6 million in 2007 to a projected 106.7 million by 2017 (Cilliers 2009). These trends pose serious challenges to governments trying to develop human resource capacity to provide health services for such a rapidly expanding population. Moreover, the rising population in Africa occurs in the context of demographic transition and a rapidly changing profile of burden of disease due, for example, to emerging and re-emerging infectious diseases such as HIV/AIDS and H1N1 influenza, from noncommunicable diseases resulting from changing lifestyles, and from climate change and other social determinants of health.

Migration

Physicians, nurses, and other health workers are migrating between public and private medicine or between countries within sub-Saharan Africa and from Africa to richer countries. Trained health workers migrate from rural to urban areas as much as they also leave the country. Others are leaving the health profession altogether to seek better-paying employment. Today's global market is increasingly porous and professionals can move freely from one country to another, just as patients can move from one country to another seeking cost-effective service delivery. The complex dynamics of international migration and the recruitment of healthcare professionals include individual choice, motivations, and attitudes to career development as well as the relative status of health workers in different country systems. The brain drain is triggered in part by pull (e.g. demands for skilled labour in countries more advanced than one's own) as well as push factors (difficulties encountered in source developing countries, including the negative effects of structural adjustment programs on health systems). In order to diminish the large numbers of migrant health professionals from sub-Saharan Africa, source countries have to reduce their push factors. Bodies such as the World Bank also play a role because their actions and policies contribute to creating and maintaining the push factors, as happened in Zambia.

An integrated response to the problems arising from health worker migration would combine preventing such migration, including mitigating the factors that drive it, and "ensuring that any improvements in the right to health are achieved without any negative repercussions to the right of health of others in source countries and without express limitation of any other rights, including freedom of movement and rights in work" (Labonté, Packer, Klassen, et al. 2006). Other suggestions address the issue of brain drain from LMICs. The option of restitution equivalent to the salaried value of health workers employed in receiving countries has been suggested as a way to reduce migration (Mensah et al. 2005). However, this has received little support from the international community. Bonding, which requires graduates to remain in service in their country of training for a number of years to repay the government-funded portion of their education, has been tried in African countries but met with very little success because of the challenges of implementation and difficulties in enforcement. For effective deterrence, a penalty must be included for breaking the bond. This option could be applied to health workers both in source and receiving countries.

Multilateral and bilateral agreements are now being tried by some agencies. For example as UN Special Rapporteur on the Right to Health, Paul Hunt (2005) emphasized that developed countries must respect the right to health in developing countries, specifically at a minimum.

> Developed countries should ensure that their human resource policies do not jeopardize the right to health in developing countries. If a developed country actively recruits health professionals from a developing country that is suffering from a shortage of health professionals in such a manner that the recruitment reduces the developing country's capacity to fulfil the right to health obligations that it owes its citizens, the developed country is prima facie in breach of its human rights responsibility of international assistance and cooperation in the context of the right to health. (Hunt 2005)

Hunt (2005) suggested that developed countries, which have a responsibility of international assistance and cooperation, should not apply "undue pressure on developing countries" to make mode 4 commitments under the General Agreement on Trade in Services that are "inconsistent with developing countries obligations arising from the right to health." Those mode 4 commitments should be revised to prevent any negative impact on the right to health for all.

The costs to sub-Saharan African source countries of brain drain have been acknowledged in numerous reports. They are the reason why WHO and the Commonwealth countries have called for urgent action to reduce the phenomenon, and why countries such as the UK and others are adopting measures to the same end (Commonwealth Health Ministers 2003; UK Department of Health 2004; WHO 2010c). The losses can be counted in terms of the direct costs incurred by African governments as investment in training health professionals who emigrate. Other costs include the loss of trained individuals to provide care and tutors to teach new health professional students, as well as the increased burden on remaining health professionals and diminished ability to provide health care.

One policy option of considerable interest to African countries is reparation or restitution, in which the receiving country would reimburse the source country. Those resources could be ploughed back into strengthening health systems particularly to support the development of human resource capacity in Africa, instead of being diverted to uses unrelated to health-worker support.

While WHO has encouraged the concept of reparation, the challenging practical question remains of how to estimate loss on a country-by-country basis. There are two possibilities for a reasonable determination, one based on the amount of out-migration and the other based on calculating the health impact of that out-migration.

The second—and arguably the fairest, although a more difficult approach in practical terms—retains the focus of an assessment specific to each country but also weights the relative importance of the resources lost. Some countries need their health workers more than others. Moreover, some health workers are worth more than others. For example, the loss of a health specialist involved in training other health professionals may be greater than the loss of one who is not, as the long-term impact of losing individuals who build capacity is significant. In Africa, rural physicians are hard to retain, and therefore may be worth more to that country than urban physicians. Other factors to be taken into account in setting the amount of compensation per health worker include amount of experience, rural or urban experience, the specific discipline and its relative importance within the given country, the ability of the country to replace the individual, and the expected remaining years of service.

Ethical Issues in Health Workforce Development

Populations in African countries have generally failed to hold their governments accountable for providing a well-functioning heath workforce that is available and accessible and that provides quality health care. Decisions by African states about equitable workforce development are inevitably caught up in ethical dilemmas because such decisions are not value free, particularly with regard to resource allocation in severely resource-constrained environments. The policy of most governments is to provide free care, which, in reality, is accessible only to a privileged few. This means that rather than fulfil their responsibilities in health service delivery and health care, governments provide care that is below the standard feasible in an efficient and fair system even with severe resource constraints.

It will require a lot of advocacy from civil society and the population at large, assisted by the academia and possibly global support, to wake up governments so they can play their rightful roles in working toward achieving an adequate workforce. The standard of care must reflect the level of available resources, but at some point the scarcity of resources turns into substandard care (Cash 2005). Indeed, as Richard Cash writes, "it would be unethical ... to impose first-world standards in training health personnel, if the result were to limit access to care to a fortunate few."

Cash (2005) has raised a number of questions relevant to health workforce development that help to illuminate the ethical dilemmas faced by the developing world. What should be the standard of care to which health workers are trained, and is it ethically acceptable for a country to support the kind of training that focuses on resource-intensive procedures that will not be equitably accessible in that country? How can each country ensure that those responsible for health care are adequately trained to deliver it? How can they make sure that workers are regularly recertified and remain up to date with emerging new knowledge? Is it ethically defensible for society to train people and then not support them in delivering quality services? Is it ethical for a state to train additional health workers but fail to absorb them in either the public or private sector, even while there might be staffing gaps in the health system or large groups of citizens without access to health services? Should health workers and training institutions be diverted from those areas of the country that are unable to provide adequate care? What minimum ethical principles regarding standards of care should be taught? Is it an ethical issue that healthcare professionals whose training was supported by public funds are leaving their countries in sub-Saharan Africa because their fundamental rights to work, to an adequate standard of living and to security, as well as others, are not secured? How should practitioners of alternative medicine be certified? Is it proper and ethical to treat traditional practitioners differently from those trained in the allopathic system?

Decisions taken by high-income countries may be of questionable ethical integrity with regard to developing the health workforce of African countries. Despite the fact that high-income countries may have adequate resources to train enough health workers of their own needs, they have often depended on unethical recruitment from poor African countries that have personnel shortages. On a positive side, these challenges are now the object of discussion in many international forums, including WHO, the European Union, and the Organisation for Economic Co-operation and Development. One unresolved question remains of how to handle recruitment by one African country from another.

Codes have been advocated for but the world is yet to commit to their wide-scale implementation, and Africa is yet to benefit from their application. The Commonwealth laid the foundation in 2003 when health ministers agreed on voluntary guidelines for the international recruitment of healthcare professionals in a manner intended to mitigate the negative impacts of such recruitment on services in source countries (Commonwealth Health Ministers 2003). The Commonwealth Code of Practice has been signed primarily by developing country members rather than the countries importing health workers and the latter are reluctant to make a formal commitment to provide compensation or reparations. The United Kingdom was the first country to produce international recruitment guidelines based on ethical principles and the first to develop a code of practice for international recruitment that stipulates that the National Health Service (NHS) should not actively recruit from developing countries unless there is agreement with the government of the country (NHS Employers 2012). The code lists countries from which healthcare professionals should not be recruited, which comprises all developing countries, including South Africa.

The UK also signed a memorandum of understanding (MOU) with South Africa for the ethical recruitment of healthcare professionals. The MOU facilitates exchanges between the two countries and provides for South African healthcare personnel to spend time-limited education and practice periods in organizations providing NHS services. Clinical staff from the UK work alongside healthcare personnel in South Africa, with particular emphasis on the rural areas. The MOU also provides for a twinning scheme between South African and UK hospitals, which has allowed 30 South African nurses to be placed in the UK for theoretical and practical training while senior nurses from the UK have worked in South Africa as mentors. This approach is contributing to development of health capacity in South Africa on mutually agreed terms.

Multilateral and Bilateral Agreements

The NEPAD health strategy specifically refers to the necessity of developing some form of bilateral or multilateral agreement to manage the brain drain of professionals from African countries. There have been some multilateral and bilateral initiatives to support the return of indigenous nationals through the provision of financial support with an attractive salary on return home guaranteed for several years. The Ghana–Netherlands Healthcare Project has been cited as an example of a bilateral success story. Its objectives are to transfer knowledge, skills, and experiences through short-term assignments and projects and practical internships for Ghanaians and to develop a centre for the maintenance of medical equipment in Ghana. It is meant to allow Ghanaian health professionals to offer services, conduct research, and implement projects within Ghana. Canada has had discussions with South Africa to determine the basis for, and value of, drafting an MOU between the two countries similar to the one South Africa has with the UK.

Observance of Health Workers Rights as a Prerequisite for Strengthening Human Resource Capacity

One of the underlying impediments to the development of effective health capacity in African countries is the failure to respect the human rights of persons, particularly health workers. African governments should pay greater attention to human right issues not only for entire populations but also specifically as they relate to health workers. The human right to health is embodied in a variety of international declarations, covenants, and plans of action. For example, article 12 of the International Covenant of Economic, Social, and Cultural Rights proclaims that "every human being is entitled to the enjoyment of the highest attainable standard of health" and specifically obligates states to ensure availability, accessibility, and quality services (Committee on Economic 2000). Therefore, individual countries have a duty to ensure the progressive realization of the full enjoyment of the right to health by their citizens.

African countries often fail to ensure adequate implementation of article 23(1) of the Universal Declaration of Human Rights, adopted in 1948, which declares that "everyone has the right to work, to free choice of employment, to just and favourable conditions of work and to protection against unemployment" (UN 1948). Article 25(1) further recognizes that "everyone has the right to a standard of living adequate for the health and well-being of himself and of his family, including food, clothing, housing and medical care and necessary social services, and the right to security in the event of unemployment, sickness, disability, widowhood, old age or other lack of livelihood in circumstances beyond his control." Healthcare professionals in sub-Saharan Africa are frequently unable to obtain work, or, if they do, are paid below a decent living wage, which is often delayed. It can be very difficult for health workers to support themselves and their families better than other workers who have no skills. Moreover, in many cases there is no social security system to support workers in the event of unemployment, illness, and retirement. There may also be no adequate protection at the workplace to provide safe and healthy working conditions, thus posing a threat to personal security.

Ensuring Sustainability of Capacity-strengthening Efforts

To succeed and become sustainable, initiatives should be decided upon, owned, and implemented by the countries themselves. Africa should avoid being held hostage to policy priorities decided by the donor community and the dominant institutions of global economic and financial governance. Most of the existing efforts are initiated by the global North. Innovative approaches to solving Africa's health worker crisis must also ensure that the health system as a whole is not dysfunctional. Otherwise health workers will not make up for the system's deficiencies. As long as Africa is as is, it is difficult to talk of existence of a just and equitable world. Countries have to commit increasing resources to achieve improvements in health workforce performance. LMICs will, for many years, sometimes require international support to initiate or develop and to maintain desirable workforce plans and programs. Further funding from international agencies such as the Global Fund to Fight AIDS, Tuberculosis, and Malaria, the GAVI Alliance, and the World Bank is necessary to support scaling up collaboration among countries and to reverse the deficits in human resources that hinder health system strengthening in much of the developing world. Having health workers (both paid and unpaid community health workers) with appropriate skills is essential but not enough in itself to bring about changes in health service delivery. There is need for a functioning health system, and financial and other resources are required for this to happen. The health workforce is a fundamental element of any functioning health system. "All countries have to deal with the challenges of ensuring an appropriate supply and distribution of health workers, maintaining adequate levels of training, retaining health professionals, and managing their motivation and performance" (Jimba 2009). It is necessary for rich countries to contribute to increasing the capacity of poor African countries for training, recruiting, and retaining their own health personnel.

References

Beaglehole, Robert and Derek Yach (2003). "Globalisation and the Prevention and Control of Non-Communicable Disease: The Neglected Chronic Diseases of Adults." *Lancet* 362(9387): 903–8.

Berer, Marge (2009). "Task-Shifting: Exposing the Cracks in Public Health Systems." *Reproductive Health Matters* 17(33): 4–8. Available online: www. rhmjournal.org.uk/publications/editorials/RHM33.pdf (October 2012).

Bryce, Jennifer, Nancy Terreri, Cesar G. Victora, et al. (2006). "Countdown to 2015: Tracking Intervention Coverage for Child Survival." *Lancet* 368(9541): 1067–76.

Cash, Richard (2005). "Ethical Issues in Health Workforce Development." *Bulletin of the World Health Organization* 83: 280–84. Available online: www.who.int/ bulletin/volumes/83/4/280.pdf (October 2012).

Chen, Lincoln (2009). "Beyond Rhetoric: The Quest for Practical Success in Global Health." *Lancet* 374(9700): 1491–2. Available online: www.thelancet. com/journals/lancet/article/PIIS0140-6736%2809%2961890-0/fulltext (October 2012).

Cilliers, Jakkie (2009). "Climate Change, Population Pressure, and Conflict in Africa." ISS Paper 178, January, Institute for Security Studies, Pretoria. Available online: www.issafrica.org/uploads/PAPER178.PDF (October 2012).

Cohen, Jon (2006). "The New World of Global Health." *Science* 311(5758): 162–7.

Commission for Africa (2005). "Our Common Interest." Report of the Commission for Africa, London. Available online: www.commissionforafrica.info/2005-report (October 2012).

Commission on Macroeconomics and Health (2001). "Macroeconomics and Health: Investing in Health for Economic Development." World Health Organization, Geneva. Available online: www.cid.harvard.edu/archive/cmh/cmhreport.pdf (October 2012).

Committee on Economic, Social, and Cultural Rights (2000). "The Right to the Highest Attainable Standard of Health." August 11, United Nations Economic and Social Council, Geneva. Available online: www.unhchr.ch/tbs/doc.nsf/(symbol)/E.C.12.2000.4.En (October 2012).

Commonwealth Health Ministers (2003). "Commonwealth Code of Practice for the International Recruitment of Health Workers." May 18, Geneva. Available online: www.thecommonwealth.org/shared_asp_files/uploadedfiles/%7B7BDD970B-53AE-441D-81DB-1B64C37E992A%7D_CommonwealthCodeofPractice.pdf (October 2012).

Corkery, Joan (2000). "Public Service Reforms and Their Impact on Health Sector Personnel in Uganda." In *Public Service Reforms and their Impact on Health Sector Personnel: Case Studies on Cameroon, Colombia, Jordan, Philippines, Poland, Uganda*, International Labour Organization, ed. Geneva: pp. 236–84.

De Vos, Pol (2005). "'No One Left Abandoned': Cuba's National Health System since the 1959 Revolution." *International Journal of Health Services* 35(1): 189–207.

De Vos, Pol, Wim De Ceukelaire, Mariano Bonet, et al. (2007). "Cuba's International Cooperation in Health: An Overview." *International Journal of Health Services* 37(4): 761–6.

De Vos, Pol, Pedro Murlá, Armando Rodriguez, et al. (2005). "Shifting the Demand for Emergency Care in Cuba's Health System." *Social Science and Medicine* 60(3): 609–16.

Dodgson, Richard, Kelley Lee, and Nick Drager (2002). "Global Health Governance: A Conceptual Review." London School of Hygiene and Tropical Medicine, London. Available online: www.bvsde.paho.org/texcom/cd050853/dodgson.pdf (October 2012).

Fink, Sheri (2002). "International Efforts Spotlight Traditional, Complementary, and Alternative Medicine." *American Journal of Public Health* 92(11): 1734–9. Available online: ajph.aphapublications.org/doi/abs/10.2105/AJPH.92.11.1734 (October 2012).

Garrett, Laurie (1994). *The Coming Plague: Newly Emerging Diseases in a World Out of Balance*. New York: Farrar, Strauss and Giroux.

Global Health Workforce Alliance (2008). "The Kampala Declaration and Agenda for Global Action." World Health Organization, Geneva. Available online: www.who.int/workforcealliance/Kampala%20Declaration%20and%20Agenda%20web%20file.%20FINAL.pdf (October 2012).

High-Level Panel on Threats, Challenges, and Change (2004). "A More Secure World: Our Shared Responsibility." United Nations, New York. Available online: www.un.org/secureworld/ (October 2012).

Homer-Dixon, Thomas (2001). *The Ingenuity Gap: Can We Solve the Problems of the Future?* Toronto: Vintage.

Hunt, Paul (2005). "The Right of Everyone to the Enjoyment of the Highest Attainable Standard of Physical and Mental Health." Report of the United Nations Special Rapporteur on the Right to Health. A/60/348. Available online: daccess-dds-ny.un.org/doc/UNDOC/GEN/N05/486/77/PDF/N0548677.pdf (October 2012).

Institute of Medicine (2005). *Healers Abroad: Americans Responding to the Human Resource Crisis in HIV/AIDS*. Washington, DC: National Academies Press.

Jimba, Masamine (2009). "Opportunities for Overcoming the Health Workforce Crisis." In *Global Action for Health System Strengthening: Policy Recommendations to the G8*. Tokyo: Japan Center for International Exchange, pp. 27–58. Available online: www.jcie.org/researchpdfs/takemi/ch2.pdf (October 2012).

Joint Learning Initiative (2004). "Human Resources for Health: Overcoming the Crisis." Harvard University, Cambridge, MA. Available online: www.who.int/hrh/documents/JLi_hrh_report.pdf (October 2012).

Kruk, Margaret Elizabeth and Lynn P. Freedman (2008). "Assessing Health System Performance in Developing Countries: A Review of the Literature." *Health Policy* 85(3): 263–76.

Labonté, Ronald, Corinne Packer, Nathan Klassen, et al. (2006). *The Brain Drain of Health Professionals from Sub-Saharan Africa to Canada*. Cape Town: Southern African Migration Project. Available online: www.queensu.ca/samp/sampresources/samppublications/mad/MAD_2.pdf (October 2012).

Lage, Agustin (2008). "Connecting Immunology Research to Public Health: Cuban Biotechnology." *Nature Immunology* 9: 109–12.

Lagomarsino, Gina, David de Ferranti, Ariel Pablos-Mendez, et al. (2009). "Public Stewardship of Mixed Health Systems." *Lancet* 374(9701): 1577–8.

Lagomarsino, Gina, Stefan Nachuk, and Sapna Singh Kundra (2009). "Public Stewardship of Private Providers in Mixed Health Systems." Synthesis report from the Rockefeller Foundation–sponsored Initiative on the Role of the Private Sector in Health Systems in Developing Countries, Rockefeller Foundation, Washington, DC. Available online: www.rockefellerfoundation.org/uploads/files/0d777898-d2eb-461d-a973-5f7d5d979544-public.pdf (October 2012).

Lee, Kelley, Kent Buse, and Suzanne Fustukian, eds (2002). *Health Policy in a Globalising World*. Cambridge: Cambridge University Press.

Liese, Bernhard, Nathan Blanchet, and Gilles Dussault (2003). "Background Paper: The Human Resource Crisis in Health Services in Sub-Saharan Africa." World Bank, Washington, DC. Available online: www-wds.worldbank.org/servlet/WDSContentServer/WDSP/IB/2003/10/31/000112742_20031031161656/additional/310436360_20050276022409.pdf (October 2012).

Márquez, Miguel (2009). "Health-Workforce Development in the Cuban Health System." *Lancet* 374(9701): 1574–5.

Mensah, Kwadwo, Maureen Mackintosh, and Leroi Henry (2005). "The 'Skills Drain' of Health Professionals from the Developing World: A Framework for Policy Formulation." Medact, London. Available online: www.medact.org/content//Skills%20drain/Mensah%20et%20al.%202005.pdf (October 2012).

Ministers of Foreign Affairs of Brazil, France, Indonesia, Norway, Senegal, South Africa, and Thailand (2007). "Oslo Ministerial Declaration—Global Health: A Pressing Foreign Policy Issue of Our Time." *Lancet* 369(9580): 2159. Available online: www.who.int/trade/events/Oslo_Ministerial_Declaration. pdf (October 2012).

NHS Employers (2012). "Code of Practice for International Recruitment." Leeds, April 24. Available online: www.nhsemployers.org/recruitmentandretention/internationalrecruitment/code-of-practice/pages/code-practice-international-recruitment.aspx (October 2012).

Nishtar, Sania (2007). "Politics of Health Systems: WHO's New Frontier." *Lancet* 370(9591): 935–6.

Novotny, Thomas E., Ilona Kickbusch, Hannah Leslie, et al. (2008). "Global Health Diplomacy: A Bridge to Innovative Collaborative Action." *Global Forum Update on Research for Health* 5: 41–5.

Omaswa, Francis (2009). "Message from the Executive Director." Global Health Workforce Alliance. Available online: www.who.int/workforcealliance/forum/1_agenda4GAction_final.pdf (October 2012).

Omer, Mohamed Ibrahim Ali (2005). "Can Medical Education Rise to the Challenge of the African Crisis?" *Annals of Tropical Paediatrics* 25(4): 227–41.

Ooms, Gorik, Wim Van Damme, Brook Baker, et al. (2008). "The 'Diagonal' Approach to Global Fund Financing: A Cure for the Broader Malaise of Health Systems?" *Globalization and Health* 4(6). doi: 10.1186/1744-8603-4-6. Available online: www.globalizationandhealth.com/content/4/1/6 (October 2012).

Philips, Mit, Rony Zachariah, and Sarah Venis (2008). "Task Shifting for Antiretroviral Treatment Delivery in Sub-Saharan Africa: Not a Panacea." *Lancet* 371(9613): 682–4.

Plsek, Paul E. (2001). "Complexity, Leadership, and Management in Healthcare Organisations." *British Medical Journal* 323(7315): 746–9.

Reich, Michael R., Keizo Takemi, Marc J. Roberts, et al. (2008). "Global Action on Health Systems: A Proposal for the Toyako G8 Summit." *Lancet* 371(9615): 865–9.

Roemer, Milton I. (1991). *National Health Systems of the World.* Vol. 1: The Countries. New York: Oxford University Press.

Sanders, David, Ehi Igumbor, Uta Lehmann, et al. (2009). "Public Health in Africa." In *Global Public Health: A New Era*, Robert Beaglehole and Ruth Bonita, eds. New York: Oxford University Press, pp. 161–84.

Spiegel, Jerry M. (2006). "Commentary: Daring to Learn from a Good Example and Break the 'Cuba Taboo.'" *International Journal of Epidemiology* 35(4): 825–6. Available online: ije.oxfordjournals.org/content/35/4/825.full (October 2012).

Tandon, Yash (2008, 1 April). "UNCTAD XII: Negotiating 'Diplomatic Truths.'" *South Bulletin* (12). Available online: www.southcentre.org/ index.php?option=com_docman&task=doc_download&gid=833&Itemid= (October 2012).

Taylor, Allyn L. (2004). "Governing the Globalization of Public Health." *Journal of Law, Medicine, and Ethics* 32(3): 500–508. Available online: digitalcommons. law.umaryland.edu/fac_pubs/58/ (October 2012).

Taylor, Allyn L. and Lawrence O. Gostin (2008). "Global Health Law: A Definition and Grand Challenges." *Public Health Ethics* 1(1): 53–63. Available online: papers.ssrn.com/sol3/papers.cfm?abstract_id=1272424 (October 2012).

Thompson, Drew (2005). "China's Soft Power in Africa: From the 'Beijing Consensus' to Health Diplomacy." *China Brief* 5(21). Available online: csis. org/files/media/csis/pubs/051013_china_soft_pwr.pdf (October 2012).

Toledo Romani, Maria E., Veerle Vanlerbergh, Dennis Perez, et al. (2007). "Achieving Sustainability of Community-Based Dengue Control in Santiago de Cuba." *Social Science and Medicine* 64(4): 976–88.

United Kingdom. Department of Health (2004). "Code of Practice for the International Recruitment of Healthcare Professionals." December, London. Available online: www.dh.gov.uk/prod_consum_dh/groups/dh_digitalassets/@ dh/@en/documents/digitalasset/dh_4097734.pdf (October 2012).

United Nations (1948). "Universal Declaration of Human Rights." Available online: www.un.org/en/documents/udhr (October 2012).

United Nations (2011). "The Millennium Development Goals Report 2009." New York. Available online: www.un.org/millenniumgoals/pdf/MDG_ Report_2009_ENG.pdf (October 2012).

United Nations Population Fund (2011). "The State of the World Population 2011." Geneva. Available online: foweb.unfpa.org/SWP2011/reports/EN-SWOP2011-FINAL.pdf (October 2012).

Vujicic, Marko, Kelechi Ohiri, and Susan Sparkes (2009). *Working in Health: Financing and Managing the Public Sector Health Workforce.* Washington, DC: World Bank. Available online: www.who.int/workforcealliance/ knowledge/publications/partner/workinginhealth_vujicic_worldbank_2009. pdf (October 2012).

World Bank (2012a). "Data: Sub-Saharan Africa." Washington, DC. Available online: data.worldbank.org/region/sub-saharan-africa (October 2012).

World Health Organization (2006). "The World Health Report 2006: Working Together for Health." World Health Organization, Geneva. Available online: www.who.int/whr/2006/en/ (October 2012).

World Health Organization (2007). "Everybody's Business: Strengthening Health Systems to Improve Health Outcomes—WHO's Framework for Action." World Health Organization, Geneva. Available online: www.who.int/healthsystems/ strategy/everybodys_business.pdf (October 2012).

World Health Organization (2010). "WHO Global Code of Practice on the International Recruitment of Health Personnel." WHA63.16, May 21, World

Health Organization, Geneva. Available online: apps.who.int/gb/ebwha/pdf_
files/WHA63/A63_R16-en.pdf (October 2012).

World Health Organization (2012). "World Health Statistics 2012." Geneva. Available
online: www.who.int/healthinfo/EN_WHS2012_Full.pdf (October 2012).

World Health Organization Regional Office for Africa (2000). "Promoting the Role
of Traditional Medicine in Health Systems: A Strategy for the African Region."
AFR/RC50/9, March 9, Brazzaville. Available online: www.afro.who.int/index.
php?option=com_docman&task=doc_download&gid=872&Itemid=2111
(October 2012).

Chapter 9

The WHO Global Code of Practice on the International Recruitment of Health Personnel: The Evolution of Global Health Diplomacy

Allyn L. Taylor and Ibadat S. Dhillon[1]

The loss of highly skilled personnel, colloquially referred to as brain drain, has been a central concern of developing countries for the last half century. Despite a call by developing countries, limited international structure has emerged to manage the gains and losses equitably from the largely asymmetric movement of skilled workers.

Over this last decade, in the context of a renewed focus on health systems and greater awareness to the scope of the global health workforce shortage—with an estimated four and a half million additional health workers needed immediately—developing country concerns related to the international migration of health workers, particularly of those whose training is publicly subsidized, have regained prominence. The demand for health workers in middle- and high-income countries is escalating and is increasingly met through reliance on foreign health workers, very often from low-income countries.

The migration of health workers to middle- and high-income countries is exacerbating existing inequities in the distribution in the global health workforce and further compromising health systems in some of the poorest countries in the world. As illustration, while themselves struggling with serious health workforce shortages, over half the potential physician workforce of Angola, Antigua and Barbuda, Grenada, Guyana, Haiti, Liberia, Mozambique, Saint Vincent and the Grenadines, Sierra Leone, Tanzania, and Trinidad and Tobago currently serves the populations of the countries that are members of the Organisation for Economic Cooperation and Development ([OECD] 2007).

---

1 The opinions expressed herein are those of the authors alone and do not necessarily reflect the views of the World Health Organization or Realizing Rights. This chapter has been adapted from an article by the authors entitled "The WHO Global Code of Practice on the International Recruitment of Health Personnel: The Evolution of Global Health Diplomacy," *Global Health Governance Journal*, November 21, 2011.

The challenge associated with health worker migration at its core points to a lack of coherence between the global health-related development agenda and the domestic health workforce policies of many donor countries. Ameliorating the negative effects of health worker migration necessitates an international structure to further dialogue and guide cooperation among and within states on issues related to the international recruitment and migration of health workers (Robinson and Clark 2008). Without serious engagement on these issues, improvements to health in low-income countries, as well as significant donor investments and credibility, are placed in jeopardy.

The May 2010 adoption by the World Health Assembly (WHA) of the World Health Organization (WHO) Global Code of Practice on the International Recruitment of Health Personnel puts in place a global architecture, including the identification of ethical norms as well as institutional and legal arrangements, to guide international cooperation on the issue of health worker migration and serves as a platform for continuing dialogue. It articulates "principles and practices" critical to the improvement of the global health system (WHO 2010b). Only the second code of its kind promulgated by WHO, the process toward the development of the code evidences a growing maturity of global health diplomacy. Multilateral agreement among all 194 WHO member states has been achieved on an issue of long-standing concern to developing countries, one that until recently was viewed as irreconcilable with the interests of high-income countries. The choice of a non-binding approach to address an issue that is dynamic, complex, and highly sensitive also reflects more nuanced understanding by members of the nature and utility of binding and non-binding international legal instruments to further global health.

This article analyses the history of the negotiations of the code and the significance of this new instrument for global health diplomacy and global health governance.

The Global Migration of Health Personnel

The global health workforce shortage and inequitable distribution of health workers among and within countries has reached crisis proportions. Launching a United Nations Decade of Human Resources for Health, *The World Health Report 2006: Working Together for Health* made prominent the extent of the global health workforce crisis (WHO 2006). According to WHO, 57 countries face critical health workforce shortages, with a total deficit of 2.4 million physicians, nurses, and midwives. These shortfalls are greatest in sub-Saharan Africa—the recognized epicentre of the global health workforce crisis. Sub-Saharan Africa bears 24 percent of the world's disease burden, but has only 3 percent of health workers and less than 1 percent of the world's financial resources to respond to this burden. The disparity in global access to health personnel almost defies comprehension (WHO 2006). As a particularly striking example, in Malawi approximately 0.2 physicians serve a population of a 10,000 people, while in the

United States 24.2 doctors serve a similar sized population (WHO 2012). Rural populations everywhere, but especially in low-income countries, suffer most directly from shortages as the health personnel that are available tend to cluster in urban areas.

Compounding existing shortages and inequitable distribution of the health workforce, the past few decades have witnessed expansion in the international migration of health workers, with patterns of migration becoming increasingly complex. Aging populations in high-income countries, new medical technologies, increased specialization of health services, as well as emerging hubs of healthcare delivery in regions such as in the Gulf States and South-East Asia, are driving up the demand for health workers globally. In addition to the increasing magnitude of the international migration of health workers and associated adverse effects on developing country health systems, there is increasing concern related to the mechanisms of international recruitment and the inequitable treatment of emigrant health personnel in the host country. It is also understood that the movement emigrant health personnel exhibit is highly dynamic and not limited to specific set of countries or geographic regions.

The OECD (2007) identified that 18 percent of physicians and 11 percent of nurses working in OECD countries are foreign born and that the international migration of health workers to OECD countries is increasing. The OECD points to evidence that the number of overseas-educated physicians who passed the third step of the US Medical Licensing Examination—a prerequisite to practising as a physician in the US—increased by 70 percent between 2001 and 2008. It is estimated that the United States, already the largest global employer of health workers, will have a physician shortage of approximately 63,000 by 2015—with many calling for increased reliance on foreign-trained physicians to meet this demand (Association of American Medical Colleges 2010). Similar increases in reliance on foreign health workers, alongside escalating future demands, can be seen in other OECD countries, including notably Australia and Canada.

The increasing demand and reliance on foreign health workers is not simply limited to OECD members. Already the vast majority of health workers practising in the Gulf Cooperation Council Countries (GCC) of Bahrain, Kuwait, Oman, Qatar, Saudi Arabia, and United Arab Emirates are emigrants, with estimates that 75 percent of the physicians and 79 percent of the nurses practising in the region are foreign expatriates. Moreover, it has been estimated that demand for healthcare services in the GCC countries is expected to increase by 240 percent in the next two decades, the highest of any region in the world, further increasing demand for health personnel (Mourshed et al. 2007).

Pull factors, including targeted recruitment efforts, as well as financial and other incentives from wealthy destination states, combine with push factors in source countries such as low wages, poor and unstable working environment, and dilapidated public health systems, are contributing to the international migration of health workers. As health workers seek job opportunities at home and abroad, in a dynamic and increasingly globalized health labour market, the problem of acute shortages of health workers, particularly as affecting rural populations, remains significant (WHO 2006).

While there is significant debate on the causes for and long-term economic effects of health worker migration from low-income countries, there is little doubt that the emigration of health workers is resulting in unsustainable gaps in the public health systems in many developing countries. As identified earlier over 50 percent of the physicians from Angola, Antigua and Barbuda, Grenada, Guyana, Haiti, Liberia, Mozambique, Saint Vincent and the Grenadines, Sierra Leone, Tanzania, and Trinidad and Tobago practise as expatriates in OECD countries. A World Bank (2009) report on nurse emigration patterns from English-speaking Caribbean countries evidences similar high levels of emigration for nurses from the region. The World Bank identifies that there are currently three times as many English-speaking Caribbean-trained nurses working abroad, primarily in Canada, the United Kingdom, and the United States, than in the region itself. The World Bank additionally reports that 30 percent of approved nursing positions in the region are vacant and that the demand for nurses in the English-speaking countries in that region is expected to increase significantly over the next 15 years.

Addressing the myriad challenges associated with the international recruitment and migration of health workers will not in itself solve the shortages and inequitable distribution of health workers present in low-income countries. The reasons for these shortages are many, including lack of training capacity, limited civil service budgets and public sector fiscal space, limited managerial capacity, weak information systems, and significant internal migration to the private and the nongovernmental sector. The international migration of health workers, particularly the current and estimated future reliance on foreign health workers in wealthy countries, does however point to a mutual or shared responsibility for destination countries to engage in dialogue with and to support health systems in countries facing severe health workforce shortages. The above described trends associated with the international recruitment and migration of health workers in particular highlights the need for a coordinated and global approach to mobilizing action in this area.

The Development of the WHO Global Code of Practice

Initiation of the WHO Global Code Process

In order to advance a global framework for dialogue and cooperation among states on international health worker recruitment issues, in 2004 the WHA adopted Resolution 57.19, which mandated that the development of a non-binding code of practice on the international recruitment of health workers in consultation with member states and all relevant partners. The resolution marked the first time that the WHA had invoked the WHO's constitutional authority to develop a non-binding code since the 1981 International Code of Marketing of Breast Milk Substitutes.

The WHO global code process was preceded by a number of initiatives to address international health worker recruitment concerns on a country-by-country, multilateral, or transnational basis. Over the last decade countries have adopted a number of non-binding instruments aimed at tackling the challenges associated with international health worker recruitment, including the Commonwealth Code of Practice on the International Recruitment of Health Workers, the Pacific Code of Practice for the International Recruitment of Health Workers in the Pacific Region, and the UK National Health Service Code of Practice for the International Recruitment of Healthcare Professionals. There has also been a proliferation of non-binding instruments adopted under the auspices of professional associations and unions, such as the World Medical Association, the International Council of Nurses, and the European Federation of Public Service Unions. Bilateral agreements between source and destination countries that formalize ongoing dialogue and address rights and responsibilities in ethical international recruitment also multiplied over the 10 years prior to the adoption of the WHO Global Code of Practice on the International Recruitment of Health Personnel (Dhillon et al. 2010).

Existing voluntary codes of practice and other similar non-binding instruments have been widely criticized as weak and ineffective in addressing the core challenges of health worker migration and its impact on health systems. Critics have argued, for example, that such non-binding instruments have been largely ineffective in limiting health worker migration from poor countries or protecting the human rights of health workers because they lacked meaningful mechanisms to collect data and to monitor national compliance (Willetts and Martineau 2004). In addition, unlike the WHO code, none of the earlier instruments set forth a global approach necessary to addressing a global problem or mobilized the funding required for implementation.

Despite early support for the development of a WHO global code, the initiative lacked political support, resources, and policy direction. However, in early 2008, the code effort re-emerged as the issues surrounding health systems and health worker recruitment rose in stature in the global health policy agenda of states. Development and drafting of the code were led by WHO's Human Resources for Health Division and a potential framework for the proposed code was first presented by the division at the Global Forum on Human Resources for Health in Kampala in March 2008.

The efforts of the Health Worker Migration Initiative, a partnership between Realizing Rights, the Global Health Workforce Alliance (GHWA), and WHO were also critical to the renewed focus on developing the code. The Health Worker Migration Initiative is composed of two closely linked entities: the Global Policy Advisory Council, whose secretariat is Realizing Rights, and the Technical Working Group, whose secretariat was the Human Resources for Health Division. The idea of the partnership, linking rigorous research and evidence with high-level political leadership and engagement, emerged in 2006 on the occasion of the UN General Assembly (UNGA) Special Session on Migration and Development. The initiative was officially launched during the WHA in 2007 as a formal initiative of Realizing Rights, GHWA, and WHO.

The Global Policy Advisory Council, co-chaired by Mary Robinson, former president of Ireland and UN High Commissioner for Human Rights, and Francis Omaswa, executive director of GHWA, played a significant role in supporting the development of the global code. The council is composed of 40 high-level sitting and former policy makers from sending and receiving countries, as well as high-level representatives from international organizations. It includes current and former ministers of labour, development, and health, as well as high-level representatives from WHO, the International Labour Organization, and the International Organization for Migration. The council aimed to further mutually acceptable solutions to the issue of health worker migration in a manner that honours both the right to health and freedom of movement. Through its members and meetings, it provided both political and technical support to the work of the Human Resources for Health Division in the development of the Code.

Despite growing support for international co-operation, many observers continued to dismiss the potential contribution that a non-binding code of practice could make to issues surrounding international health worker recruitment. It was argued that the proposed code was not "legal" or could have no impact in state practice because it would be technically non-binding as a matter of international law. To respond to such concerns, as well as galvanize stakeholder interest, at its May 2008 meeting in Geneva, the Global Policy Advisory Council commissioned a paper to facilitate critical discussion on the potential strengths of non-binding instruments in international legal practice and how the proposed code could best be structured and negotiated to advance global consensus and action on international health worker migration issues (Taylor 2008b). In addition, in March and April 2008 WHO, GHWA, and Realizing Rights hosted a two-week Online Global Dialogue to further disseminate this information and to engage discussion on the potential value and content of the code. The online dialogue included 749 participants from 102 countries.

Preparation of First Draft Text and Early Stages in the Negotiation Process

Technical legal work and the preparation of the first draft of the code commenced in earnest in July 2008 at WHO headquarters in Geneva immediately after the final declaration of the G8 Toyako Summit in Japan. The draft of the code prepared under the auspices of WHO's Human Resources for Health Division, headed by Manuel Dayrit, was ready for consideration by member states by the end of August in 2008.

The first draft of the global code endeavoured to establish global architecture for national and international dialogue and action on international health worker recruitment and migration. The brief first draft, consisting of 11 articles, did not aim to address and resolve all of the substantive issues raised by the international recruitment of health personnel or the substantial challenges to the health systems of low-income states raised by health worker migration. Rather, the goal was to set forth a brief, straightforward framework and platform for substantive negotiations. It was expected that WHO members would negotiate more detailed commitments in the final text of the code or in later instruments.

Notably, the first draft did aim to respond to criticisms of other non-binding instruments by recommending voluntary measures to promote national compliance. Consistent with contemporary international practice in other realms of international law and the recommendations of the paper commissioned by the council in May 2008, the first and all the following drafts of the code recommended a robust and transparent framework for global governance, including voluntary mechanisms for effective and periodic information sharing, reporting, and supervision of implementation (Taylor 2008a, 2008b).

In September 2008, the WHO secretariat launched a web-based global public hearing on the first draft of the proposed code. In addition, the draft text was presented by the WHO Human Resources for Health Department and considered at WHO regional committee meetings in September and October 2008 in Europe, South-East Asia, and the Western Pacific. The council also met for two days in September 2008, with members including the chair of the WHO executive board reviewing the text line by line and providing specific input through the online process. Based on the input provided by the regional committee meetings, the global public hearing, and the comments provided by the council, the secretariat prepared a second draft of the proposed code in November 2008.

The second draft was considered by the executive board in January 2009 at one regular session and at one closed informal session. While there was wide agreement on many parts of the text, there was also a divergence on some key aspects that reflected the underlying complexity of the issues and differences among states surrounding health worker recruitment and migration. For example, a number of industrialized countries, including the US and Hungary on behalf of the European Union, expressed concern that the code was overly prescriptive for a non-binding instrument. Japan, the US, and other delegations intervened that provisions on monitoring and implementation were inappropriate for a non-binding instrument. In contrast, however, a number of countries, including Mauritania on behalf of the WHO Regional Office for Africa (WHO/AFRO), as well as Malawi and South Africa, emphasized that the code needed "teeth" and to be enforced. As a further example, WHO/AFRO members, Sri Lanka, and others expressed the view that the code must also include mechanisms to compensate developing countries for the migration of health workers to high-income states. Other participants, in particular some destination states, indicated that bilateral support was a preferred alternative and that a compensatory mechanism should not be included in the code.

Notably, many member states, including Mauritania on behalf of WHO/AFRO, Hungary on behalf of the EU, Brazil, Djibouti, Bahamas, and China expressed the view that the second draft paid insufficient attention to the impact of migration on the health systems of developing countries. Some delegations also argued that it overemphasized the rights of health workers at the expense of the health systems of source states and could be interpreted as encouraging migration.

In recognition of the important differences among countries on issues surrounding health worker recruitment, there was widespread agreement that the draft code required further consultation among members and subsequent revision before it could be forwarded to the WHA for negotiation and adoption. At the same time, some state delegates privately expressed the view that delaying negotiation and adoption of the code for one year could create a more fertile negotiating environment by allowing time for a new US presidential administration to take office and establish policy that might be more supportive of the code effort. Consequently, it was agreed that the secretariat should initiate a consultative process on the draft, including consideration at the WHO regional committee meetings in the fall of 2009 before the issue of the code would be revisited by the executive board in January 2010.

Following the January 2009 executive board session, issues related to the code were considered in national, regional, and international meetings in preparation for fall 2009 regional committee sessions. Some members held national consultations, and some regional offices convened regional and sub-regional meetings. In addition, a draft WHO code was highlighted in international settings. In July 2009, at the L'Aquila Summit the G8 countries encouraged WHO to develop a code of practice on the international recruitment of health personnel by 2010, and the ministerial declaration of the 2009 High-Level Segment of the United Nations Economic and Social Council called for the finalization of a WHO code. In September and October 2009, all six regional committees discussed the key issues relating to a code.

The secretariat revised the text and prepared a third draft in order to take into account the views and comments expressed by members of the executive board in January 2009 and the outcome of the subsequent sessions of the regional committees (WHO 2010a). In particular, the code was deftly revised to strengthen the emphasis of the text considerably on the interests and concerns of source countries in the health worker migration process and, at the same time, incorporate the views of destination states by, among other things, softening the perceived "prescriptive" language of the draft text.

In January 2010 the draft code was once again before the executive board. While some states expressed disagreement with some aspects of the draft text, or proposed mechanisms for improvement, it was unanimously agreed that the draft code was a good basis for negotiation and should be forwarded to the May 2010 WHA for negotiation and possible adoption. Mauritania on behalf of the WHO/AFRO states, Hungary on behalf of the EU, Canada, Samoa, Moldova, Russia, New Zealand, India, Bangladesh, Paraguay, France, Switzerland, Bahamas, Japan, Oman, South Africa, Zimbabwe, and Iran all spoke in favour of forwarding the draft for negotiations.

Alongside the formal WHO process, council members and others supported a political process to both inform and engage states in support of a substantive

WHO code. Norway's leadership, both in its capacity as a member state and as an active member of the council, was invaluable in this process. The council, through its meetings and partnerships, additionally worked to highlight the content and importance of a WHO code to both source and destination members. Particular emphasis was placed on engaging constructively with US president Barack Obama's incoming administration. Mary Robinson and others reached out to the highest level of the American government, including to the president through his advisors, on numerous occasions to encourage support for the WHO code.

While it was African countries that championed the call for development of the code, their engagement with the initial drafts of the proposed text was relatively limited. The council endeavoured over the course of the development process to inform and engage source countries, particularly sub-Saharan African countries, with the text. A week before formal negotiations at the WHA in May 2010, Norway and the WHO Regional Office for Europe (WHO/EURO) supported the council to host a two-day inter-regional dialogue to discuss the text and contentious issues of the code. Norway in particular supported the council in ensuring strong representation of African countries at the meeting. The meeting included 55 participants from 32 countries, with 15 from Africa. Some of the governments represented at the meeting included South Africa, Norway, the US, Botswana, Ghana, Uganda, Kenya, Brazil, Zimbabwe, the UK, France, Hungary, and Spain (which held the EU presidency)—many of which were to play a leading role in code negotiations. The two-day meeting was perhaps most important in familiarizing some participants with the text and underlying points of contention associated with the draft code before formal negotiations took place, as not all of the members had participated in the executive board deliberations over the past two years. The participants were united in recognizing that the areas of contention could not be allowed to jeopardize adoption of the code.

Negotiation of the Global Code at the 2010 World Health Assembly

The 63rd WHA, on its opening day of May 17, 2010, established a drafting committee open to all members to negotiate the text of the code of practice that had been forwarded by the executive board in January. It was chaired by an experienced negotiator, Viroj Tangcharoensathien of Thailand, with the support of the WHO secretariat, led by Manuel Dayrit, the director of the WHO Human Resources for Health Division. The final text was negotiated over three days during the World Health Assembly, including a final negotiating session that lasted until 4:30 AM on May 20.

More than 30 countries participated in the global negotiations, including representatives of many of the key players in the global health recruitment debate, such as the South Africa, Norway, the US, Botswana, Switzerland, Uganda, Kenya, Brazil, Thailand, Zimbabwe, New Zealand, Australia, Canada, and the EU, represented by Spain (as well as some of its members such as the UK, France, Belgium, and Germany). Notably missing from the drafting group were countries such as India and Japan that had been vocal participants in debates at the executive board and the regional committees.

While there remained important differences among countries, under the keen stewardship of Viroj, the negotiating group forged a consensus document that contained voluntary recommendations on many of the issues relating to international recruitment of health personnel. The draft was negotiated by first identifying the key issues in dispute and then proceeding through the text provision by provision until consensus was achieved.

Global health workforce recruitment and migration constitute a complex and multidimensional global health challenge and a number of the critical issues that had challenged the development of the text throughout the negotiation process were central to the debates of the drafting group. However, as the draft text had been revised several times prior to the WHA by the secretariat, the differences among countries had been considerably narrowed. Consequently, the final text of the code can be fairly described as only subtly different from the last draft prepared by the secretariat: it reflects fine differences in tone and precision, but there were only limited substantive changes.

A recurring issue in the discussions leading up to the WHA and the drafting group itself was the perceived "prescriptive" nature of the voluntary code. As already described, during the executive board debates a number of high-income countries argued that the tone of the draft was too prescriptive or mandatory for a non-binding instrument. Most of the high-income countries present in the drafting sessions joined in support for modifying the text during the WHA, including Canada, New Zealand, Spain on behalf of the EU, the US, and Monaco. Without any objection from low-income states, the draft was revised to eliminate terms such as "standards" and "comply." At the same time, member commitments under the code were modified throughout the text from the word "should" to terms such as "should consider" or "should encourage." It can well be argued that since the code is non-binding and only makes recommendations to governments that these subtle changes have no impact on the substance of the code and are likely to make no meaningful difference in state practice. However, the case can also be made that such changes, by undermining the precision of the commitments in the text, could potentially have an impact on or even soften the sense of duty among members to comply with the underlying norms in the code.

Another key issue that arose during the consultations on the draft code was whether the instrument should narrowly focus on establishing voluntary principles and practices related to international recruitment or whether the scope of the instrument should be broadened to address the impact of health worker migration on health systems generally. Revisions during the drafting committee did not fully clarify this issue. Early in the drafting group, high-income states tailored the text, particularly the objectives in Section 1, to focus exclusively on recruitment and leave out the larger issues of migration. However, a careful reading of the final text reveals that broad issues of health workforce migration, the brain drain from developing countries, comprises a substantial part of the text. For example,

Article 5 focuses on general issues surrounding health system sustainability and Articles 6 and 7 are centred on the collection and exchange of information on health personnel migration.

An important area of concurrence among high- and low-income states during the drafting process revolved around human rights issues under Article 4 of the code. As already described, issues surrounding how to honour the right of developing countries to strengthen their health systems and the rights of health workers to migrate to countries that wish to admit and employ them was a long-standing concern. During the WHA deliberations, the right to health of source countries became the dominant concern in this balance as interests among high-income and low-income participating states aligned. Consistent with international human rights law and pre-existing codes, such as the Commonwealth and the Pacific Codes of Practice, the draft code included the human rights of health workers in Article 4 to fairness and equality of treatment in several articles. High-income countries modified the language in this article by, among other things, subjecting rights to "applicable law." The effort of high-income countries to limit the broad recognition of rights aligned with the interests of developing countries that had long argued that the draft code had prioritized the rights of workers at the expense of the health systems of developing countries.

Another key area on which there was significant discussion during the negotiations was the way in which the code should reflect and encourage an appropriate balance between the interests of source states and destination states. The United States led a wide consensus to modify the draft text in Article 5 to address issues of "health workforce development and sustainability" rather than "mutuality of benefit," reflecting more of a change in tone and not substance. Other modifications proposed by destination states, however, highlighted the interests of high-income countries. One important area of divergence was whether the code should promote bilateral and other arrangements among source and destination states. While low-income states had emphasized the importance of such agreements in discussions leading up to the WHA, the draft language calling upon states to abstain from active international recruitment unless there exist equitable agreements to support recruitment activities was deleted from the final text.

Throughout most of the negotiation process at the WHA, high-income states, particularly the participating EU states, Canada, the US, and New Zealand, dominated the interventions and advanced recommendations for change in the draft. Developing countries, particularly the delegates from African states, frequently remained silent during discussions of the substantive provisions of the draft, with Norway and Brazil often voicing the position of source countries. However, an important change occurred after midnight on May 20 as the delegates moved from negotiations of the substantive aspects of the code to discussions of the detailed procedural mechanisms involving data collection, information exchange, monitoring, and implementation, and as the ranks of negotiators thinned from a high of more than 30 participating states to a core group of delegates from just over 20 states. As described above, a number of high-income states had strongly opposed the secretariat's detailed inclusion of these critical procedural and institutional mechanisms in the voluntary instrument. An information document prepared by the secretariat, consisting of members' proposals to the draft, evidenced that countries such as Canada, the EU, and the US preferred that such provisions be strictly circumscribed or deleted (WHA 2010). However, starting with the deliberations on data collection the delegations from African states, including South Africa, Zimbabwe, Kenya, and Botswana, established a united front in favour of maintaining the strong legal and institutional provisions in the draft against all efforts to modify and limit such provisions. In the end, the detailed legal, institutional, and data sharing provisions established in the final text remained substantively unchanged from the draft prepared by the secretariat.

In addition, while some developing countries had long pushed for strengthening the financial mechanisms to promote "compensation" from destination states to source states during the early stages of the code process, there was no effort to negotiate more detailed commitments on financial provisions in the final negotiations. Indeed, there was a keen recognition among developing country delegates at the WHA that high-income states would simply not agree to deeper provisions on financial support to developing countries. As the delegate of Brazil essentially noted, the code effort should not be held back by lack of agreement on compensation and that perhaps, in the future, there could be meaningful discourse on compensation.

The three-day negotiation of the WHO Global Code of Practice occurred during what was a well-attended and highly charged World Health Assembly. The agenda of the WHA included the negotiation of contentious issues in other substantive and procedural areas. It also saw US president Barack Obama's Global Health Initiative promoted by the US delegation. While negotiations on the Global Code were occurring at Committee A, which is responsible for programmatic issues, there were negotiations on WHO governance structures, in particular the process to appoint the director-general, occurring in Committee B, which is responsible for budget and managerial issues. Delegates to the Global Code negotiations were highly sensitive to shifts in alliances due to negotiation positions taken on other subjects.

The linkages between the various different sessions at the WHA and their impact on the code negotiations were especially evident during discussions hosted by the United States on the Global Health Initiative on the second day of the assembly. This session was open to all members and other participants and observers, including civil society. The United States found its efforts to highlight the good works of the Global Health Initiative hampered as delegates as well as other participants specifically and repeatedly brought up the challenges of health worker migration and the US negotiating position in the closed "room next door."

The drafting committee's final text of the code was brought forward on May 21 to Committee A for further discussion before it was to be accepted by the committee as final. Many of the negotiators from both source and destination countries privately expressed the view that they remained apprehensive that the process could still be derailed by ongoing discussion and negotiation at Committee A. However, the Global Code of Practice elicited no such discussion. Once accepted for adoption, there was spontaneous applause by all present in the room. According to observers, the applause reflected both the magnitude and urgency of the challenge of health worker migration, as well as the ability to achieve multilateral agreement on such a complex and sensitive subject. It should be noted that at the beginning of the development process there was considerable debate and little agreement on whether health worker migration was even resulting in negative effects to health systems in developing countries and whether consensus could ever be achieved on the proposed code.

The WHO Global Code of Practice on the International Recruitment of Health Personnel was officially adopted on May 21, 2010 at the closing session of the 63rd World Health Assembly (WHO 2010b). Director-General Margaret Chan (2010) identified the adoption of the code as one of the major achievements of the assembly, referring to it as a "real gift to public health, everywhere."

The WHO Global Code of Practice

The final text of the Global Code includes a preamble and 10 articles: objectives; nature and scope; guiding principles; responsibilities, rights, and recruitment practices; health workforce development and health systems sustainability; data gathering and research; information exchange; implementation of the code; monitoring and institutional arrangements; and partnerships, technical collaboration and financial support.

The WHO Global Code's preamble and first three articles, Objectives, Nature and Scope, and Guiding Principles, provide the context and define the scope of the Code effort. The code is a voluntary instrument that articulates global ethical norms—"principles and practices"—for the international recruitment and migration of health workers. Moreover, the code explicitly seeks to further dialogue and cooperation among and within member states on these issues. The preamble and first two articles make especially prominent the focus on supporting health systems, particularly in developing countries, countries with economies in transition, and small island states. The code's guiding principles reaffirm its focus on supporting health systems in developing countries, including the need to provide technical and financial assistance for health personnel development, affirm the human right to the highest attainable standard of health, call for a better "managed approach" to the international recruitment of health workers, call also for the development of sustainable health workforce in all countries, and point to the need to protect and fulfil the rights of health workers that do emigrate.

Article 4, Responsibilities, Rights, and Recruitment Practices, articulates the ethical responsibilities of stakeholders to ensure fair recruitment and equitable treatment practices as relevant to emigrant health workers. It also calls on recruiters and employers to be aware of and not seek to recruit health workers with existing domestic contractual obligations, and for health workers to be transparent about their contractual obligations.

Article 5, Health Workforce Development and Health Systems Sustainability, is at the core of the Global Code. It discourages active recruitment from countries with critical health workforce shortages and encourages utilization of code norms as a guide when entering into bilateral, regional, and multilateral arrangements to further international cooperation and coordination. It identifies the need to develop and support circular migration policies between countries of source and destination and encourages countries to develop sustainable health systems that, as far as possible, would allow for domestic health services demand to be met by domestic human resources. It also emphasizes the importance of a multi-sectoral approach in addressing the issues and places particular focus on the need to develop health workforce policies and incentives in all countries that support the retention of health workers in underserved areas.

The code's sixth article, Data Gathering and Research, responds to the significant lack of data and research in the area of health personnel migration, particularly as it affects health systems. It urges members, with support from WHO, to strengthen their efforts in this area and to translate data collected and research into effective policies and planning related to the health workforce. In the field of health worker migration, improvement in the data gathering and research efforts is necessary for a number of critical reasons. The formulation of effective policies addressing the drivers, trends, and impacts of health worker migration needs to be grounded in a sound evidence base, yet the current state of that evidence base is fragmented. The challenges involved in data collection and analysis are compounded by a lack of consistency in the definition of relevant data items among countries. Consequently, a major contribution of the code is to provide a legal framework for data collection.

The next three articles—Information Exchange, Implementation of the Code, and Monitoring and Institutional Arrangements—focus on the process related to implementation and monitoring. These articles are perhaps most important to the future success of the code. They incorporate legal and institutional mechanisms to promote cooperation and implementation of the code that are more robust than similar mechanisms found in some contemporary treaties, including the Framework Convention on Tobacco Control.

Article 7, Information Exchange, provides structure for the exchange of information with regard both to health personnel migration and to health systems, including by calling on member states, as feasible, to maintain an updated database of laws and regulation related to recruitment and migration, to maintain updated data related to health personnel, and to designate a national authority responsible for information exchange. Moreover, the designated national authority is asked to report on data and on relevant laws and regulations to WHO every three years for purposes of information exchange with other members, with an initial report to be filed two years following adoption of the code.

Article 8, Implementation of the Code, while relevant to all stakeholders, places primary responsibility on WHO member states to publicize and implement the code. It specifically calls on members to maintain a record of all recruiters authorized to operate within their jurisdiction, to endeavour to utilize only those recruiting agencies that comply with the guiding principles of the code, and to assess the magnitude of active recruitment from countries facing critical health workforce shortages, as well as the impact of circular migration.

Article 9, Monitoring and Institutional Arrangements, defines the process of member reporting to the WHO secretariat and WHO reporting to the World Health Assembly. Members are called upon to report activities undertaken, progress made, and difficulties encountered in implementing the code every three years, starting in 2012. Notably, non-state actors have a critical role to play in the implementation regime as they are also called upon to report their observations on implementation to the secretariat. Based upon member state and other reports, the director general is also called upon to submit a report every three years to the WHA on the status of the code and recommendations for its strengthening. These reporting mechanisms are designed to keep the topic of health worker migration and the code on the active agenda of member states, WHO, and civil society. Importantly, while members are encouraged to report to WHO, WHO's reporting on the code is not voluntary. The director-general also must support the information exchange network, develop guidelines and recommendation as specified by the code, and maintain liaison with relevant regional and international organizations, as well as concerned nongovernmental organizations in support of implementation. Moreover, the article also explicitly identifies the code as a dynamic text that is to be updated based on the changing nature and impact of the issues it aims to address.

The final article, Article 10, relates to partnerships, technical collaboration, and financial support. Relatively general, it again stresses the need for global cooperation to support implementation of the code, with a particular focus on providing technical and financial support to strengthen health personnel development in countries facing critical health workforce shortages.

The WHO Global Code is neither a perfect text nor a solution to the challenges associated with health worker migration. The substantive norms it espouses remain relatively general and are advanced in a soft manner to member states. It should be recognized, however, that the WHO Global Code was never intended to be the final answer or encompass the whole solution to the challenges associated with health worker migration. Rather, the goal of the drafters was to establish a global platform that could provide a framework for continuing dialogue and cooperation among states on what is undoubtedly a topic of significant complexity and sensitivity. The Global Code, in particular the key legal and institutional arrangements, does provide a robust instrument for ongoing global cooperation that may lead to a deepening of commitment over time.

While the long-term impact of the Global Code is yet undetermined, there are already some positive developments that have resulted from the process of negotiation and adoption. First, and foremost, the long-ignored issue of health-worker migration is now centrally on the global political agenda. This has been made most evident by inclusion of the code, as well as some of its relevant norms, in the outcome document of the 2010 UN Millennium Development Goals (MDGs) Summit (UN 2010). The legal and institutional arrangements present in the Global Code will further ensure that the issue remains on the WHA agenda for the foreseeable future, with reporting by the director general mandated every three years.

Moreover, one of the historic challenges to addressing the challenges associated with the international recruitment and migration of health personnel has been the need for and difficulty in engaging with the various sectors within a national government. These include the ministries of foreign affairs and international development, health, labour, education, and immigration. Prior to negotiations, only a few countries—notably Norway and the Philippines—had engaged in a whole-of-government approach in reflecting on the issue of health worker migration. In the process of developing a negotiating position, a number of additional states engaged across these multiple sectors within their government. This process of engagement is itself important, with the networks created potentially an important step toward greater internal coherence and meaningful implementation of the norms articulated by the code.

Lessons Learned for Future Negotiations:
The Evolution of Global Health Diplomacy

This chapter has provided a detailed analysis of the WHO Global Code negotiations. In any political context, the organization of negotiations is a question of political mapping that must respond to political realities and resource constraints. Issues, interests, and strategies need to be organized to reduce complexity and promote coalition building and consensus. As this review of the negotiation and drafting process reveals, certain aspects of the legislative process contributed to the success of the Global Code endeavour.

The lessons to be learned from the negotiations go beyond the mere spectrum of the nuts and bolts of international negotiation processes, however, and provide some deeper insight into the evolution in global health diplomacy over the past decade. The senior author of this chapter (Allyn Taylor) initiated the idea of the Framework Convention on Tobacco Control (FCTC), the first treaty negotiated under the auspices of WHO, with Ruth Roemer, and was a legal adviser to WHO during the negotiations of that agreement as well as during the negotiations of the Global Code (see Roemer et al. 2005). A comparison of the negotiating processes of the code and the FCTC clearly is not a scientific endeavour that can fully reveal transformations in global health diplomacy over the past decade. Among other things, there are important differences between the two processes, including the fact that the analysis involves a comparison of the negotiations of a binding instrument and a non-binding one. As described further below, the experience of the code negotiations does appear to evidence some growing maturity and, perhaps, an evolution, in global health diplomacy at WHO among the different actors in the process: the secretariat, civil society, and, most importantly, member states.

The WHO Process: Introduction of a Simple Draft Text and Maintaining Control of Drafting Process

An important factor contributing to the success of the code negotiation process is that the WHO secretariat introduced a simple negotiating text early and maintained control of drafting the text until formal negotiations at the World Health Assembly in 2010. At first instance, a key strategy was to establish concise and carefully drafted commitments for states to bargain over and flush out. In addition, secretariat control over the drafting process helped prevent the document from spiralling out of control.

The first draft of the code and process of developing subsequent drafts can be contrasted sharply with the negotiating experience during the FCTC. During the FCTC negotiations, the first draft text prepared by the secretariat for the negotiating chair contained an entire catalogue of potential substantive obligations (Intergovernmental Negotiating Body on the WHO Framework Convention on Tobacco Control 2001). In addition, during the process of negotiating the FCTC in six formal rounds of negotiations open to all member states, each and every recommendation made by member states, sometimes amounting to nothing other than mere wording and stylistic differences, were incorporated into the draft. This produced remarkably complex texts and unnecessarily prolonged negotiating sessions. In the case of the code, the secretariat contributed to advancing negotiations by maintaining control of the drafting process and incorporating the key themes proposed by members and not verbatim text during the early stages of the negotiation process.

The WHO Process: Staging the Negotiations

Negotiations tend to be marked by a series of stages that narrow the agenda and differences among countries. There is no one formula for successful negotiations, and different structures can be used. In some respects, the code negotiations are a good example of sequencing in that secretariat draft text went through several political scrubs by a small group of state representatives at the WHO regional committees and the WHO executive board before it was opened up for broader negotiation for all WHO members at the WHA. Consequently, the text was largely acceptable before it was opened up to broad negotiations. However, a critical last stage of the negotiation process involved the members taking control and ownership of the document in the final negotiations at the WHA.

Cementing broad stakeholder participation and, therefore, ownership is critical in any negotiation process. A cautionary tale is provided by some international negotiations that fail to incorporate effective participation by relevant stakeholders, particularly states. For example, in the case of the UN Guidelines on Internal Displacement, the draft text was developed by an expert group and never negotiated by governments. When the guidelines were brought for adoption to UNGA, certain countries complained that they lacked legitimacy because states had not been involved in drafting them. Such objections were overcome only by the arguments that the guidelines merely reflected existing international law and did not set forth new standards.

With that said, it should be recognized that the code negotiation process was also hampered by the absence of a truly global negotiation prior to the WHA in May 2010. Issues relating to health worker recruitment and migration reveal important political divides among high-income and low-income states. Although the code was considered in various international forums and by regional committees prior to the WHA negotiations, no formal global consultation was necessary to advance consensus, and to move the text and the agreement forward prior to the World Health Assembly in May 2010.

Political Leadership

Political leadership is a critical factor in international negotiations to broker deals and bring innovative thinking. Leadership can come from many sources, including the executive head of an international organization, as was the case of Mostafa Tolba for many years at the United Nations Environment Programme. It can also be brought by states. Notably, it is often mid-sized countries such as Australia, Canada, Switzerland, New Zealand, and Norway that have provided leadership in areas ranging from the environment to health.

In context of the Global Code negotiations, Norway led the way among the states. Recognizing the challenges associated with health worker migration, it had previously engaged across its ministries to make coherent its domestic need for foreign health workers with its international development efforts. In February 2009, Norway released its internal policy coherence strategy. However, Norway also recognized that unilateral action alone could not meaningfully address the global nature of the challenge. As such, it was a strong advocate for development of the WHO Global Code of Practice. Moreover, Norway was cognizant throughout the process of its own unique economic position and the need to engage other champions, particularly source countries.

In addition to country leadership, a strong chair is an essential ingredient of effective negotiations. The code negotiations were expertly steered throughout the WHA process by Viroj Tangcharoensathien of Thailand.

The Role of Civil Society

The unique partnership among WHO's Human Resources for Health Division, GHWA, and Realizing Rights was integral to the development of the Global

Code. Realizing Rights' formation of the Global Policy Advisory Council, an independent body and authority, in particular, allowed for a channel that could run parallel to the formal process in shaping and advancing negotiations. The council, through its secretariat, members, and meetings, was able to complement the WHO secretariat's efforts by reaching out to specific member states and hosting an inter-regional discussion in order to clarify and further consensus on contentious issues. The code effort reflects a new type of civil society participation in global health negotiations at WHO. Through the Health Worker Migration Initiative partnership, Realizing Rights, an organization with experience in global governance, was involved with the code development from the very inception of the process. Realizing Rights' method of work focused on supporting its partners and member state capacity to move forward mutually acceptable solutions. Moreover, Realizing Rights staff—led by Mary Robinson—had knowledge and experience in international law and global negotiations and was able to bring this depth to council meetings and contacts with member states. Robinson's ability to convene and engage stakeholders and key decision makers was undoubtedly an important additional asset.

Notably, neither the council nor or its secretariat were ever directly involved in drafting the text of the code or the formal negotiation process, but rather worked with states to provide detailed commentary on draft text and raised awareness and support for the code. Moreover, enabled by the technical legal work of the WHO secretariat, the council was able to point to an actual vision and action that political leadership, from both source and destination countries, could further.

The role of civil society in the negotiation of the code stands in contrast with that of the negotiation of the FCTC from 1998 to 2003. Civil society played a much more limited role in participating and guiding the FCTC negotiations, primarily because of its lack of expertise and experience in international law making and the limited opportunities to work with member states and WHO in closed negotiation sessions that dominated the negotiation process. Of course, the FCTC was the first binding treaty negotiated at WHO. Civil society organizations participating in the treaty negotiations were largely domestic tobacco control organizations, with no experience in international law and negotiations. In recent years, however, through the Framework Convention Alliance, civil society acquired depth and experience in the international law-making process, and has played an increasingly important role in guiding the implementation of the FCTC.

WHO Members and the Evolution of Diplomatic Capacity

Similar to the apparent growth in legal capacity among members of civil society, the code negotiations provide evidence of a deepening or maturing of diplomatic capacity to engage in global health negotiations among low-income country delegations. Indeed, there was a striking difference between delegations engaged in the FCTC negotiations and the code negotiations. During the FCTC negotiations, the vast majority of low-income delegations were new to international law negotiation process. Those delegations were composed of representatives from health ministries accompanied by junior mission lawyers, or had no lawyers at all. Such inexperienced delegates were simply and frequently out-lawyered by the experienced negotiators, including highly skilled international lawyers, from high-income states.

The difference in negotiating capacity, including legal expertise, largely, though not exclusively, explains the textual outcome of the FCTC that consists of soft substantive obligations and shallow institutional and procedural mechanisms. A lack of realistic assessment about the scope of the treaty and the depth of commitments haunted the negotiations of the FCTC from the very beginning of the process. Health ministers from low-income countries clearly thought it possible to have deep and wide substantive commitments on tobacco control without losing any participants. During the final days of the negotiations, high-income states were able to negotiate substantially softer substantive commitments in the 17 articles of the text that set forth tobacco control commitments. But, at the same time that low-income delegations focused on the substantive obligations, they neglected attention to the key legal procedural and institutional mechanisms necessary in a framework convention to strengthen and deepen the regime over time. Although a robust procedural framework had been set forth by the secretariat in the drafts of the FCTC, many of the key legal and institutional mechanisms of global governance were deleted from the text in a side meeting open to all members in the final negotiations round in 2003, in which no developing countries participated. The FCTC has, in practice, been remarkably successful in a number of respects (Taylor 2013). But an important consequence of a lack of negotiation experience among delegates from low-income countries is a framework convention with uniquely shallow procedural and institutional mechanisms.

In contrast, in the code negotiations, the character of the state delegations in the WHA negotiations differed markedly and was reflected in the negotiations and the final text. Delegations from developing countries, particularly sub-Saharan Africa, consisted of senior diplomats and highly experienced international lawyers. They came to the table with a keen understanding of what agreement was possible and targeted critical areas of negotiations. Unlike with the FCTC negotiations, these delegations, recognizing the realities of underlying politics of the negotiations, spent precious little time trying to hammer out deep substantive commitments to limit recruitment or create compensatory mechanisms. Rather, the skilled delegates and veteran negotiators focused attention on the critical legal and institutional mechanisms of information exchange and monitoring and reporting that are necessary to maintain the legal regime and, perhaps, deepen it over time.

The differences in character of the negotiating teams at the FCTC and Global Code negotiations may reflect a deepening of interest in global health among WHO members and an evolution of global health negotiations. As global health has risen on the political agenda, more and more states may be identifying global health negotiations as a priority and bringing more experienced diplomats and lawyers to the table. If this is the case, it is a welcome development to balance the negotiation dynamics and put high-income and low-income countries on a more even footing in terms of negotiating expertise, although not, of course, negotiating power. However, the limited participatory scope of the code negotiations may mean that it is too soon to draw a definitive conclusion of whether those negotiations reflect a genuine evolution in global health diplomacy.

The Evolution of Global Health Governance: The Potential Contribution of Non-binding Instruments to Global Health Governance

Recent developments in global health diplomacy have led to increasing calls for the negotiation and codification of international legal mechanisms to provide a framework for global health cooperation. The experience of the Global Code illustrates the important and largely overlooked contribution that non-binding instruments can make to global health diplomacy and may serve as a model for future global health law negotiations (Taylor et al. 2003).

There has been academic interest in the role of international legal instruments for global health cooperation for almost 20 years (Taylor 1992). Yet international law has traditionally been neglected as a tool of global health policy. Of course, the contemporary reality is altogether different. Over the last decade or so, the field of global health has undergone transformations that have been widely described as revolutionary. Aggressive globalization, among other factors, has lifted global health from an issue of political neglect to an issue of political prominence among state and non-state actors. As health has emerged on the foreign policy agenda, so has interest in international law as a tool for health policy.

Today there is an evolving array of binding and non-binding instruments in global health governance. Notably, however, consistent with other international legal realms, the pattern that is beginning to emerge is a marked preference for binding global health law instruments. This preference for expanding treaty law appears among state actors, civil society, and academia and is reflected in the proliferation of proposals for new global health treaties over the last decade. The rising demand for treaties may reflect, in part, the perceived credibility of treaties and the widely held view that non-binding instruments are weak and ineffective.

Undoubtedly, there is no alternative to treaties when states want to make credible commitments. However, treaties are not the only source of norms in the international system. It is increasingly recognized that the challenges of global governance demand faster and more flexible approaches to international cooperation than can be provided by traditional and heavily legalized strategies. Consequently, in other realms of international concern ranging from the environment to arms control the world community is increasingly turning to the creation of non-binding international norms.

Like binding international instruments, non-binding instruments have important strengths and limitations as international legal tools. Chief among the limitations of non-binding instruments is the fact that such voluntary agreements are not subject to international law and, in particular, its fundamental principle of *pacta sunt servanda*. There are no rules of international law that regulate or supplement non-binding instruments like the Vienna Convention on the Law of Treaties. Moreover, many non-binding instruments are purposefully designed as way stations or even permanent detours from hard, binding legal commitments. Consequently, many if not most non-binding instruments are purely rhetorical and have no impact on state practice.

However, non-binding instrument have some important advantages as a mechanism for international cooperation and can, at times, make an important contribution to shaping state behaviour. The experience negotiating the Global Code demonstrates some of the key advantages of non-binding instruments. For example, a core characteristic of non-binding instruments is their flexibility. Flexibility is an essential component of international negotiations. Non-binding agreements can facilitate compromise and agreement may be easier to achieve than binding instruments, especially when states jealously guard their sovereignty since non-binding standards do not involve formal legal commitments. Notably, the FCTC was negotiated in six separate rounds of two-week negotiation sessions open to all WHO members over five years, while the Global Code was negotiated in just a fraction of that time. In addition, by removing concerns about legal non-compliance, non-binding instruments may, at times, promote deeper commitments with stricter compliance mechanisms than comparable binding instruments. Notably, the code incorporates procedural mechanisms to advance implementation that are more potent than those incorporated in the FCTC. While both the FCTC and the Global Code set forth a shallow substantive framework, the code sets forth a deep legal and institutional framework.

Given the strength of the Global Code as an international legal instrument and the effectiveness of the code negotiation process, non-binding instruments deserve much greater attention in future global health diplomacy efforts.

Conclusion

The summer of 2010 witnessed adoption of the WHO Global Code of Practice on the International Recruitment of Health Personnel. This is only the second instrument of its kind promulgated by WHO—almost three decades after adoption of the International Code of the Marketing of Breast Milk Substitutes. The adoption of the Global Code both provides evidence of the gauntlet of a process associated with promulgating global health law at WHO and suggests evolution in the capacity of the WHO secretariat, member states, and civil society to engage in global health law making.

Spurred by the urgency of the problem and increased global attention on strengthening health systems, WHO members have come together to make available a unique and potentially powerful instrument to begin addressing the challenges associated with the international recruitment and migration of health workers. Various factors contributed to the successful development and adoption of the Global Code, including an innovative partnership among the WHO secretariat, GHWA, and Realizing Rights, as well as the choice of a simple negotiating text, the sequencing of negotiations, and political leadership from both member states and individuals. Of particular note, the choice of a non-binding instrument to address these challenges reflects recognition of the political realities and complexities associated with the issue, as well as an understanding of the role of such instruments in shaping state behaviour.

Long ignored, the issue of health worker migration is and, thanks to the code's reporting requirements, will remain on the global health agenda for the foreseeable future. African governments, underrepresented in global negotiations, played a key role in addressing an issue of significant concern to African health systems. Reflecting on the adoption of the code, one African government representative at the WHA said that the issue of health worker migration long "under the table, is now squarely on the table."

It should also be recalled that the WHO Global Code was adopted in the context of a strong spirit of multilateralism and goodwill among member states. Despite that goodwill and multilateral spirit, there is a real danger that the norms articulated in the code, due in part to their voluntary nature, will not be reflected in national and international laws, policies, and programs. Although heralded as a "real gift to public health everywhere," the success of the Global Code will ultimately be judged by whether its norms are implemented and lead to real improvement in the lives of individuals and communities of those most affected. Work to this end is underway and must be supported and intensified. Nothing less than progress toward the health-related MDGs and donor credibility is at stake.

References

Association of American Medical Colleges (2010). "AAMC Releases New Physician Shortage Estimates Post-Reform." News Alert, September 30, Washington, DC. Available online: www.aamc.org/newsroom/ newsreleases/2010/150570/100930.html (October 2012).

Chan, Margaret (2010). "Agreements at World Health Assembly a Gift to Public Health." Closing remarks at the 63rd World Health Assembly, Geneva, May 21. Available online: www.who.int/dg/speeches/2010/WHA_closing_20100521/ en (October 2012).

Dhillon, Ibadat S., Margaret E. Clark, and Robert Kapp (2010). "Innovations in Cooperation: A Guidebook on Bilateral Agreements to Address Health Worker Migration." May Aspen Institute. Available online: www.aspeninstitute.org/ sites/default/files/content/docs/pubs/Bilateral%20Report_final%20code.pdf (October 2012).

Intergovernmental Negotiating Body on the WHO Framework Convention on Tobacco Control (2001). "Chair's Text of a Framework Convention on Tobacco

Control." A/FCTC/INB2/2, January 9, World Health Organization, Geneva. Available online: extranet.who.int/iris/restricted/bitstream/10665/75408/1/e2inb2.pdf (October 2012).

Mourshed, Mona, Viktor Hediger, and Toby Lambert (2007). "Gulf Cooperation Council Health Care: Challenges and Opportunities." In *Global Competitiveness Reports*. McKinsey and Company, pp. 55–64. Available online: members. weforum.org/pdf/Global_Competitiveness_Reports/Reports/chapters/2_1.pdf (October 2012).

Organisation for Economic Co-operation and Development (2007). "Immigrant Health Workers in OECD Countries in the Broader Context of Highly Skilled Migration." In *International Migration Outlook*. Paris: pp. 161–228. Available online: www.oecd.org/migration/internationalmigrationpoliciesanddata/41515701.pdf (October 2012).

Robinson, Mary and Peggy Clark (2008). "Forging Solutions to Health Worker Migration." *Lancet* 371(9613): 691–3.

Roemer, Ruth, Allyn L. Taylor, and Jean Lariviere (2005). "Origins of the WHO Framework Convention on Tobacco Control." *American Journal of Public Health* 95(6): 936–8. Available online: www.ncbi.nlm.nih.gov/pmc/articles/PMC1449287/ (October 2012).

Taylor, Allyn L. (1992). "Making the World Health Organization Work: A Legal Framework for Universal Access to the Conditions for Health." *American Journal of Law and Medicine* 18: 301–46.

Taylor, Allyn L. (2008a). "The Draft WHO Code of Practice on the International Recruitment of Health Personnel." *American Society of International Law Insights* 12(23).

Taylor, Allyn L. (2008b). "The Proposed WHO Code of Practice on Health Worker Migration: Issues of Form, Substance, and Negotiation." Paper presented at the Health Work Migration Global Policy Advisory Council Meeting, 18 May.

Taylor, Allyn L. (2013). "Global Health Law." In *Global Health Diplomacy: Concepts, Issues, Actors, Instruments, Fora, and Cases*, Ilona Kickbusch, Graham Lister, Michaela Told, et al., eds. New York: Springer.

Taylor, Allyn L., Douglas W. Bettcher, and Richard Peck (2003). "International Law and the International Legislative Process: The WHO Framework Convention on Tobacco Control." In *Global Public Goods for Health: Health Economic and Public Health Perspectives*, Richard Smith, Robert Beaglehole, David Woodward, et al., eds. Oxford: Oxford University Press, pp. 212–30.

United Nations (2010). "Keeping the Promise: United to Achieve the Millennium Development Goals." Outcome document of the 56th session, October 19, New York. Available online: www.un.org/en/mdg/summit2010/pdf/outcome_documentN1051260.pdf (October 2012).

Willetts, Annie and Tim Martineau (2004). "Ethical International Recruitment of Health Professionals: Will Codes of Practice Protect Developing Country Health Systems?," Liverpool School of Tropical Medicine. Available online:

www.medact.org/content/health/documents/brain_drain/Martineau%20 codesofpracticereport.pdf (October 2012).

World Bank (2009). "The Nurse Labor and Education Markets in the English-Speaking CARICOM: Issues and Options for Reform." Report No. 48988-LAC, Washington, DC. Available online: siteresources.worldbank.org/ INTJAMAICA/Resources/The_Nurse_Labor_Education_Market_Eng.pdf (October 2012).

World Health Assembly (2010). "International Recruitment of Health Personnel: Draft Global Code of Practice." A63/INF.DOC./2, April 15, World Health Organization, Geneva. Available online: apps.who.int/gb/ebwha/pdf_files/ WHA63/A63_ID2-en.pdf (October 2012).

World Health Organization (2006). "The World Health Report 2006: Working Together for Health." World Health Organization, Geneva. Available online: www.who.int/whr/2006/en/ (October 2012).

World Health Organization (2010a). "International Recruitment of Health Personnel: Draft Global Code of Practice. Report by the Secretariat." A63/8, April 15, World Health Organization, Geneva. Available online: apps.who.int/ gb/ebwha/pdf_files/WHA63/A63_8-en.pdf (October 2012).

World Health Organization (2010b). "WHO Global Code of Practice on the International Recruitment of Health Personnel." WHA63.16, May 21, World Health Organization, Geneva. Available online: apps.who.int/gb/ebwha/pdf_ files/WHA63/A63_R16-en.pdf (October 2012).

World Health Organization (2012). "World Health Statistics 2012." Geneva. Available online: www.who.int/healthinfo/EN_WHS2012_Full.pdf (October 2012).

PART V
Conclusion

Chapter 10

Moving Health Sovereignty: Global Challenge, African Perspective

Hany Besada, Andrew F. Cooper, Franklyn Lisk, and John Kirton

Nowhere does global health present a greater challenge than in Africa. The exploration of health governance in Africa has often been conducted in isolation, focusing on problems particular to Africa. The chapters in this volume respond to a growing need to develop a global health agenda that addresses the growing health crisis in Africa through reflecting on possible governance responses to the current health crisis in Africa, at both the national and regional levels, with some emphasis on exploring the broader implications for health governance in emerging governance models. Thus the chapters address Africa's several health-sector issues identified by the five steps of the analytical framework presented in Chapter 1.

Central to the discussion of health governance is the issue of sovereignty. Debate has arisen over who has jurisdiction over health sovereignty and the role that foreign influence and participation should play in the health sector. The contributors to this volume all agree that health issues in Africa transcend national borders, and, with globalization shifting the power from the national to the international level, the state has been challenged as the ultimate authority.

Health provides a lens into a particular challenge for orthodox concepts of state sovereignty. As Sampford forcefully reminds us in his overview chapter, this challenge is based on the fact that health—akin to the global financial crisis and climate change—is an issue that cannot be dealt with within traditional boundaries. At the core of his analysis is the understanding that many of the most intractable governance problems occur when inadequacies at one level of governance are reinforced and exacerbated by inadequacies at other levels.

Globalization also has had far-reaching implications for health systems in Africa. By intensifying the economic and social interconnectivity between countries, it has provided more employment opportunities for healthcare workers and greater integration of healthcare services, exchange of medical information, transfer of skills, information, medical products, and standards of practice as well as resources and avenues for responding to challenges in the health sector.

As Rudi Robinson argues, in chapters 3 and 4, it is not the prevalence but the scale of this dynamic that grabs attention. There is nothing intrinsically new about the movement of health professionals from poor to rich countries. High-level health experts have always been internationally mobile, regardless of their country of origin. What is new is the emergence of an international healthcare labour market that provides increased opportunities for an ever larger number of health professionals from poor countries to seek mobility in response to pull factors on the demand side and push factors on the supply side.

Increasing the cross-border flow of people, commodities, and capital has affected the emergence of infectious disease and facilitated the international mobility of healthcare workers, most often from poor countries to rich countries. This in turn has contributed to the already existing deficit in the healthcare labour force in poor countries and has increased the speed and scope for disease to spread through increasingly porous borders.

As healthcare workers have been recruited to work outside their country of origin, the healthcare sector in Africa, particularly in sub-Saharan Africa, has faced diminishing capacity of an already underfunded, under-resourced sector. This lack of capacity has been neglected by government, donor agencies, and global health initiatives. To address this gap, the chapters in this book explore possibilities for policy innovations at the national and regional levels. Arguing that a skilled, well-resourced health workforce is required to confront raging epidemics and poor service delivery in poor African countries, the authors contend that it is necessary to address the structure of the labour market for international healthcare workers in order to minimize the costs and maximize benefits of their migration.

Robinson argues that the best way forward is through a co-development framework as an alternative approach to "stay-at-home" strategies for managing the international mobility of health professionals from sub-Saharan Africa to member countries of the Organisation for Economic Co-operation and Development (OECD). Such an approach emphasizes balancing stakeholders' interests, promoting brain gain as opposed to brain drain, breaking the monopoly of OECD countries' domestic agenda over integration policies, creating policy and institutional coherence, promoting partnerships, and, most importantly, shifting the integration paradigm from exclusion to inclusion.

In Chapter 5, Anita Davis provides an overview of international migration patterns and the important relationship between migrants' legal status, and access to healthcare services. In doing so, she refers to critical infectious diseases that are important to public health in order to illustrate the need for states to provide migrants and mobile populations access to health and social services—irrespective of their legal status as a way of inclusion, and promoting good health governance for the host community. There is a great need for more evidence-based policies in migration, health, and development.

Although Jane Adar is concerned in Chapter 6 with the mobility of people migrating from South to North or South to South as increasing the brain drain of qualified health professionals from developing countries to developed countries, she does so with a specific focus on this dynamic as further weakening of already weak health systems. This is particularly true in the context of the fight against the HIV/AIDS epidemic.

Adar discusses the integration of traditional medicine from the perspective that it plays a role in increasing access to universal HIV/AIDS prevention programs, treatment, care, and support through its integration into mainstream healthcare systems. Her chapter concentrates on the reasons why traditional medicine must be integrated into health systems in the African region, and then describes the formats in which systems of integration have taken place. The establishment of rules governing traditional medicine provide a framework for developing the practice while ensuring safety measures are respected.

While these arguments may differ in terms of the level at which they stress that policy innovation needs to be emphasized, all the authors in this volume emphasize the necessity for policy makers to develop policy coherence in interdependent sectors and create integrated initiatives at different levels of governance. Some authors emphasize the implementation of national health policies, with global leadership, while others focus on the necessity for regional and international institutions to formulate policies and initiatives to govern the health sector that national African governments are unable to address.

This collection underscores the role that other sectors and stakeholders can play, such as traditional medicine and the private sector, as well as highlights the necessity for creating partnerships between researchers, nongovernmental organizations, regional bodies, United Nations agencies, civil society, academia, and national governments.

By way of contrast, in Chapter 7 Mengsteab Tesfayohannes lays the priority on a radical reform of the current archaic and inefficient healthcare governance and management system at the national level, which he sees as the main source for the continuing brain drain of qualified healthcare professionals. There must be coordination in formulating and implementing policies and strategies relating to the healthcare systems. As Tesfayohannes notes, the countries in the Horn of Africa are obliged ensure that qualified packages of financial and non-financial incentives are in place to respond realistically to the needs of healthcare professionals.

Nelson Sewankambo's Chapter 8 confirms the need to continue to privilege to the Millennium Development Goals (MDGs) for Africa. Each of the eight MDGs relate to health outcomes either directly or indirectly. Africa, however, should not target the MDGs in isolation but with an eye to successes from within and outside the continent. Nevertheless, it should avoid being held hostage to policy priorities decided by the donor community and the dominant institutions of global economic and financial governance.

In terms of innovation at the global level, Chapter 9's discussion by Allyn L. Taylor and Ibadat S. Dhillon of the Global Code of Practice on the International Recruitment of Health Personnel developed by the World Health Organization (WHO) offers a different form of innovation at the architectural level of global governance. As they attest, this is a classic illustration of how global health workforce recruitment and migration has become a complex and multidimensional global health challenge. Although the Global Code was never intended to be the final answer, it does point to the need to establish a global platform that could provide a framework for continuing dialogue and cooperation among states on an important and sensitive subject.

As a package, the chapters in this book identify an array of challenges that will impede the formulation of successful innovative health policies. At the national level, health systems in Africa have suffered neglect and underfunding, with adequate health made available only to wealthier urban populations. There is a dearth of policy coherence in African countries and a lack of ability for African countries to work together to govern regional health systems, combined with an isolationist foreign policy with regard to health. At the international level, there is a deficiency of policies in developed countries that address the resource strain facing developing countries when healthcare workers seek more lucrative employment in the North and a lack of initiatives that focus on responding to health issues.

This collection serves to illuminate the potential for greater innovation in health governance in Africa, despite these considerable challenges. Health governance that combines intersectoral national development strategies and regional and global bodies will most effectively address the global health concerns plaguing Africa. There is hope in the mandate and goals of donors, international organizations, and national governments, which in combination with international initiatives and plans such as the MDGs and the WHO's Global Code of Practice on the International Recruitment of Health Personnel have galvanized action.

Bibliography

Abu-Laban, Yasmeen and Christina Gabriel (2002). *Selling Diversity: Immigration, Multiculturalism, Employment Equity, and Globalization*. Peterborough: Broadview Press.

Adams Jr., Richard H. (2003). "International Migration, Remittances and the Brain Drain: A Study of 24 Labor Exporting Countries." World Bank, Washington, DC. Available online: go.worldbank.org/FOFTG7F4V0 (October 2012).

Addis, Adeno (2004). "The Thin State in Thick Globalism: Sovereignty in the Information Age." *Vanderbilt Journal of Transnational Law* 37(1): 1–107.

Adelman, Howard, ed. (2008). *Protracted Displacement in Asia: No Place to Call Home*. Aldershot: Ashgate.

Adelman, Jeremy (2006). *Sovereignty and Revolution in the Iberian Atlantic*. Princeton, NJ: Princeton University Press.

Adredo, Dejene (2000). "Human Capital Flight from Africa: An Assessment of Brain Drain from Ethiopia." In *Brain Drain and Capacity Building in Africa*, Sibry J.M. Tapsoba, Sabiou Kassoum, Pascal V. Houenou, et al., eds. United Nations Economic Commission for Africa, pp. 122–47. Available online: idl-bnc.idrc.ca/dspace/bitstream/10625/28020/1/118149.pdf (October 2012).

African Union (2005). "Plan of Action on the AU Decade of Traditional Medicine (2001–2010): Implementation of the Decision of the Lusaka Summit of Heads of State and Government." October 10–12, Gabarone. Available online: www.africa-union.org/Social%20Affairs/African%20Ministers%20of%20Health%202005/PLAN%20OF%20ACTION-TRADITIONAL%20MEDICINE.pdf (October 2012).

African Union (2005). "Report of the Meeting of Experts from Member States on the Definition of the African Diaspora." April 11–12, Addis Ababa. Available online: www.africa-union.org/organs/ecossoc/Report-Expert-Diaspora%20Defn%2013april2005-Clean%20copy1.doc (October 2012).

African Union (2007). "Africa Health Strategy: 2007–2015." April 9–13, Johannesburg. Available online: www.africa-union.org/root/UA/Conferences/2007/avril/SA/9-13%20avr/doc/en/Health_Strategy_Min_Draft.pdf (October 2012).

Aginam, Obijifor (2004). "Salvaging Our Global Neighbourhood: Critical Reflections on the G8 Summit and Global Health Governance in an Interdependent World." *Law, Social Justice, and Global Development* 1. Available online: www2.warwick.ac.uk/fac/soc/law/elj/lgd/2004_1/aginam (October 2012).

Aiken, Linda H., James Buchan, Julie Sochalski, et al. (2004). "Trends in International Nurse Migration." *Health Affairs* 23(3): 69–77. Available online: content.healthaffairs.org/content/23/3/69.full (October 2012).

Alkire, Sabina and Lincoln Chen (2002). "'Medical Exceptionalism' in International Migration: Should Doctors and Nurses Be Treated Differently?" In *Globalizing Migration Regimes: New Challenges to Transnational Cooperation*, Kristof Tamas and Joakim Palme, eds. Aldershot: Ashgate, pp. 100–117.

Alliance for Ethical International Recruitment Practices (2011). "Voluntary Code of Ethical Conduct for the Recruitment of Foreign-Educated Health Professionals to the United States." April, Washington, DC. Available online: www. fairinternationalrecruitment.org/images/uploads/THE%20CODE%281%29. pdf (October 2012).

AMES (2010). "Partnership for Eritrea: Graduate Medical Education Program." April 18. Available online: www.samss.org/samss.upload/ wysiwyg/Presentations%20from%20AMES/Eritrea%20-%20George%20 Washington%20Postgrad.pdf (October 2012).

Anarfi, John K. (1993). "Sexuality, Migration, and AIDS in Ghana: A Socio-Behavioural Study." *Health Transition Review* 3: 45–67.

Angola Press Agency (2010). "Health Minister Says War Hindered HIV/Aids Spread in Nation." March 19.

Annan, Kofi (2000). "UN Secretary General Kofi Annan's Closing Remarks to the Ministerial." June 27, Council for a Community of Democracies, Warsaw. Available online: www.ccd21.org/pdf/annan_warsaw_closing_remarks.pdf (October 2012).

Annan, Kofi (2000). "'We the Peoples': The Role of the United Nations in the 21st Century." United Nations, New York. Available online: www.un.org/ millennium/sg/report/ (October 2012).

Anyangwe, Stella C. and Chipayeni Mtonga (2007). "Inequities in the Global Health Workforce: The Greatest Impediment to Health in Sub-Saharan Africa." *International Journal of Environmental Research and Health* 4(2): 93–100. Available online: www.mdpi.org/ijerph/papers/ ijerph2007040002.pdf (October 2012).

Appleby, Joyce (1992). *Liberalism and Republicanism in the Historical Imagination*. Cambridge, MA: Harvard University Press.

Araia, Ghelawdewos (2001). "Development Policy Shift for Africa." *African Link Magazine*. Available online: www.africanidea.org/african_development.html (October 2012).

Arcand, Jean-Louis (2001). "Undernourishment and Economic Growth: The Efficiency Cost of Hunger." FAO Economic and Social Development Paper No. 147. Available online: www.fao.org/docrep/003/X9280E/X9280E00. HTM (October 2012).

Association of American Medical Colleges (2010). "AAMC Releases New Physician Shortage Estimates Post-Reform." News Alert,

September 30, Washington, DC. Available online: www.aamc.org/newsroom/newsreleases/2010/150570/100930.html (October 2012).

Australian Health Workforce Advisory Committee and Australian Medical Workforce Advisory Committee (2005). "A Models of Care Approach to Health Workforce Planning." Health Workforce Information Paper No. 1, March, Sydney. Available online: www.ahwo.gov.au/documents/Publications/2005/A%20models%20of%20care%20approach%20to%20health%20workforce%20planning.pdf (October 2012).

Australian Nursing and Midwifery Council (2007). "Position Statement: Ethical Recruitment of Internationally Qualified and Registered Nurses and Midwives." August, Canberra. Available online: www.anmc.org.au/userfiles/file/guidelines_and_position_statements/Ethical%20Recruitment%20of%20Internationally%20Qualified%20and%20Registered%20Nurses%20and%20Midwives.pdf (October 2012).

Awases, Magda, Akpa R. Gbary, Jennifer Nyoni, et al. (2004). "Migration of Health Professionals in Six Countries: A Synthesis Report." World Health Organization Regional Office for Africa. Available online: info.worldbank.org/etools/docs/library/206860/Migration%20study%20AFRO.pdf (October 2012).

Bach, Stephen (2006). "International Mobility of Health Professionals: Brain Drain or Brain Exchange?," United Nations University World Institute for Development Economics Research. Available online: www.wider.unu.edu/publications/working-papers/research-papers/2006/en_GB/rp2006-82/_files/78091786133112658/default/rp2006-82.pdf (October 2012).

Baldacchino, Godfrey, Sarath Chandrasekere, and Pat Saunders (2007). "Internationally Educated Health Professions in Atlantic Canada." *Canadian Issues: Foreign Credential Recognition* (Spring): 104–7. Available online: canada.metropolis.net/pdfs/cdn_issues_CITC_spring07.pdf (October 2012).

Barro, Robert J. (1996). "Health and Economic Growth." Prepared for the Pan American Health Organization, November. Available online: www.paho.org/english/hdp/hdd/barro.pdf (October 2012).

Bayly, C.A. (2003). *The Birth of the Modern World, 1780–1914: Global Connections and Comparisons.* Malden, MA: Blackwell Publishing.

BBC News (2007). "Key Facts: Africa to Europe Migration." July 2. Available online: news.bbc.co.uk/2/hi/europe/6228236.stm (October 2012).

Beaglehole, Robert and Derek Yach (2003). "Globalisation and the Prevention and Control of Non-Communicable Disease: The Neglected Chronic Diseases of Adults." *Lancet* 362(9387): 903–8.

Beine, Michel, Frederic Docquier, and Hillel Rapaport (2001). "Brain Drain and Economic Growth: Theory and Evidence." *Journal of Development Economics* 64: 275–89.

Benton, Lauren (2002). *Law and Colonial Cultures: Legal Regimes in World History, 1400–1900.* Cambridge: Cambridge University Press.

Berer, Marge (2009). "Task-Shifting: Exposing the Cracks in Public Health Systems." *Reproductive Health Matters* 17(33): 4–8. Available online: www.rhmjournal.org.uk/publications/editorials/RHM33.pdf (October 2012).

Berhan, Yifru (2008). "Medical Doctors Profile in Ethiopia: Protection, Attrition, and Retention. In Memory of 100 Years Ethiopian Modern Medicine and the New Ethiopian Millennium." *Ethiopian Medical Journal* 46(1): 1–77.

Biddlecom, Ann E. and Martin Brockerhoff (1999). "Migration, Sexual Behavior, and the Risk of HIV in Kenya." *International Migration Review* 33(4): 833–56.

Biesma, Regien G., Ruairí Brugha, Andrew Harmer, et al. (2009). "The Effects of Global Health Initiatives on Country Health Systems: A Review of the Evidence from HIV/AIDS Control." *Health Policy and Planning* 24: 239–52.

Bilder, Richard (1994). "Perspectives on Sovereignty in the Current Context: An American Viewpoint." *Canada-United States Law Journal* 20: 9–17. Available online: ssrn.com/abstract=1551964 (October 2012).

Bodeker, Gerard, Donna Kabatesi, Rachel King, et al. (2000). "A Regional Task Force on Traditional Medicine and AIDS." *Lancet* 355(9211): 1284.

Boelen, Charles and Jeffery E. Hack (1995). "Defining and Measuring Social Accountability of Medical Schools." World Health Organization, Geneva. Available online: whqlibdoc.who.int/hq/1995/WHO_HRH_95.7.pdf (October 2012).

Boyd, Monica and Grant Schellenberg (2005). "Re-accreditation Demands and Skilled Labor Flows: The Paradoxes of Professional Migration." Paper presented at the International Population Conference of the International Union for the Scientific Study of Population, 18–23 July, Tours, France. Available online: iussp2005.princeton.edu/papers/50333 (October 2012).

Brand, Ronald A. (2008). "Sovereignty: The State, the Individual, and the International Legal System in the Twenty First Century." *Hastings International and Comparative Law Review* 25: 279–95. Available online: ssrn.com/abstract=1214210 (October 2012).

Bratton, Michael and Nicholas van de Walle (1997). *Democratic Experiments in Africa: Regime Transitions in Comparative Perspective*. Cambridge: Cambridge University Press.

Brooks, Rosa Ehrenreich (2005). "Failed States, or the State as Failure?" *University of Chicago Law Review* 72(4): 1159–96.

Brown, Mercy (2000). "Using Intellectual Diaspora to Reverse the Brain Drain: Some Useful Examples." In *Brain Drain and Capacity Building in Africa*, Sibry J.M. Tapsoba, Sabiou Kassoum, Pascal V. Houenou, et al., eds. United Nations Economic Commission for Africa, pp. 92–109. Available online: idl-bnc.idrc.ca/dspace/bitstream/10625/28020/1/118149.pdf (October 2012).

Bryce, Jennifer, Nancy Terreri, Cesar G. Victora, et al. (2006). "Countdown to 2015: Tracking Intervention Coverage for Child Survival." *Lancet* 368(9541): 1067–76.

Buchan, James (2006, 27 January). "International Recruitment of Health Professionals." *British Medical Journal*. doi: 10.1136/bmj.330.7485.210.

Buchan, James (2008). "How Can the Migration of Health Service Professionals Be Managed So As to Reduce Any Negative Effects on Supply?," World Health Organization, Copenhagen. Available online: www.euro.who.int/__ data/assets/pdf_file/0006/75453/E93414.pdf (October 2012).

Buchan, James (2008). "New Opportunities: United Kingdom Recruitment of Filipino Nurses." In *The International Migration of Health Workers: A Global Health System?*, John Connell, ed. New York: Routledge, pp. 47–61.

Buchan, James and Delanyo Dovlo (2004). "International Recruitment of Health Workers to the UK: A Report for DFID." Department for International Development Health Systems Resource Centre, London. Available online: www.equinetafrica.org/bibl/docs/BUChres310108.pdf (October 2012).

Buchan, James and Barbara McPake (2007). "The Impact of the Department of Health, England, Code of Practice on International Recruitment of Health Professionals." June. Available online: www.aspeninstitute.org/sites/default/files/content/images/Impact%20of%20the%20Department%20of%20 Health%20England%20Code%20of%20Practice%20on%20International%20 Recruitment.pdf (October 2012).

Buchan, James and Fiona O'May (1999). "Globalisation and Healthcare Labour Markets: A Case Study from the United Kingdom." *Human Resources for Health Development Journal* 3(3): 199–209. Available online: www.who.int/hrh/en/HRDJ_3_3_04.pdf (October 2012).

Bueno de Mesquita, Judith and Matt Gordon (2005). "The International Migration of Health Workers: A Human Rights Analysis." Medact, London. Available online: www.medact.org/content/Skills%20drain/Bueno%20de%20 Mesquita%20and%20Gordon.pdf (October 2012).

Camilleri, Joseph A. and Jim Falk (1992). *End of Sovereignty? The Politics of a Shrinking and Fragmenting World.* Aldershot: Elgar.

Canadian Institute for Health Information (2007). "Health Care in Canada 2007." Ottawa. Available online: secure.cihi.ca/free_products/hcic2007_e.pdf (October 2012).

Carballo, Manuel and Mourtala Mboup (2005). "International Migration and Health." Paper prepared for the Policy Analysis and Research Programme, September, Global Commission on International Migration. Available online: www.iom.int/jahia/webdav/site/myjahiasite/shared/shared/mainsite/policy_ and_research/gcim/tp/TP13.pdf (October 2012).

Cárdenas, Emilio J. and María Fernanda Cañás (2002). "The Limits of Self-Determination." In *The Self-Determination of Peoples: Community, Nation, and State in an Interdependent World*, Wolfgang Danspeckgruber, ed. Boulder, CO: Lynne Rienner Publishers, pp. 101–18.

Cash, Richard (2005). "Ethical Issues in Health Workforce Development." *Bulletin of the World Health Organization* 83: 280–84. Available online: www.who.int/bulletin/volumes/83/4/280.pdf (October 2012).

Central Intelligence Agency (2012). "The World Factbook." Washington, DC. Available online: www.cia.gov/library/publications/the-world-factbook (October 2012).

Cerna, Lucie (2007). "The Politics of Coalitions for High-Skilled Immigration Policies in Europe and North America." Paper presented at the Midwest Political Science Association Conference, 12 April, Chicago. Available online: www.allacademic.com/meta/p199328_index.html (October 2012).

Chabal, Patrick and Jean-Pascal Daloz (1999). *Africa Works: Disorder as Political Instrument*. Bloomington, IN: Indiana University Press.

Chan, Margaret (2010). "Agreements at World Health Assembly a Gift to Public Health." Closing remarks at the 63rd World Health Assembly, Geneva, May 21. Available online: www.who.int/dg/speeches/2010/WHA_closing_20100521/ en (October 2012).

Chanda, Rupa (2002). "Trade in Health Services." *Bulletin of the World Health Organization* 80(2): 158–63. Available online: www.who.int/bulletin/ archives/80(2)158.pdf (October 2012).

Chatora, Rufaro (2003). "An Overview of the Traditional Medicine Situation in the African Region." *African Health Monitor* 4(1): 4–7. Available online: www.afro.who.int/index.php?option=com_docman&task=doc_ download&gid=501&ItemId=2111 (October 2012).

Chen, Lincoln (2009). "Beyond Rhetoric: The Quest for Practical Success in Global Health." *Lancet* 374(9700): 1491–2. Available online: www.thelancet. com/journals/lancet/article/PIIS0140-6736%2809%2961890-0/fulltext (October 2012).

Chesterman, Simon (2001). *Just War or Just Peace? Humanitarian Intervention and International Law*. Oxford: Oxford University Press.

Chesterman, Simon, Michael Ignatieff, and Ramesh Thakur, eds (2005). *Making States Work: State Failure and the Crisis of Governance*. Tokyo: United Nations University Press.

Chicha, Marie-Thérèse and Éric Charest (2008). "L'intégration des immigrés sur le marché du travail à Montréal: Politiques et enjeux." *Choix IRPP* 14(2). Available online: www.irpp.org/fr/choices/archive/vol14no2.pdf (October 2012).

Chikanda, Abel (2004). "Skilled Health Professionals' Migration and Its Impact on Health Delivery in Zimbabwe." Policy and Society Working Paper No. 4, Centre on Migration, University of Oxford. Available online: hdl. handle.net/10646/48 (October 2012).

Chikanda, Abel (2005). "Nurse Migration from Zimbabwe: Analysis of Recent Trends and Impacts." *Nursing Inquiry* 12(3): 162–75.

Chou, Meng-Hsuan (2006). "EU and the Migration-Development Nexus: What Prospects for EU-Wide Policies?" Working Paper No. 37, Centre on Migration, Policy, and Society, University of Oxford. Available online: www.compas. ox.ac.uk/fileadmin/files/Publications/working_papers/WP_2006/WP0637- Chou.pdf (October 2012).

Cilliers, Jakkie (2009). "Climate Change, Population Pressure, and Conflict in Africa." ISS Paper 178, January, Institute for Security Studies, Pretoria. Available online: www.issafrica.org/uploads/PAPER178.PDF (October 2012).

Clapham, Christopher (1996). *Africa and the International System: The Politics of State Survival*. Cambridge: Cambridge University Press.

Clark, Paul F., James B. Stewart, and Darlene A. Clark (2006). "The Globalization of the Labour Market for Health-Care Professionals." *International Labour Review* 145(1/2): 37–64.

Clemens, Michael A. and Gunilla Pettersson (2007). "A New Database of Health Professional Emigration from Africa." Working Paper No. 95, August, Center for Global Development. Available online: www.cgdev.org/files/9267_file_CGDWP95_Feb_2007.pdf (October 2012).

Coghlan, Benjamin, Pascal Ngoy, Flavien Mulumba, et al. (2009). "Update on Mortality in the Democratic Republic of Congo: Results from a Third Nationwide Survey." *Disaster Medicine and Public Health Preparedness* 3: 88–96.

Cohen, Jon (2006). "The New World of Global Health." *Science* 311(5758): 162–7.

Collier, Paul (2007). *The Bottom Billion: Why the Poorest Countries Are Failing and What Can Be Done About It*. Oxford: Oxford University Press.

Collin, Jeff, Kelley Lee, and Karen Bissell (2005). "Negotiating the Framework Convention on Tobacco Control: An Updated Politics of Global Health Governance." In *The Global Governance Reader*, Rorden Wilkinson, ed. New York: Routledge.

Commission for Africa (2005). "Our Common Interest." Report of the Commission for Africa, London. Available online: www.commissionforafrica.info/2005-report (October 2012).

Commission of the European Communities (2003). "Communication from the Commission to the Council, the European Parliament, the European Economic and Social Committee, and the Committee of the Regions on Immigration, Integration, and Employment." COM (2003) 336 final, June 3, Brussels. Available online: eur-lex.europa.eu/LexUriServ/LexUriServ.do?uri=COM:2003:0336:FIN:EN:PDF (October 2012).

Commission on Macroeconomics and Health (2001). "Macroeconomics and Health: Investing in Health for Economic Development." World Health Organization, Geneva. Available online: www.cid.harvard.edu/archive/cmh/cmhreport.pdf (October 2012).

Commission on Social Determinants of Health (2008). *Closing the Gap in a Generation: Health Equity through Action on the Social Determinants of Health. Final Report of the Commission on Social Determinants of Health*. Geneva: World Health Organization. Available online: www.who.int/social_determinants/thecommission/finalreport/en/index.html (October 2012).

Committee on Economic, Social, and Cultural Rights (2000). "The Right to the Highest Attainable Standard of Health." August 11, United Nations Economic and Social Council, Geneva. Available online: www.unhchr.ch/tbs/doc.nsf/ (symbol)/E.C.12.2000.4.En (October 2012).

Commonwealth Health Ministers (2003). "Commonwealth Code of Practice for the International Recruitment of Health Workers." May 18, Geneva. Available online: www.thecommonwealth.org/ shared_asp_files/uploadedfiles/%7B7BDD970B-53AE-441D-81DB-1B64C37E992A%7D_CommonwealthCodeofPractice.pdf (October 2012).

Cooper, Andrew F. and John J. Kirton, eds (2009). *Innovation in Global Health Governance: Critical Cases.* Farnham: Ashgate.

Cooper, Andrew F., John J. Kirton, and Ted Schrecker, eds (2007). *Governing Global Health: Challenge, Response, Innovation.* Aldershot: Ashgate.

Corkery, Joan (2000). "Public Service Reforms and Their Impact on Health Sector Personnel in Uganda." In *Public Service Reforms and their Impact on Health Sector Personnel: Case Studies on Cameroon, Colombia, Jordan, Philippines, Poland, Uganda*, International Labour Organization, ed. Geneva: pp. 236–84.

Cosnard, Michel (2003). "Sovereign Equality—'The *Wimbledon* Sails On.'" In *United States Hegemony and the Foundations of International Law*, Michael Byers and George Nolte, eds. Cambridge: Cambridge University Press.

Crawford, James (1979). *The Creation of States in International Law.* New York: Clarendon Press.

Dayton-Johnson, Jeff, Louka T. Katseli, Gregory Maniatis, et al., eds (2007). *Gaining from Migration: Towards a New Mobility System.* Paris: Organisation for Economic Co-operation and Development. Available online: www. migrationpolicy.org/pubs/Gaining_from_Migration.pdf (October 2012).

De Haas, Hein (2010). "Migration and Development: A Theoretical Perspective." *International Migration Review* 44(1): 227–64.

De Vos, Pol (2005). "'No One Left Abandoned': Cuba's National Health System since the 1959 Revolution." *International Journal of Health Services* 35(1): 189–207.

De Vos, Pol, Wim De Ceukelaire, Mariano Bonet, et al. (2007). "Cuba's International Cooperation in Health: An Overview." *International Journal of Health Services* 37(4): 761–76.

De Vos, Pol, Pedro Murlá, Armando Rodriguez, et al. (2005). "Shifting the Demand for Emergency Care in Cuba's Health System." *Social Science and Medicine* 60(3): 609–16.

Deaton, Angus (2004). "Health in an Age of Globalization." Working Paper 10669, National Bureau of Economic Research, Cambridge, MA. Available online: www.nber.org/papers/w10669 (October 2012).

Deloitte PLC (2009). "A Report on Healthcare Quality." Deloitte Development LLC.

Dhillon, Ibadat S., Margaret E. Clark, and Robert Kapp (2010). "Innovations in Cooperation: A Guidebook on Bilateral Agreements to Address Health Worker Migration." May, Aspen Institute. Available online: www.aspeninstitute.org/ sites/default/files/content/docs/pubs/Bilateral%20Report_final%20code.pdf (October 2012).

Diallo, Khassoum (2004). "Data on the Migration of Health-Care Workers: Sources, Uses, and Challenges." *Bulletin of the World Health Organization* 82(8): 601–7. Available online: www.who.int/bulletin/volumes/82/8/601.pdf (October 2012).

Docquier, Frederic and Abdeslam Marfouk (2004). "Measuring the International Mobility of Skilled Workers (1990–2000): Release 1.0." World Bank, Washington, DC. doi: 10.1596/1813-9450-3381. Available online: elibrary.worldbank.org/content/workingpaper/10.1596/1813-9450-3381 (October 2012).

Dodgson, Richard, Kelley Lee, and Nick Drager (2002). "Global Health Governance: A Conceptual Review." London School of Hygiene and Tropical Medicine, London. Available online: www.bvsde.paho.org/texcom/cd050853/dodgson.pdf (October 2012).

Dovlo, Delanyo (2003). "The Brain Drain and Retention of Health Professionals in Africa." Case study prepared for a conference on "Improving Tertiary Education in Sub-Saharan Africa: Things That Work!" 23–25 September, Accra. Available online: www.medact.org/content/health/documents/brain_drain/Dovlo%20-%20brain%20drain%20and%20retention.pdf (October 2012).

Dovlo, Delanyo (2004). "The Brain Drain in Africa: An Emerging Challenge to Health Professionals' Education." *Journal of Higher Education in Africa* 2(3): 1–18. Available online: www.codesria.org/IMG/pdf/02-dovlo.pdf (October 2012).

Dovlo, Delanyo and Tim Martineau (2004). "A Review of the Migration of Africa's Health Professionals." JLI Working Paper 4–4, Ministry of Health, Ghana.

Dumont, Jean-Christophe, Pascal Zurn, Jody Church, et al. (2008). "International Mobility of Health Professionals and Health Workforce Management in Canada: Myths and Realties." Working Paper No. 40, Organisation for Economic Co-operation and Development, Paris. Available online: www.oecd.org/canada/41590427.pdf (October 2012).

Easterly, William and Yaw Nyarko (2008). "Is the Brain Drain Good for Africa?" Global Working Paper 18, Brookings Institution. Available online: www.brookings.edu/research/papers/2008/03/brain-drain-easterly (October 2012).

Edokat, Tofah (2000). "Effects of Brain Drain on Higher Education in Cameroon." In *Brain Drain and Capacity Building in Africa*, Sibry J.M. Tapsoba, Sabiou Kassoum, Pascal V. Houenou, et al., eds. United Nations Economic Commission for Africa, pp. 174–85. Available online: idl-bnc.idrc.ca/dspace/bitstream/10625/28020/1/118149.pdf (October 2012).

European Centre for Disease Prevention and Control (2009). "ECDC Interim Guidance: Uses of Specific Pandemic Influenza Vaccines During the H1N1 2009 Pandemic." August, Stockholm. Available online: ecdc.europa.eu/en/publications/publications/0908_gui_pandemic_influenza_vaccines_during_the_h1n1_2009_pandemic.pdf (October 2012).

Fink, Sheri (2002). "International Efforts Spotlight Traditional, Complementary, and Alternative Medicine." *American Journal of Public Health* 92(11): 1734–9.

Available online: ajph.aphapublications.org/doi/abs/10.2105/AJPH.92.11.1734 (October 2012).

Fiorina, Carly (2001). "Policymaking in an Internet Age." Speech delivered at the "Progress and Freedom Foundation Summit," August 19, Aspen. Available online: www.hp.com/hpinfo/execteam/speeches/fiorina/aspen_01.html (October 2012).

Fogel, Robert W. (2002). "Nutrition, Physiological Capital, and Economic Growth." Lecture prepared for presentation at the Senior Policy Seminar on Health, Human Capital, and Economic Growth: Theory, Evidence, and Policies of the Pan American Health Organization and the Inter American Development Bank, October 3. Available online: www.paho.org/english/HDP/HDD/fogel.pdf (October 2012).

Forcier, Mélanie B., Steven Simoens, and Antonio Giuffrida (2004). "Impact, Regulation, and Health Policy Implications of Physician Migration in OECD Countries." *Human Resources for Health* 2(12). doi: 10.1186/1478-4491-2-12. Available online: www.human-resources-health.com/content/2/1/12 (October 2012).

Franck, Thomas (1992). "The Emerging Right to Democratic Governance." *American Journal of International Law* 86: 46–91.

Frank, Reanne (2008). "Migradollars as a Form of Health Insurance? The Relationship between U.S. Migration, Remittances, and Health Care in Mexico." Paper presented at the annual meeting of the American Sociological Association, 31 July, Boston. Available online: www.allacademic.com/meta/p242491_index.html (October 2012).

Frank, Reanne and Robert A. Hummer (2002). "The Other Side of the Paradox: The Risk of Low Birth Weight among Infants of Migrant and Nonmigrant Households within Mexico." *International Migration Review* 36(3): 746–65. doi: 10.1111/j.1747-7379.2002.tb00103.x.

Fritzen, Scott A. (2007). "Strategic Management of the Health Workforce in Developing Countries: What Have We Learned?" *Human Resources for Health* 5(4). doi: 10.1186/1478-4491-5-4. Available online: www.human-resources-health.com/content/5/1/4 (October 2012).

Galeotti, Mark (1995). "Cross-Border Crime in the Former Soviet Union." Boundary and Territory Briefing, vol. 1, no. 5, International Boundaries Research Unit, University of Durham.

Gallup, John Luke and Jeffrey Sachs (1998). "The Economic Burden of Malaria." October, Center for International Development at Harvard. Available online: www.earth.columbia.edu/sitefiles/file/about/director/pubs/mal_wb.pdf (October 2012).

Gandhi, Neel R., Anthony Moll, A. Willem Sturm, et al. (2006). "Extensive Drug Resistant Tuberculosis as a Cause of Death in Patients Co-infected with Tuberculosis and HIV in a Rural Area of South Africa." *Lancet* 368(9547): 1575–80. Available online: ftp.cdc.gov/pub/nchstp/tb/

who_cc_latvia/present/Articles/Gandhi_XDR%20TB%20HIV%20in%20 KZN_Lancet.pdf

Gardner, Bob (2008). "Health Equity Discussion Paper." Toronto Central Local Health Integration Network. Available online: www.torontocentrallhin.on.ca/ uploadedFiles/Home_Page/Report_and_Publications/Health%20Equity%20 Discussion%20Paper%20v1.0.pdf (October 2012).

Garrett, Laurie (1994). *The Coming Plague: Newly Emerging Diseases in a World Out of Balance*. New York: Farrar, Strauss and Giroux.

George Washington University (2009). "GW Helps African Nation Double Its Pediatricians." Washington, DC, December 15. Available online: gwtoday. gwu.edu/gw-helps-african-nation-double-its-pediatricians (October 2012).

Gerlinger, Thomas and Rolf Schmucker (2007). "Transnational Migration of Health Professionals in the European Union." *Cadernos de Saúde Pública* 23(2): S184–S92. Available online: www.scielosp.org/pdf/csp/ v23s2/07.pdf (October 2012).

Giddens, Anthony (2000). *The Third Way and Its Critics*. Cambridge: Polity Press.

Girardin, Brigitte (2006). "And If Immigration Benefitted Everyone?" *Les Echos*, April 12. Available online: www.ambafrance-ca.org/spip.php?article1151 (October 2012).

Global Health Workforce Alliance (2008). "The Kampala Declaration and Agenda for Global Action." World Health Organization, Geneva. Available online: www.who.int/workforcealliance/Kampala%20Declaration%20and%20 Agenda%20web%20file.%20FINAL.pdf (October 2012).

Goma, Lameck (1990). "The African Brain Drain: Investment in and Utilization of Human Capital." In *Capacity Building and Human Resource Development*, Alexander A. Kwapong and Barry Lesser, eds. Halifax: Lester Pearson Institute for International Development.

Grande, Edgar and Louis W. Pauly, eds (2005). *Complex Sovereignty: Reconstituting Political Authority in the Twenty-first Century*. Toronto: University of Toronto Press.

Grant, Mary L. (1999). "Evidence of New Immigrant Assimilation in Canada." *Canadian Journal of Economics* 32(4): 930–55. Available online: economics. ca/cgi/xms?jab=v32n4/04.pdf (October 2012).

Gushulak, Brian D., Liane Macdonald, and Douglas W. MacPherson (2007). "Health and Foreign Policy: Influences of Migration and Population Mobility." *Bulletin of the World Health Organization* 85(3): 200–206. Available online: www.who.int/bulletin/volumes/85/3/06-036962.pdf (October 2012).

Gushulak, Brian D. and Douglas W. MacPherson (2006). *Migration Medicine and Health: Principles and Practice*. Hamilton: BC Decker.

Hagopian, Amy, Matthew J. Thompson, Meredith Fordyce, et al. (2004). "The Migration of Physicians from Sub-Saharan Africa to the United States of America: Measures of the African Brain Drain." *Human Resources for Health* 2(17). doi: 10.1186/1478-4491-2-17. Available online: www.human-resources-health.com/content/2/1/17 (October 2012).

Hall, Lisbeth and Pim Martens (2000). "Malaria on the Move: Human Population Movement and Malaria Transmission." *Emerging Infectious Diseases* 6(2): 103–9. Available online: wwwnc.cdc.gov/eid/content/6/2/contents.htm (October 2012).

Harbeson, John W., Raymond F. Hopkins, and David Smith, eds (1994). *Responsible Governance: The Global Challenge.* Lanham, MD: University Press of America.

Helman, Gerald B. and Steven R. Ratner (1992–93). "Serving Failed States." *Foreign Policy* 89 (Winter): 3–20.

Henderson, Lyn N. and Jim Tulloch (2008). "Incentives for Retaining and Motivating Health Workers in Pacific and Asian Countries." *Human Resources for Health* 6(18). doi: 10.1186/1478-4491-6-18. Available online: www.human-resources-health.com/content/pdf/1478-4491-6-18.pdf (October 2012).

Henkin, Louis (1993). "The Mythology of Sovereignty." *American Society of International Law Newsletter*, March.

High-Level Panel on Threats, Challenges, and Change (2004). "A More Secure World: Our Shared Responsibility." United Nations, New York. Available online: www.un.org/secureworld/ (October 2012).

Hildebrandt, Nicole and David J. McKenzie (2005). "The Effects of Migration on Child Health in Mexico." Policy Research Working Paper No. 3573, World Bank, Washington, DC. doi: 10.1596/1813-9450-3573. Available online: elibrary.worldbank.org/content/workingpaper/10.1596/1813-9450-3573 (October 2012).

Homedes, Núria and Antonio Ugalde (2005). "Human Resources: The Cinderella of Health Sector Reform in Latin America." *Human Resources for Health* 3(1). doi: 10.1186/1478-4491-3-1. Available online: www.human-resources-health.com/content/3/1/1 (October 2012).

Homer-Dixon, Thomas (2001). *The Ingenuity Gap: Can We Solve the Problems of the Future?* Toronto: Vintage.

Homsy, Jaco, Rachel King, Joseph Tenywa, et al. (2004). "Defining Minimum Standards of Practice for Incorporating African Traditional Medicine into HIV/AIDS Prevention, Care, and Support: A Regional Initiative in Eastern and Southern Africa." *Journal of Alternative and Complementary Medicine* 10(5): 905–10.

Hunt, Paul (2005). "The Right of Everyone to the Enjoyment of the Highest Attainable Standard of Physical and Mental Health." Report of the United Nations Special Rapporteur on the Right to Health. A/60/348. Available online: daccess-dds-ny.un.org/doc/UNDOC/GEN/N05/486/77/PDF/N0548677.pdf (October 2012).

Independent International Commission on Kosovo (2000). *The Kosovo Report: Conflict, International Response, Lessons Learned.* doi: 10.1093/0199243093.001.0001. Available online: www.oxfordscholarship.com/view/10.1093/0199243093.001.0001/acprof-9780199243099 (October 2012).

Institute of Medicine (2001). *Crossing the Quality Chasm: A New Health System for the 21st Century.* Washington, DC: National Academy Press.

Institute of Medicine (2005). *Healers Abroad: Americans Responding to the Human Resource Crisis in HIV/AIDS.* Washington, DC: National Academies Press.

Intergovernmental Negotiating Body on the WHO Framework Convention on Tobacco Control (2001). "Chair's Text of a Framework Convention on Tobacco Control." A/FCTC/INB2/2, January 9, World Health Organization, Geneva. Available online: extranet.who.int/iris/restricted/bitstream/10665/75408/1/e2inb2.pdf (October 2012).

International Commission on Intervention and State Sovereignty (2001). "The Responsibility to Protect: Report of the International Commission on Intervention and State Sovereignty." December. Available online: responsibilitytoprotect.org/ICISS%20Report.pdf (October 2012).

International Conference on Primary Health Care (1978). "Declaration of Alma-Ata." Alma-Ata, September 12. Available online: www.who.int/publications/almaata_declaration_en.pdf

International Organization for Migration (2004). "Glossary on Migration." Geneva. Available online: publications.iom.int/bookstore/free/IML_1_EN.pdf (October 2012).

International Organization for Migration (2004). "Migrant Health for the Benefit of All." MC/INF/275, November 8, Geneva. Available online: www.iom.int/jahia/webdav/shared/shared/mainsite/about_iom/en/council/88/MC_INF_275.pdf (October 2012).

International Organization for Migration (2005). *The Berne Initiative: International Agenda for Migration Management.* Geneva: International Organization for Migration. Available online: publications.iom.int/bookstore/free/IAMM.pdf (October 2012).

International Organization for Migration (2005). "Policy Approaches to Migration and Development." MC/INF/281, November 9, International Organization for Migration, Geneva. Available online: www.iom.int/jahia/webdav/site/myjahiasite/shared/shared/mainsite/policy_and_research/policy_documents/MCINF281.pdf (October 2012).

International Organization for Migration (2005). "World Migration Report 2005: Costs and Benefits of International Migration." Geneva. Available online: publications.iom.int/bookstore/free/wmr_2005.pdf (October 2012).

International Organization for Migration (2007). "Migration and the Right to Health: A Review of European Community Law and Council of Europe Instruments." Geneva. Available online: publications.iom.int/bookstore/free/IML_12_EN.pdf (October 2012).

Jimba, Masamine (2009). "Opportunities for Overcoming the Health Workforce Crisis." In *Global Action for Health System Strengthening: Policy Recommendations to the G8.* Tokyo: Japan Center for International Exchange, pp. 27–58. Available online: www.jcie.org/researchpdfs/takemi/ch2.pdf (October 2012).

Johnson, Maureen (2007). "The Challenge of Achieving Health Equity in Africa." International Development Research Centre, Ottawa. Available online: www.idrc.ca/EN/Resources/Publications/Pages/ArticleDetails. aspx?PublicationID=702 (October 2012).

Joint Learning Initiative (2004). "Human Resources for Health: Overcoming the Crisis." Harvard University, Cambridge, MA. Available online: www.who.int/ hrh/documents/JLi_hrh_report.pdf (October 2012).

Josselin, Daphné and William Wallace, eds (2001). *Non-State Actors in World Politics.* Houndmills: Palgrave Macmillan.

Kabene, Stefane M., Carole Orchard, John M. Howard, et al. (2006). "The Importance of Human Resources Management in Health Care: A Global Context." *Human Resources for Health* 4(20). doi: 10.1186/1478-4491-4-20. Available online: www.human-resources-health.com/content/4/1/20 (October 2012).

Kasilo, Ossy M.J. (2003). "Enhancing Traditional Medicine Research and Development in the African Region." *African Health Monitor* 4(1): 15–18. Available online: www.afro.who.int/index. php?option=com_docman&task=doc_download&gid=501&ItemId=2111 (October 2012).

Kayombo, Edmund J., Febronia C. Uiso, Zakaria H. Mbwambo, et al. (2007). "Experience of Initiating Collaboration of Traditional Healers in Managing HIV and AIDS in Tanzania." *Journal of Ethnobiology and Ethnomedicine* 3(6). doi: 10.1186/1746-4269-3-6. Available online: www.ethnobiomed.com/ content/3/1/6 (October 2012).

Keal, Paul (2003). *European Conquest and the Rights of Indigenous Peoples: The Moral Backwardness of International Society.* Cambridge: Cambridge University Press.

Kebede, Derege, ed. (2010). *African Health Monitor.* Special Issue 14: African Traditional Medicine Day, August 31. Available online: ahm.afro.who.int/ special-issue14/ahm-special-issue-14.pdf

Kelsen, Hans (2005). *Pure Theory of Law.* Clark, NJ: Lawbook Exchange.

Kirton, John J., ed. (2009). *Global Health.* Farnham: Ashgate.

Kondro, Wayne (2006, 21 November). "Pulse: Trends in Physician Supply." *Canadian Medical Association Journal* 175(11): 1362. doi: 10.1503/ cmaj.061434.

Kotler, Philip and Nancy R. Lee (2009). *Up and Out of Poverty: The Social Marketing Solution.* Upper Saddle River, NJ: Pearson Education.

Krasner, Stephen (2003–2004). "The Hole in the Whole: Sovereignty, Shared Sovereignty, and International Law." *Michigan Journal of International Law* 25(4): 1075–101.

Krasner, Stephen (2005). "The Case for Shared Sovereignty." *Journal of Democracy* 16(1): 69–83.

Krisch, Nico (2003). "More Equal Than the Rest? Hierarchy, Equality, and US Predominance in International Law." In *United States Hegemony and the*

Foundations of International Law, Michael Byers and George Nolte, eds. Cambridge: Cambridge University Press.

Kruk, Margaret Elizabeth and Lynn P. Freedman (2008). "Assessing Health System Performance in Developing Countries: A Review of the Literature." *Health Policy* 85(3): 263–76.

Labonté, Ronald and Corinne Packer (2006). "Globalisation and the Health Worker Migration Crisis." Draft, Institute for Population Health, University of Ottawa, Ottawa.

Labonté, Ronald, Corinne Packer, and Nathan Klassen (2006). "Managing Health Professional Migration from Sub-Saharan Africa to Canada: A Stakeholder Inquiry into Public Options." *Human Resources for Health* 4(22). doi: 10.1186/1478-4491-4-22. Available online: www.human-resources-health.com/content/4/1/22 (October 2012).

Labonté, Ronald, Corinne Packer, Nathan Klassen, et al. (2006). *The Brain Drain of Health Professionals from Sub-Saharan Africa to Canada.* Cape Town: Southern African Migration Project. Available online: www.queensu.ca/samp/sampresources/samppublications/mad/MAD_2.pdf (October 2012).

Laganà, Giulia (2007). "Co-development: 'Win-Win' Solution for All or Burden-Shifting Opportunity for the Developed World?," Solidar, Brussels. Available online: cms.horus.be/files/99931/MediaArchive/migration/Solidar_co_development_paper.pdf (October 2012).

Lage, Agustin (2008). "Connecting Immunology Research to Public Health: Cuban Biotechnology." *Nature Immunology* 9: 109–12.

Lagomarsino, Gina, David de Ferranti, Ariel Pablos-Mendez, et al. (2009). "Public Stewardship of Mixed Health Systems." *Lancet* 374(9701): 1577–8.

Lagomarsino, Gina, Stefan Nachuk, and Sapna Singh Kundra (2009). "Public Stewardship of Private Providers in Mixed Health Systems." Synthesis report from the Rockefeller Foundation–sponsored Initiative on the Role of the Private Sector in Health Systems in Developing Countries, Rockefeller Foundation, Washington, DC. Available online: www.rockefellerfoundation.org/uploads/files/0d777898-d2eb-461d-a973-5f7d5d979544-public.pdf (October 2012).

Larson, Brooke (2004). *Trials of National Making: Liberalism, Race, and Ethnicity in the Andes, 1810–1910.* Cambridge: Cambridge University Press.

Lee, Kelley, Kent Buse, and Suzanne Fustukian, eds (2002). *Health Policy in a Globalising World.* Cambridge: Cambridge University Press.

Liese, Bernhard, Nathan Blanchet, and Gilles Dussault (2003). "Background Paper: The Human Resource Crisis in Health Services in Sub-Saharan Africa." World Bank, Washington, DC. Available online: www-wds.worldbank.org/servlet/WDSContentServer/WDSP/IB/2003/10/31/000112742_20031031161656/additional/310436360_20050276022409.pdf (October 2012).

Linklater, Andrew (1998). *The Transformation of Political Community: Ethical Foundations of the Post-Westphalian Era.* London: Polity Press.

Lochhead, Clarence (2003). "The Transition Penalty: Unemployment among Recent Immigrants to Canada." Canadian Labour and Business Centre.

Available online: www.clbc.ca/files/Reports/Fitting_In/Transition_Penalty_e-CLBC.pdf (October 2012).

Loescher, Gil (1992). "Refugee Movements and International Security." *Adelphi Papers* 32(268): 3–8. doi: 10.1080/05679329208449097.

Lorenzo, Fely Marilyn E., Jaime Galvez-Tan, Kriselle Icamina, et al. (2007, July). "Nurse Migration from a Source Country Perspective: Philippine Country Case Study." *Health Services Research* 42(3): 1406–18. doi: 10.1111/j.1475-6773.2007.00716.x.

Lowell, B. Lindsay and Allan Findlay (2001). "Migration of Highly Skilled Persons from Developing Countries: Impact and Policy Responses." Synthesis Report. International Migration Papers No. 44., International Labour Organization, Geneva. Available online: www.ilo.org/public/english/protection/migrant/download/imp/imp44.pdf (October 2012).

Márquez, Miguel (2009). "Health-Workforce Development in the Cuban Health System." *Lancet* 374(9701): 1574–5.

Martineau, Tim, Karola Drecker, and Peter Bundred (2002). "Briefing Note on International Migration of Health Professionals: Levelling the Playing Field for Developing Country Health Systems." Liverpool School of Tropical Medicine, Liverpool.

McAuliffe, Eilish and Malcolm Maclachlan (2005). "'Turning the Ebbing Tide': Knowledge Flows and Health in Low-income Countries." *Higher Education Policy* 18(3): 231–52.

McCorquodale, Robert (2000). "Concepts: Self-Determination." In *Self-Determination in International Law*, Robert McCorquodale, ed. Aldershot: Ashgate.

McCoy, David, Sara Bennett, Sophie Witter, et al. (2008). "Salaries and Incomes of Health Workers in Sub-Saharan Africa." *Lancet* 371(9613): 675–81. Available online: www.thelancet.com/journals/lancet/article/PIIS0140-6736%2808%2960306-2/abstract (October 2012).

McDougal, Myres S., Harold D. Lasswell, and W. Michael Reisman (1967). "The World Constitutive Process of Authoritative Decision." *Faculty Scholarship Series,* Paper 675. Available online: digitalcommons.law.yale.edu/fss_papers/675/

Meeus, Wilma (2003). "'Pull' Factors in International Migration of Health Professionals: An Analysis of Developed Countries' Policies Influencing Migration of Health Professionals." Unpublished master's thesis, University of the Western Cape, Cape Town. Available online: etd.uwc.ac.za/usrfiles/modules/etd/docs/etd_gen8Srv25Nme4_8927_1216732945.pdf (October 2012).

Mejia, Alfonso and Helena Pizurki (2005). "Migration of Health Personnel." World Health Organization Regional Office for the Western Pacific, Manila.

Mensah, Kwadwo, Maureen Mackintosh, and Leroi Henry (2005). "The 'Skills Drain' of Health Professionals from the Developing World: A Framework for Policy Formulation." Medact, London. Available online: www.medact.org/content//Skills%20drain/Mensah%20et%20al.%202005.pdf (October 2012).

Mexican Commission on Macroeconomics and Health (2004). "Investing in Health for Economic Development." Instituto de Políticas Públicas y Estudios del Desarrolo, Mexico City.

Meyer, Jean-Baptiste (2001). "The Brain Drain: New Aspects of the South/North Exodus." *ACP-EU Courier* 187 (July/August).

Mills, Edward, Curtis Cooper, Dugald Seely, et al. (2005). "African Herbal Medicines in the Treatment of HIV: *Hypoxis* and *Sutherlandia*. An Overview of Evidence and Pharmacology." *Nutrition Journal* 4(19). doi: 10.1186/1475-2891-4-19. Available online: www.nutritionj.com/content/4/1/19 (October 2012).

Mills, Edward, Sonal Singh, Kumanan Wilson, et al. (2006). "The Challenges of Involving Traditional Healers in HIV/AIDS Care." *International Journal of STD & AIDS* 17(6): 360–63. doi: 10.1258/095646206777323382.

Ministers of Foreign Affairs of Brazil, France, Indonesia, Norway, Senegal, South Africa, and Thailand (2007). "Oslo Ministerial Declaration—Global Health: A Pressing Foreign Policy Issue of Our Time." *Lancet* 369(9580): 2159. Available online: www.who.int/trade/events/Oslo_Ministerial_Declaration. pdf (October 2012).

Mourshed, Mona, Viktor Hediger, and Toby Lambert (2007). "Gulf Cooperation Council Health Care: Challenges and Opportunities." In *Global Competitiveness Reports*. McKinsey and Company, pp. 55–64. Available online: members. weforum.org/pdf/Global_Competitiveness_Reports/Reports/chapters/2_1.pdf (October 2012).

Mullan, Fitzhugh (2005). "The Metrics of the Physician Brain Drain." *New England Journal of Medicine* 353: 1810–18. Available online: www.nejm.org/doi/full/10.1056/NEJMsa050004 (October 2012).

Munga, Michael A. and Deogratius R. Mbilinyi (2008). "Non-financial Incentives and the Retention of Health Workers in Tanzania." Equinet Discussion Paper No. 61. Available online: www.equinetafrica.org/bibl/docs/DIS61HRmunga. pdf (October 2012).

Mutume, Gumisai (2003). "Reversing Africa's 'Brain Drain': New Initiatives Tap Skills of African Expatriates." *African Recovery* 17(2).

Nair, Sami (1997). "Rapport de bilan et d'orientation sur la politique de codéveloppement liée aux flux migratoires." Paris. Available online: www. ladocumentationfrancaise.fr/rapports-publics/984000139/index.shtml (October 2012).

Newland, Kathleen (2003). "Migration as a Factor in Development and Poverty Reduction." Migration Policy Institute. Available online: www. migrationinformation.org/feature/display.cfm?ID=136 (October 2012).

Newland, Kathleen (2004). "Migration as a Factor in Development and Poverty Reduction: The Impact of Rich Countries' Immigration Policies on the Prospects of the Poor." In *Impact of Rich Countries' Policies on Poor Countries: Towards a Level Playing Field in Development Cooperation*,

Robert Picciotto and Rachel Weaving, eds. New Brunswick NJ: Transaction Publisher, pp. 187–214.

Newman, Edward and Joanne van Selm, eds (2004). *Refugees and Forced Displacement: International Security, Human Vulnerability, and the State.* Tokyo: United Nations University Press.

NHS Employers (2012). "Code of Practice for International Recruitment." Leeds, April 24. Available online: www.nhsemployers.org/recruitmentandretention/ internationalrecruitment/code-of-practice/pages/code-practice-international- recruitment.aspx (October 2012).

Nishtar, Sania (2007). "Politics of Health Systems: WHO's New Frontier." *Lancet* 370(9591): 935–6.

Novotny, Thomas E., Ilona Kickbusch, Hannah Leslie, et al. (2008). "Global Health Diplomacy: A Bridge to Innovative Collaborative Action." *Global Forum Update on Research for Health* 5: 41–5.

Ntuli, Antoinette (2003). "Equity in the Distribution of Health Personnel." Equinet, Harare. Available online: www.equinetafrica.org/bibl/docs/ HRHdiscussiondoc.pdf (October 2012).

Nugent, Jeffrey B. and Seung-jae Yhee (2002). "Small and Medium Enterprises in Korea: Achievements, Constraints and Policy Issues." *Small Business Economics* 18(1–3): 85–119.

Nwankwo, Sonny and Darlington Richards (2004). "Institutional Paradigm and the Management of Transitions: A Sub-Sahara African Perspective." *International Journal of Social Economics* 31(1/2): 111–30.

Nyberg-Sorensen, Ninna, Nicholas Van Hear, and Poul Engberg-Pedersen (2002). "The Migration-Development Nexus Evidence and Policy Options." July, International Organization for Migration, Geneva. Available online: iom.ch/ jahia/webdav/site/myjahiasite/shared/shared/mainsite/published_docs/serial_ publications/mrs_8.pdf (October 2012).

Nyumbu, Mutinta, E. Bwalya, and N. Orabaton (2000). "Referral Practices among Zambian Traditional Health Practitioners to Health Delivery Points: Has the HIV/AIDS Pandemic Changed the Practice." 13th International AIDS Conference, 9–14 July, Durban. Available online: ww1.aegis.org/conferences/ iac/2000/WePeD4730.html (October 2012).

Odongo, Eunice A. (2002). "Women Fighting AIDS in Kenya, Traditional Medicine and HIV/AIDS." 14th International AIDS Conference, 7–12 July, Durban. Available online: www.iasociety.org/Abstracts/A9559.aspx (October 2012).

Ogbaharya, Daniel G. (2008). "(Re-)Building Governance in Post-Conflict Africa: The Role of the State and Informal Institutions." *Development in Practice* 18(3): 395–402.

Ogilvie, Linda, Judy E. Mill, Barbara Astle, et al. (2007). "The Exodus of Health Professionals from Sub-Saharan Africa: Balancing Human Rights and Societal Needs in the Twenty-First Century." *Nursing Inquiry* 14(2): 114–24.

Omae, Kenichi (1990). *The Borderless World: Power and Strategy in the Interlinked Economy.* New York: HarperBusiness.

Omaswa, Francis (2009). "Message from the Executive Director." Global Health Workforce Alliance. Available online: www.who.int/workforcealliance/forum/1_agenda4GAction_final.pdf (October 2012).

Omer, Mohamed Ibrahim Ali (2005). "Can Medical Education Rise to the Challenge of the African Crisis?" *Annals of Tropical Paediatrics* 25(4): 227–41.

Ooms, Gorik, Wim Van Damme, Brook Baker, et al. (2008). "The 'Diagonal' Approach to Global Fund Financing: A Cure for the Broader Malaise of Health Systems?" *Globalization and Health* 4(6). doi: 10.1186/1744-8603-4-6. Available online: www.globalizationandhealth.com/content/4/1/6 (October 2012).

Organisation for Economic Co-operation and Development (2003). "Policy Coherence: Vital for Global Development." *OECD Observer*. Available online: www.oecd.org/pcd/20202515.pdf (October 2012).

Organisation for Economic Co-operation and Development (2007). "Immigrant Health Workers in OECD Countries in the Broader Context of Highly Skilled Migration." In *International Migration Outlook*. Paris: pp. 161–228. Available online: www.oecd.org/migration/internationalmigrationpoliciesanddata/41515701.pdf (October 2012).

Østergaard-Nielsen, Eva (2005). "Co-development Policies and the Role of Migrants' Transnational Networks." Abstract for intervention at Roundtable on "Migrations and Development: Transnational Networks, Remittances, Civil Society, and Human Capital Potential," 19–21 September.

Owira, Peter M.O. and John A.O. Ojewole (2008). "'African Potato' (*Hypoxis hemerocallidea* corm): A Plant-Medicine for Modern and 21st Century Diseases of Mankind? A Review." *Phytotherapy Research* 23(2): 147–52. doi: 10.1002/ptr.2595.

Padarath, Ashnie, Charlotte Chamberlain, David McCoy, et al. (2003). "Health Personnel in Southern Africa: Confronting Maldistribution and Brain Drain." Equinet Discussion Paper No. 3. Available online: www.equinetafrica.org/bibl/docs/DIS3hres.pdf (October 2012).

Peabody, John W., Mario M. Taguiwalo, David A. Robalino, et al. (2006). "Improving the Quality of Care in Development Countries." In *Disease Control Priorities in Developing Countries*, Dean T. Jamison, Joel G. Breman, Anthony R. Measham, et al., eds. Washington, DC: World Bank. Available online: www.ncbi.nlm.nih.gov/books/NBK11790/#A10280 (October 2012).

Peltzer, Karl, Nolwandle Mngqundaniso, and Gebrewold Petros (2006). "HIV/AIDS/STI/TB Knowledge, Beliefs, and Practices of Traditional Healers in KwaZulu-Natal, South Africa." *AIDS Care* 18(6): 608–13.

Peltzer, Karl, Natalie F. Preez, Shandir Ramlagan, et al. (2008). "Use of Traditional Complementary and Alternative Medicine for HIV Patients in KwaZulu-Natal, South Africa." *BMC Public Health* 8(255). doi: 10.1186/1471-2458-8-255. Available online: www.biomedcentral.com/1471-2458/8/255 (October 2012).

People's Health Movement, Medact, and Global Equity Gauge Alliance (2005). *Global Health Watch 2005–2006: An Alternative World Health Report.* New York: Zed Books.

Philips, Mit, Rony Zachariah, and Sarah Venis (2008). "Task Shifting for Antiretroviral Treatment Delivery in Sub-Saharan Africa: Not a Panacea." *Lancet* 371(9613): 682–4.

Picciotto, Robert (2004). "Institutional Approaches to Policy Coherence for Development." Room Document 2, May 18–19, Organisation for Economic Co-operation and Development, Paris. Available online: www.oecd.org/pcd/31659358.pdf (October 2012).

Pillay, Yogan and Percy Mahlati (2008). "Health-Worker Salaries and Incomes in Sub-Saharan Africa." *Lancet* 371(9613): 632–4. Available online: www.thelancet.com/journals/lancet/article/PIIS0140-6736%2808%2960283-4/fulltext (October 2012).

Pittman, Patricia, Amanda Folsom, Emily Bass, et al. (2007). "US-Based International Nurse Recruitment: Structure and Practices of a Burgeoning Industry." Report on Year I of the Project International Recruitment of Nurses to the United States: Toward a Consensus on Ethical Standards of Practice, November. Available online: www.intlnursemigration.org/assets/pdfs/Report-on-Year-I.pdf (October 2012).

Plsek, Paul E. (2001). "Complexity, Leadership, and Management in Healthcare Organisations." *British Medical Journal* 323(7315): 746–9.

Pope, Cynthia, Renée T. White, and Robert Malow, eds (2009). *HIV/AIDS: Global Frontiers in Prevention/Intervention.* New York: Routledge.

Prahalad, C.K. (2010). *The Fortune at the Bottom of the Pyramid: Eradicating Poverty Through Profits.* Upper Saddle River, NJ: Pearson Education.

Puckree, Threethambal, Melody Mkhize, Zama Mgobhozi, et al. (2002). "African Traditional Healers: What Health Care Professionals Need to Know." *International Journal of Rehabilitation Research* 25(4): 247–51.

Quartey, Peter, Evelyn Kwakye, and Gifty Merdiemah (2008). "The Impact of Rich Countries' Policies on Poverty in LDCs: The Case of Migrant Nurses from Ghana." *Research Monitor* 5: 19–21. Available online: cloud2.gdnet.org/CMS/getFile.php?id=rm_issue5 (October 2012).

Ragin, Charles C. (1987). *The Comparative Method: Moving Beyond Qualitative and Quantitative Strategies.* Berkeley, CA: University of California Press.

Reich, Michael R., Keizo Takemi, Marc J. Roberts, et al. (2008). "Global Action on Health Systems: A Proposal for the Toyako G8 Summit." *Lancet* 371(9615): 865–9.

Republic of Kenya. Ministry of Medical Services and Ministry of Public Health and Sanitation (2010). "Sessional Paper on National Pharmaceutical Policy." June. Available online: apps.who.int/medicinedocs/documents/s18697en/s18697en.pdf (October 2012).

Republic of Kenya. Ministry of Public Health and Sanitation (2006). "Annual Health Report." Nairobi.

Robinson, Mary and Peggy Clark (2008). "Forging Solutions to Health Worker Migration." *Lancet* 371(9613): 691–3.

Robinson, Rudi (2007). "A Framework for Benchmarking Progress on Policy Coherence in the Migration and Development Domain in OECD Countries." Unpublished.

Robinson, Rudi (2009). "Engaging African Diaspora Communities as Partners in Health System Strengthening in Their Countries of Origin." Workshop proposal, North-South Institute, Ottawa.

Rockey, Paul H. (2006). "Fixing the U.S. Physician Shortage Requires Many More Slots for Resident Physicians in Training." *Medscape General Medicine* 8(2): 52. Available online: www.ncbi.nlm.nih.gov/pmc/articles/PMC1785175/ (October 2012).

Roemer, Milton I. (1991). *National Health Systems of the World*. Vol. 1: The Countries. New York: Oxford University Press.

Roemer, Ruth, Allyn L. Taylor, and Jean Lariviere (2005). "Origins of the WHO Framework Convention on Tobacco Control." *American Journal of Public Health* 95(6): 936–8. Available online: www.ncbi.nlm.nih.gov/pmc/articles/PMC1449287/ (October 2012).

Roth, Brad R. (1999). *Governmental Illegitimacy in International Law*. Oxford: Clarendon Press.

Roth, Brad R. (2004). "The Enduring Significance of State Sovereignty." *Florida Law Review* 56(12): 1017–51.

Russett, Bruce M. (1995). *Grasping the Democratic Peace: Principles for a Post-Cold War World* Princeton, NJ: Princeton University Press.

Saltman, Richard B. and Odile Ferroussier-Davis (2000). "The Concept of Stewardship in Health Policy." *Bulletin of the World Health Organization* 78(6): 732–9. Available online: www.who.int/bulletin/archives/78%286%29732.pdf (October 2012).

Sambo, Luis G. (2003). "Integration of Traditional Medicine into National Health Systems in the African Region: The Journey So Far." *African Health Monitor* 4(1): 8–11. Available online: www.afro.who.int/index.php?option=com_docman&task=doc_download&gid=501&ItemId=2111 (October 2012).

Sampford, Charles (1989). "Coups d'États and Law." *Bulletin of the Australian Society of Legal Philosophy* 13(3): 253–86.

Sampford, Charles (1991). "Law, Institutions and the Public/Private Divide." *Federal Law Review* 20(2): 185–222.

Sampford, Charles (1999). "Sovereignty and Intervention." 19th World Congress on Philosophy of Law and Social Philosophy, 29 June, New York.

Sampford, Charles (2002). "Get New Lawyers." *Legal Ethics* 6(1): 85.

Sampford, Charles (2005). "More and More Lawyers But Still No Judges." *Legal Ethics* 8(1): 16.

Sampford, Charles (2010). "Adam Smith's Dinner." In *The Future of Financial Regulation*, Ian MacNeil and Justin O'Brien, eds. Oxford: Hart, pp. 23–40.

Sampford, Charles (2010). "Legal Ethics in a Post-Westphalian World: Building the International Rule of Law and Other Tasks." In *Reaffirming Legal Ethics: Taking Stock and New Ideas*, Kieran Tranter, Francesca Bartlett, Lillian Corbin, et al., eds. London: Routledge.

Sanders, David, Ehi Igumbor, Uta Lehmann, et al. (2009). "Public Health in Africa." In *Global Public Health: A New Era*, Robert Beaglehole and Ruth Bonita, eds. New York: Oxford University Press, pp. 161–84.

Scott, Mark L., Anna Whelan, John Dewdney, et al. (2004). "'Brain Drain' or Ethical Recruitment." *Medical Journal of Australia* 180(4): 174–6. Available online: www.mja.com.au/journal/2004/180/4/brain-drain-or-ethical-recruitment (October 2012).

Shinn, David H. (2002). "Reversing the Brain Drain in Ethiopia." Paper presented to the Ethiopian North American Health Professionals Association, November 23, Alexandria VA. Available online: chora.virtualave.net/brain-drain8.htm (October 2012).

Simoens, Steven and Jeremy Hurst (2006). "The Supply of Physician Services in OECD Countries." OECD Health Working Paper No. 21, Organisation for Economic Co-operation and Development, Paris. Available online: www.oecd.org/health/healthpoliciesanddata/35987490.pdf (October 2012).

Slaughter, Anne-Marie (2004). "Sovereignty and Power in a Networked World Order." *Stanford Journal of International Law* 40(7): 283–387.

Slaughter, Anne-Marie (2005). "Security, Solidarity, and Sovereignty: The Grand Themes of UN Reform." *American Journal of International Law* 99(7): 619–31.

Spiegel, Jerry M. (2006). "Commentary: Daring to Learn from a Good Example and Break the 'Cuba Taboo.'" *International Journal of Epidemiology* 35(4): 825–6. Available online: ije.oxfordjournals.org/content/35/4/825.full (October 2012).

Stern, Jessica (1999). *The Ultimate Terrorists*. Cambridge, MA: Harvard University Press.

Stiglitz, Joseph (2002). *Globalization and Its Discontents*. New York: W.W. Norton.

Stilwell, Barbara, Khassoum Diallo, Pascal Zurn, et al. (2003). "Developing Evidence-Based Ethical Policies on the Migration of Health Workers: Conceptual and Practical Challenges." *Human Resources for Health* 1(8). doi: 10.1186/1478-4491-1-8. Available online: www.human-resources-health.com/content/1/1/8 (October 2012).

Strange, Susan (1996). *The Retreat of the State: The Diffusion of Power in the World Economy*. Cambridge: Cambridge University Press.

Sunkel, Osvaldo (1972). "Latin American Under Development in the Year 2000." In *Economics and World Order from the 1970s to the 1990s*, Jagdish N. Bhagwati, ed. New York: Macmillan, pp. 199–231.

Talbott, Chris (2007). "Shortage of Doctors Affects Rural U.S." *Washington Post*, July 22. Available online: www.washingtonpost.com/wp-dyn/content/article/2007/07/21/AR2007072100432.html (October 2012).

Tandon, Yash (2008, 1 April). "UNCTAD XII: Negotiating 'Diplomatic Truths.'" *South Bulletin* (12). Available online: www.southcentre.org/

index.php?option=com_docman&task=doc_download&gid=833&Itemid= (October 2012).

Taylor, Allyn L. (1992). "Making the World Health Organization Work: A Legal Framework for Universal Access to the Conditions for Health." *American Journal of Law and Medicine* 18: 301–46.

Taylor, Allyn L. (2004). "Governing the Globalization of Public Health." *Journal of Law, Medicine, and Ethics* 32(3): 500–508. Available online: digitalcommons. law.umaryland.edu/fac_pubs/58/ (October 2012).

Taylor, Allyn L. (2008a). "The Draft WHO Code of Practice on the International Recruitment of Health Personnel." *American Society of International Law Insights* 12(23).

Taylor, Allyn L. (2008b). "The Proposed WHO Code of Practice on Health Worker Migration: Issues of Form, Substance, and Negotiation." Paper presented at the Health Work Migration Global Policy Advisory Council Meeting, 18 May.

Taylor, Allyn L. (2013). "Global Health Law." In *Global Health Diplomacy: Concepts, Issues, Actors, Instruments, Fora, and Cases*, Ilona Kickbusch, Graham Lister, Michaela Told, et al., eds. New York: Springer.

Taylor, Allyn L., Douglas W. Bettcher, and Richard Peck (2003). "International Law and the International Legislative Process: The WHO Framework Convention on Tobacco Control." In *Global Public Goods for Health: Health Economic and Public Health Perspectives*, Richard Smith, Robert Beaglehole, David Woodward, et al., eds. Oxford: Oxford University Press, pp. 212–30.

Taylor, Allyn L. and Lawrence O. Gostin (2008). "Global Health Law: A Definition and Grand Challenges." *Public Health Ethics* 1(1): 53–63. Available online: papers.ssrn.com/sol3/papers.cfm?abstract_id=1272424 (October 2012).

Teelucksingh, Cheryl and Grace-Edward Galabuzi (2005, November). "Impact of Race and Immigrants Status on Employment Opportunities and Outcomes in the Canadian Labour Market." *Policy Matters* (22). Available online: www. ceris.metropolis.net/wp-content/uploads/pdf/research_publication/policy_ matters/pm22.pdf (October 2012).

Teferra, Damtew (2000). "Revisiting the Doctrine of Human Capital Mobility in the Information Age." Regional Conference on Brain Drain and Capital Building in Africa, 22–24 February, Addis Ababa. Available online: www.iom. int/africandiaspora/pdf/TEFERRA.pdf (October 2012).

Teferra, Damtew (2005). "Brain Circulation: Unparalleled Opportunities, Underlying Challenges, and Outmoded Presumptions." *Journal of Studies in International Education* 9(3): 229–50.

Tettey, Wisdom J. (2003). "Africa's Options: Return, Retention, or Diaspora." May 1, Science and Development Network. Available online: www.scidev. net/en/policy-briefs/africa-s-options-return-retention-or-diaspora-.html (October 2012).

Thompson, Drew (2005). "China's Soft Power in Africa: From the 'Beijing Consensus' to Health Diplomacy." *China Brief* 5(21). Available online: csis. org/files/media/csis/pubs/051013_china_soft_pwr.pdf (October 2012).

Tilly, Charles (1990). *Coercion, Capital, and European States, AD 990–1990*. Cambridge, MA: Blackwell.

Todaro, Michael P. and Stephen C. Smith (2006). *Economic Development*. 9th ed. Boston: Pearson Addison Wesley.

Toledo Romani, Maria E., Veerle Vanlerbergh, Dennis Perez, et al. (2007). "Achieving Sustainability of Community-Based Dengue Control in Santiago de Cuba." *Social Science and Medicine* 64(4): 976–88.

Travis, Phyllida, Dominique Egger, Philip Davies, et al. (2002). "Towards Better Stewardship: Concepts and Critical Issues." WHO/EIP/DP/02.48, World Health Organization, Geneva. Available online: www.who.int/healthinfo/paper48.pdf (October 2012).

Tshibangu, K.C., Z.B. Worku, M.A. de Jongh, et al. (2004). "Assessment of Effectiveness of Traditional Herbal Medicine in Managing HIV/AIDS Patients in South Africa." *East African Medical Journal* 81(10): 499–504.

UNAIDS (2000). "Collaboration with Traditional Healers in HIV/AIDS Prevention and Care in Sub-Saharan Africa: A Literature Review." Geneva. Available online: data.unaids.org/Publications/IRC-pub01/jc299-tradheal_en.pdf (October 2012).

UNAIDS (2002). "Ancient Remedies, New Disease: Involving Traditional Healers in Access to AIDS Care and Prevention in East Africa." UNAIDS Case Study, June, Geneva. Available online: data.unaids.org/Publications/IRC-pub02/jc761-ancientremedies_en.pdf (October 2012).

UNAIDS (2005). "AIDS in Africa: Three Scenarios to 2025." Geneva. Available online: data.unaids.org/Publications/IRC-pub07/jc1058-aidsinafrica_en.pdf (October 2012).

UNICEF (2012). "Response to the Horn of Africa Emergency: A Continuing Crisis Threatens Hard-Won Gains." April, Addis Ababa. Available online: www.unicef.org/esaro/HOA_2012_Report.pdf (October 2012).

United Kingdom. Department of Health (2004). "Code of Practice for the International Recruitment of Healthcare Professionals." December, London. Available online: www.dh.gov.uk/prod_consum_dh/groups/dh_digitalassets/@dh/@en/documents/digitalasset/dh_4097734.pdf (October 2012).

United Nations (1948). "Universal Declaration of Human Rights." Available online: www.un.org/en/documents/udhr (October 2012).

United Nations (2010). "Keeping the Promise: United to Achieve the Millennium Development Goals." Outcome document of the 56th session, October 19, New York. Available online: www.un.org/en/mdg/summit2010/pdf/outcome_documentN1051260.pdf (October 2012).

United Nations (2011). "The Millennium Development Goals Report 2009." New York. Available online: www.un.org/millenniumgoals/pdf/MDG_Report_2009_ENG.pdf (October 2012).

United Nations (2012). "The Millennium Development Goals Report 2012." New York. Available online: www.undp.org/content/dam/undp/library/MDG/english/The_MDG_Report_2012.pdf (October 2012).

United Nations, Department of Economic and Social Affairs, Population Division. (2012). "Trends in International Migrant Stock: The 2008 Revision." United Nations database, POP/DB/MIG/Stock/Rev.2008, October 6. Available online: esa.un.org/migration/p2k0data.asp (October 2012).

United Nations Development Programme (2009). "Overcoming Barriers: Human Mobility and Development." United Nations, New York. Available online: hdr. undp.org/en/reports/global/hdr2009/ (October 2012).

United Nations Development Programme (2011). "Towards Human Resilience: Sustaining MDG Progress in an Age of Economic Uncertainty." United Nations, New York. Available online: www.undp.org/content/dam/undp/ library/Poverty%20Reduction/Towards_SustainingMDG_Web1005.pdf (October 2012).

United Nations Economic and Social Council (2000). "Report of the Regional Conference on Brain Drain and Capacity Building in Africa." February 24. Available online: www.iom.int/africandiaspora/pdf/Braindrain. pdf (October 2012).

United Nations High Commissioner for Refugees (2007). "2006 Global Trends: Refugees, Asylum-Seekers, Returnees, Internally Displaced and Stateless Persons." Geneva. Available online: www.unhcr.org/4676a71d4.html (October 2012).

United Nations High Commissioner for Refugees (2009). "2008 Global Trends: Refugees, Asylum-Seekers, Returnees, Internally Displaced and Stateless Persons." June 16, Geneva. Available online: www.unhcr.org/4a375c426.html (October 2012).

United Nations High Commissioner for Refugees (2012). "UNHCR Global Trends 2011: A Year of Crises." Geneva. Available online: www.unhcr. org/4fd6f87f9.pdf (October 2012).

United Nations Office of the High Commission for Human Rights (1966). "International Covenant on Economic, Social, and Cultural Rights." Available online: www2.ohchr.org/english/law/cescr.htm (October 2012).

United Nations Population Fund (2011). "The State of the World Population 2011." Geneva. Available online: foweb.unfpa.org/SWP2011/reports/EN-SWOP2011- FINAL.pdf (October 2012).

Usher, Erica (2005). "The Millennium Development Goals and Migration." International Organization for Migration, Geneva. Available online: www.iom. int/jahia/webdav/site/myjahiasite/shared/shared/mainsite/published_docs/ serial_publications/mrs20.pdf (October 2012).

von Zweck, Claudia (2006). "Enabling the Workforce Integration of International Graduates: Issues and Recommendations for Occupational Therapy in Canada." CAOT Publications ACE, Ottawa. Available online: www.caot.ca/ pdfs/wip/WIP%20Report.pdf (October 2012).

Vujicic, Marko, Kelechi Ohiri, and Susan Sparkes (2009). *Working in Health: Financing and Managing the Public Sector Health Workforce*. Washington, DC: World Bank. Available online: www.who.int/workforcealliance/

knowledge/publications/partner/workinginhealth_vujicic_worldbank_2009. pdf (October 2012).

Vujicic, Marko, Pascal Zurn, Khassoum Diallo, et al. (2004). "The Role of Wages in the Migration of Health Care Professionals from Developing Countries." *Human Resources for Health* 2(3). doi: 10.1186/1478-4491-2-3. Available online: www.human-resources-health.com/content/2/1/3 (October 2012).

Wibulpolprasert, Suwit, Cha-aim Pachanee, Siriwan Pitayarangsarit, et al. (2004). "International Service Trade and Its Implications for Resources for Health: A Case Study of Thailand." *Human Resources for Health* 2(10). doi: 10.1186/1478-4491-2-10. Available online: www.human-resources-health.com/content/2/1/10 (October 2012).

Wiessner, Siegfried and Andrew R. Willard (1999). "Policy-Oriented Jurisprudence and Human Rights Abuses in Internal Conflict: Toward a World Public Order of Human Dignity." *American Journal of International Law* 93(2): 316–34.

Willetts, Annie and Tim Martineau (2004). "Ethical International Recruitment of Health Professionals: Will Codes of Practice Protect Developing Country Health Systems?," Liverpool School of Tropical Medicine. Available online: www.medact.org/content/health/documents/brain_drain/Martineau%20 codesofpracticereport.pdf (October 2012).

Wolgin, Jerome M. (1997). "The Evolution of Economic Policymaking in Africa." *American Economic Review* 87(2): 54–7.

Woodward, David (2003). "Trading Health for Profit: The Implications of the GATS and Trade in Health Services for Health in Developing Countries." UK Partnership for Global Health. Available online: web.archive.org/ web/20031201074316/www.ukglobalhealth.org/content/Text/GATS_ Woodward.pdf (October 2012).

World Bank (2007). "World Bank Officials Engage African Diaspora in Development Efforts." Washington, DC, December 3. Available online: go.worldbank.org/TNAUDP28A0 (October 2012).

World Bank (2009). "The Nurse Labor and Education Markets in the English-Speaking CARICOM: Issues and Options for Reform." Report No. 48988-LAC, Washington, DC. Available online: siteresources.worldbank.org/ INTJAMAICA/Resources/The_Nurse_Labor_Education_Market_Eng.pdf (October 2012).

World Bank (2010). "Migration and Remittances Data." Washington, DC. Available online: go.worldbank.org/092X1CHHD0 (October 2012).

World Bank (2012a). "Data: Sub-Saharan Africa." Washington, DC. Available online: data.worldbank.org/region/sub-saharan-africa (October 2012).

World Bank (2012b). "Health Nutrition and Population Statistics." Database, Washington, DC. Available online: databank.worldbank.org/Data/Views/ VariableSelection/SelectVariables.aspx?source=Health%20Nutrition%20 and%20Population%20Statistics (October 2012).

World Bank (2012c). "World Development Indicators 2012." Washington, DC. Available online: data.worldbank.org/sites/default/files/wdi-2012-ebook.pdf (October 2012).

World Bank (2012d). "World Development Indicators and Global Development Finance." Database, Washington, DC. Available online: databank.worldbank.org/Data/Views/VariableSelection/SelectVariables.aspx?source=World%20Development%20Indicators%20and%20Global%20Development%20Finance (October 2012).

World Health Assembly (2008). "Health of Migrants." WHA61–17, May 24, World Health Organization, Geneva. Available online: apps.who.int/gb/ebwha/pdf_files/A61/A61_R17-en.pdf (October 2012).

World Health Assembly (2010). "International Recruitment of Health Personnel: Draft Global Code of Practice." A63/INF.DOC./2, April 15, World Health Organization, Geneva. Available online: apps.who.int/gb/ebwha/pdf_files/WHA63/A63_ID2-en.pdf (October 2012).

World Health Organization (2000). "The World Health Report 2000—Health Systems: Improving Performance." World Health Organization, Geneva. Available online: www.who.int/whr/2000/en (October 2012).

World Health Organization (2002). "Human Resources for Health: Developing Policy Options for Change." Draft discussion paper, November, Geneva. Available online: www.who.int/hrh/documents/en/Developing_policy_options.pdf (October 2012).

World Health Organization (2002). "WHO Traditional Medicine Strategy: 2002–2005." Geneva. Available online: apps.who.int/medicinedocs/pdf/s2297e/s2297e.pdf (October 2012).

World Health Organization (2003). "The World Health Report 2003: Shaping the Future." World Health Organization, Geneva. Available online: www.who.int/whr/2003/en/ (October 2012).

World Health Organization (2004). "Recruitment of Health Workers from the Developing World." EB114/5. Report by the Secretariat, April 19, Geneva. Available online: extranet.who.int/iris/restricted/bitstream/10665/20165/1/B114_5-en.pdf (October 2012).

World Health Organization (2004). "World Report on Knowledge for Better Health: Strengthening Health Systems." World Health Organization, Geneva. Available online: www.who.int/rpc/meetings/pub1/en/ (October 2012).

World Health Organization (2005). "Revision of the International Health Regulations." Geneva, May 23. Available online: www.who.int/entity/csr/ihr/IHRWHA58_3-en.pdf (October 2012).

World Health Organization (2006). "The World Health Report 2006: Working Together for Health." World Health Organization, Geneva. Available online: www.who.int/whr/2006/en/ (October 2012).

World Health Organization (2007). "Everybody's Business: Strengthening Health Systems to Improve Health Outcomes—WHO's Framework for Action." World

Health Organization, Geneva. Available online: www.who.int/healthsystems/ strategy/everybodys_business.pdf (October 2012).

World Health Organization (2007). "The World Health Report 2007—A Safer Future: Global Public Health Security in the 21st Century." Geneva. Available online: www.who.int/whr/2007/en (October 2012).

World Health Organization (2008). "Maximizing Positive Strategies between Health Systems and Global Health Initiatives." Geneva. Available online: www.who.int/entity/healthsystems/New-approach-leaflet-ENv2-p4p.pdf (October 2012).

World Health Organization (2008). "The World Health Report 2008—Primary Health Care (Now More Than Ever)." Geneva. Available online: www.who. int/whr/2008/en (October 2012).

World Health Organization (2010). "Country Cooperation Strategy at a Glance: Djibouti." Geneva. Available online: www.who.int/countryfocus/cooperation_ strategy/ccsbrief_dji_en.pdf (October 2012).

World Health Organization (2010). "International Recruitment of Health Personnel: Draft Global Code of Practice. Report by the Secretariat." A63/8, April 15, World Health Organization, Geneva. Available online: apps.who.int/ gb/ebwha/pdf_files/WHA63/A63_8-en.pdf (October 2012).

World Health Organization (2010). "WHO Global Code of Practice on the International Recruitment of Health Personnel." WHA63.16, May 21, World Health Organization, Geneva. Available online: apps.who.int/gb/ebwha/pdf_ files/WHA63/A63_R16-en.pdf (October 2012).

World Health Organization (2011). "Global Tuberculosis Control: WHO Report 2011." Geneva. Available online: www.who.int/tb/publications/global_ report/2011/gtbr11_full.pdf (October 2012).

World Health Organization (2011). "World Health Statistics 2011." Geneva. Available online: www.who.int/gho/publications/world_health_statistics/EN_ WHS2011_Full.pdf (October 2012).

World Health Organization (2012). "Health Systems Topics." Geneva. Available online: www.who.int/healthsystems/topics/en/ (October 2012).

World Health Organization (2012). "Tuberculosis Care and Control in Refugee and Displaced Populations." Geneva. Available online: www.who.int/tb/ challenges/refugees/en/ (October 2012).

World Health Organization (2012). "World Health Statistics 2012." Geneva. Available online: www.who.int/healthinfo/EN_WHS2012_Full.pdf (October 2012).

World Health Organization, UNAIDS, and UNICEF (2011). "Global HIV/AIDS Response: Epidemic Update and Health Sector Progress Towards Universal Access." Progress Report 2011, Geneva. Available online: whqlibdoc.who.int/ publications/2011/9789241502986_eng.pdf (October 2012).

World Health Organization Regional Office for Africa (1984). "Final Report of the Regional Committee." 34th Session of the WHO Regional Committee for Africa, September 12–19, October, Brazzaville. Available online: www.afro.

who.int/en/downloads/doc_download/5226-thirty-fourth-session-of-the-who-regional-committee-for-africa-final-report.html (October 2012).

World Health Organization Regional Office for Africa (2000). "Promoting the Role of Traditional Medicine in Health Systems: A Strategy for the African Region." AFR/RC50/9, March 9, Brazzaville. Available online: www.afro.who.int/index.php?option=com_docman&task=doc_download&gid=872&Itemid=2111 (October 2012).

World Health Organization Regional Office for Africa (2010). "Guidelines for Registration of Traditional Medicines in the WHO African Region." Brazzaville. Available online: www.afro.who.int/index.php?option=com_docman&task=doc_download&gid=6152 (October 2012).

World Tourism Organization (2012, September). "22 Million More International Arrivals in the First Half of 2012." *UNWTO World Tourism Barometer* 10(September). Available online: dtxtq4w60xqpw.cloudfront.net/sites/all/files/pdf/unwto_barom12_05_sept_excerpt.pdf (October 2012).

Yannis, Alexandros (2002). "The Concept of Suspended Sovereignty in International Law and Its Implications in International Politics." *European Journal of International Law* 13(5): 1037–52.

Zurn, Pascal, Mario R. Dal Poz, Barbara Stilwell, et al. (2002). "Imbalances in the Health Workforce." March. Available online: www.who.int/hrh/documents/en/imbalances_briefing.pdf (October 2012).

Index

GLOBAL ENVIRONMENTAL GOVERNANCE SERIES

Full series list

Corporate Responses to
EU Emissions Trading
Resistance, Innovation or Responsibility?
*Edited by Jon Birger Skjærseth and
Per Ove Eikeland*

Renewable Energy Policy
Convergence in the EU
The Evolution of Feed-in Tariffs in
Germany, Spain and France
David Jacobs

The EU as International
Environmental Negotiator
Tom Delreux

Global Energy Governance in a
Multipolar World
*Dries Lesage, Thijs Van de Graaf
and Kirsten Westphal*

Innovation in Global Health Governance
Critical Cases
*Edited by Andrew F. Cooper
and John J. Kirton*

Environmental Skepticism
Ecology, Power and Public Life
Peter J. Jacques

Transatlantic Environment and
Energy Politics
Comparative and International Perspectives
*Edited by Miranda A. Schreurs, Henrik Selin,
and Stacy D. VanDeveer*

The Legitimacy of International Regimes
Helmut Breitmeier

Governing Agrobiodiversity
Plant Genetics and Developing Countries
Regine Andersen

The Social Construction of Climate Change
Power, Knowledge, Norms, Discourses
Edited by Mary E. Pettenger

Governing Global Health
Challenge, Response, Innovation
*Edited by Andrew Cooper, John Kirton
and Ted Schrecker*

Participation for Sustainability in Trade
*Edited by Sophie Thoyer and
Benoît Martimort-Asso*

Bilateral Ecopolitics
Continuity and Change in Canadian-
American Environmental Relations
*Edited by Philippe Le Prestre
and Peter Stoett*

Governing Global Desertification
Linking Environmental Degradation,
Poverty and Participation
*Edited by Pierre Marc Johnson,
Karel Mayrand and Marc Paquin*

Sustainability, Civil Society and
International Governance
Local, North American and
Global Contributions
Edited by John J. Kirton and Peter I. Hajnal

A World Environment Organization
Solution or Threat for Effective International
Environmental Governance?
Edited by Frank Biermann and Steffen Bauer

Hard Choices, Soft Law
Voluntary Standards in Global Trade,
Environment and Social Governance
*Edited by John J. Kirton and
Michael J. Trebilcock*

The Politics of Irrigation Reform
Contested Policy Formulation and
Implementation in Asia, Africa and
Latin America
*Edited by Peter P. Mollinga
and Alex Bolding*

Governing Global Biodiversity
The Evolution and Implementation of the
Convention on Biological Diversity
Edited by Philippe G. Le Prestre

Agricultural Policy Reform
Politics and Process in the EU and US
in the 1990s
Wayne Moyer and Tim Josling

Linking Trade, Environment, and
Social Cohesion
NAFTA Experiences, Global Challenges
*Edited by John J. Kirton and
Virginia W. Maclaren*

International Equity and Global
Environmental Politics
Power and Principles in US Foreign Policy
Paul G. Harris

For Product Safety Concerns and Information please contact our
EU representative GPSR@taylor-francis.com
Taylor & Francis Verlag GmbH, Kaufingerstraße 24, 80331 München (Germany)